Administration of the Small Public Library

FOURTH EDITION

DARLENE E. WEINGAND

D1118231

AMERICAN LIBRARY ASSOCIATION
Chicago and London   2001

While extensive effort has gone into ensuring the reliability of information appearing in this book, the publisher makes no warranty, express or implied, on the accuracy or reliability of the information, and does not assume and hereby disclaims any liability to any person for any loss or damage caused by errors or omissions in this publication.

Project editor: Joan A. Grygel
Cover and text design: Dianne M. Rooney
Composition by the dotted i using Caxton and Novarese typefaces

Printed on 50-pound white offset, a pH-neutral stock, and bound in 10-point cover stock by Batson Printing.

The paper used in this publication meets the minimum requirements of American National Standard for Information Sciences—Permanence of Paper for Printed Library Materials, ANSI Z39.48-1992. ∞

Library of Congress Cataloging-in-Publication Data
Weingand, Darlene E.
    Administration of the small public library / Darlene E. Weingand.—4th ed.
      p.   cm.
    Includes bibliographical references and index.
    ISBN 0-8389-0794-6
    1. Public libraries—Administration.   2. Small libraries—Administration.
  I. Title.
  Z678.6.W44 2001
  025.1′974—dc21

                         00-059423

Printed in the United States of America.

05 04 03 02 01   5 4 3 2 1

CONTENTS

Figures   vii

Preface   ix

1   The Small Community: An Opportunity
for the Librarian   1

Characteristics of Small Communities   2

Small Communities with Specialized Customer Bases   3

The Changing Marketplace   5

Marketing/Planning: The Keystone   6

2   Library Governance   12

The Library's Legal Basis   13

Working with Local Officials   15

The Permutations of a Library Board   16

Strategies to Enhance Library Governance   26

Taking the Long View   28

3   Studying the Community
and Developing a Plan   30

The Planning Team   31

Developing Mission, Vision, Roles, and
Service Responses   32

Reconsidering Service from a Marketing Perspective   34

Conducting a Marketing Audit   36

The Study Is Over . . . Now What?   47

Creating Goals and Objectives   48

4 **From Objectives to Customer Service through Marketing   54**

What Are the Library's Products?   54

Price: Determining the Cost of Products   56

Setting Priorities   58

Levels of Service   65

Public Relations as a Service Function   68

Staff Attitudes toward Service   70

5 **Policies   73**

Changes in Policy   77

Policy Making   78

Establishing Specific Policies   79

6 **Finance   96**

Sources of Local Income   98

State and Federal Aid   101

Supplementary Funding   103

Preparing the Budget   106

Purchasing   114

Accountability   116

7 **Personnel Administration   120**

Personnel Policies   122

Personnel Functions   123

Levels of Staff   133

Compensation   137

Working Conditions   138

Continuing Education for Competence
and Advancement   140

8   Operations in Support of the Library's Products   145

Collection Management   146

Developing the Collection   154

Preparing Materials for Use   158

Collection Control   164

Circulation   167

9   Library Systems and
Cooperative Arrangements   171

Library Systems   171

State and National Networks   178

Cooperation with Other Libraries and Agencies   181

10   Outlets for Library Service
in the New Millennium   188

Electronic Access   189

The Library Building   190

Steps to Improved Library Facilities   199

Deciding to Build or Remodel   204

Costs   208

Energy Considerations   209

Furniture   210

Equipment   211

A New Building   212

Conversion and Remodeling   216

Refurbishing the Existing Building   218

Additional Distribution Options   221

APPENDIXES

A   Library Bill of Rights   233

B   Kendall Public Library Long- and Short-Range Plans 1999–2003   234

Index   249

FIGURES

1.1 Public Library Roles 8

1.2 Public Library Service Responses 8

2.1 Division of Responsibilities between Trustees and Library Director 23

3.1 The Planning Process 31

3.2 Steps in a Marketing Audit 37

3.3 Example of a SWOT Analysis 46

3.4 Example of Three Sets of Objectives 50

3.5 Action Strategies Supporting Objective Set A 51

4.1 The Product Mix 55

4.2 The Relationship between a Program Budget and a Line-Item Budget 57

4.3 Example of a Time Log 58

4.4 The Relationship between Cost and Demand 59

5.1 Sample Policy Sets 74

6.1 Developing Three Budgets 114

6.2 Interpreting and Communicating Statistics 118

7.1 Examples of Job Descriptions 124

7.2 Sample Organizational Chart 125

7.3 Sample Salary and Classification Chart 133

7.4 Relationship between Community Size and Educational Requirements for Public Library Administrators in Wisconsin 135

7.5 Maslow's Hierarchy of Needs 141

8.1 Activities in Support of the Library's Products 146

9.1 National Interlibrary Loan Code Guidelines Summary 184

10.1 The Library Board's Role in a Library Building Project 192

10.2 Generic Outline of Building Program Statement 196

viii   *Figures*

10.3 Steps to a Successful Building Program   199
10.4 Structural, Electrical, Mechanical, and Plumbing Surveys   205
10.5 Conversion Criteria   217
10.6 Images of Public Libraries   228

PREFACE

This is the fourth edition of a title that has turned out to be a staple of educational preparation for library staff in small public libraries. It has also been selected as a textbook for graduate-level library management courses in several universities. Dorothy Sinclair created the first and second editions; I took over with the third edition and now offer a fourth edition to the library community.

While quite a few years passed between the second and third editions, from 1979 to 1992, it has been only eight years from the time the third edition was published to the emergence of this new edition. This difference in publishing patterns clearly illustrates how the pace of change in libraries has quickened and how our evolving society and developing technologies continue to influence the ways libraries do business.

The preface to the third edition can still be considered a valuable insight into the evolution of library management, with its emphasis on change, marketing, the perception of library as a *business,* the movement away from *patron* to *customer,* and the broadening of the term *books* to include a wide range of information formats. This fourth edition introduces features and concepts that enhance and expand those views. Some of those new concepts include selective dissemination of information (SDI), the importance of vision, service responses, multiple objective sets, the relationship between cost and demand, grantsmanship, program budgeting, and non-monetary compensation.

The importance of using management techniques in even the smallest public library is essential to effective library service. The old paradigm of libraries as being worthy of adequate funding levels because of their status as a public good can no longer carry the day. While this essential value is still true, accountability is paramount in the minds of funding authorities, and the library that demonstrates an essential involvement in the life of the community, with clear responses to identified community needs, is the library that will earn sufficient resources to continue and expand its role.

Even as the library is recognized as a service-oriented institution, the current emphasis on customer service is a phenomenon that is both difficult to fathom and yet perfectly understandable. Difficult because one might expect library staff to be intrinsically tuned into customer service as a core philosophy since, after all, the public library is a service organization; however, this heightened interest suggests that staff apparently perceive considerable room for improvement. Understandable because customer satisfaction— or the lack of it—can play the pivotal card in an organization's quest for success.

Therefore, this new edition will once again highlight the importance of marketing and other management tools as key to effective administration of the small public library. Public libraries in communities of all sizes serve as the window to the global information exchange for their citizens. Marketing strategies and a focus on customer service are the newest tools for library managers as the new century dawns. The value of customer service excellence will be presented as the context within which the library manager should frame decision making. While there is no guaranteed road to achieving centrality in the life of a community, these approaches offer a high probability of a positive outcome.

The twenty-first century is here. There will undoubtedly be even more changes affecting the small public library than occurred in the last century, for the rate of change continues to increase. It is a challenge to adapt, embrace, and work with these changes. I am confident in the public library's ability to do so. It will be an exciting time.

1 The Small Community

An Opportunity for the Librarian

oday's librarian, unlike predecessors of prior decades, may elect to work in a broad spectrum of work settings. There is no longer a mandate, or even an overarching tradition, to work in an institution called a library. However, this current reality by no means suggests that libraries are on the decline; rather, it presents an ever-expanding window of opportunity to work in a variety of capacities in what may now be viewed as the information industry.

For those information workers who do prefer the library as a setting for their talents and energies, the public library offers unique challenges and rewards. It will always be true that some librarians seek employment in large public libraries, since heavily populated areas offer more plays, concerts, and other cultural advantages. However, small communities present equally attractive, but different, possibilities. While the smaller community's range of cultural events cannot compete with those of the big city environment, the human closeness and interaction, slower pace, and proximity to nature add special dimensions to the quality of life, and many librarians find such an environment decidedly appealing.

In addition, working in a small library, one learns a variety of tasks and has the opportunity to make many decisions that may not come the way of the junior staff member in a large library for years. To work with a board, to create and implement a budget, to recommend policy, to select a wide range of materials, to order furniture and equipment, to automate or update an existing system, to interview and hire new staff—these are some of the tasks that the administrator of a small library undertakes on a daily basis. While librarians in larger libraries will work with much larger collections, give service in greater depth, or specialize in subject or age levels, they will seldom have the variety of experiences of their counterparts in a small library.

Characteristics of Small Communities

While small communities differ from one another, there are some common characteristics. These characteristics make working in a library in this setting a very special and rewarding experience.

Personal relationships are stronger in a small community. People tend to know one another, to be on first-name terms, and to participate in the community's affairs. This friendliness and involvement give the librarian many opportunities to know and to serve. There may, however, be problems that would be somewhat obscured in a larger community: Individuals may expect special attention; the board may not always act officially as a body and individual members may be accustomed to issuing orders; votes on both the board and the community's governing bodies may depend on personal relationships; or cliques may develop. These human characteristics are by no means unknown in larger communities, but they can be more difficult in the informal climate of a small community.

These communities have a "small is beautiful" attitude. Smallness creates its own defenders. Residents may have come to the community to escape some of the problems of larger places and take pride in having done so. Smallness, too, can be an excellent characteristic, but for a library it can have its pitfalls. A community that is self-consciously a village may have in mind certain architectural qualities for its new (or old) library building and may fiercely avoid any attempt to organize and expand the library in a way that will seem to diminish its informality, friendliness, and small town flavor. While its citizens, unlike small town residents of generations past, now have sophisticated television, cable, VCRs, computers, shopping centers, and other amenities—to the extent that there is very little difference between them and the urban dweller—they may still affect a certain homespun quality. In such a situation, the librarian needs to find ways to adapt desirable changes to the local self-image without sacrificing substance.

Dislike of change is a human characteristic found everywhere, but it is perhaps stronger in some small communities. There may be a tendency to ignore world and national problems, however urgent, because they are not immediately represented in the community—although the emergence of television and other media is making a global village out of planet Earth, and such isolationism is less and less common. Yet, dislike of change itself continues in every community, for the known is always preferred to the unknown, and it is the creative librarian who can guide customers into uncharted waters (such as an online catalog) with a minimum of discomfort.

Members of smaller communities often have a great interest in details. Participation of the entire community in its concerns may cause residents to become preoccupied with details that city dwellers might overlook. This has the potential to be a mixed blessing. While citizen interest is a definite plus, staff in small libraries have been called to account for purchasing a colored typewriter (or computer) rather than a black or gray one, for discarding books still in good physical condition, and for removing old pictures and objects. It is important that such citizen concerns be acknowledged and understood; however, it can be challenging for the librarian to put—and keep—these concerns in the proper perspective.

Life in a small community can be delightful for the librarian who can appreciate and build upon the unique strengths and opportunities. As with all jobs, the match between the work environment and the individual's personality and expectations needs to be considered. An appropriate match results in mutual benefit to all concerned.

Small Communities with Specialized Customer Bases

The characteristics described previously are those that may be found, to a degree, in a rural community or a town some distance from a metropolitan area—one that offers a normal cross section of community life. There are other communities whose libraries are also "small" by this book's definition, that will have variations.

The Suburban Community

Within metropolitan areas are frequently found small incorporated communities that have determinedly maintained their identities. Their budgets and libraries tend to be small, their services as limited as those of the more rural small community. Their populations, however, tend to be less diversified. They may be "bedroom" communities, many of whose citizens work, shop, and seek entertainment in the city and return home only to sleep— at least according to the stereotype. These residents may be more homogeneous than citizens of the separate small town that provides its own services, jobs, and diversions. Here, a librarian will be "small" among a group of professionals in larger institutions. There will be opportunities for cooperation, reciprocal use, and other benefits that are available, but not as readily accessible, to a smaller community. Yet, even these statements must be tempered with the knowledge that public and multitype library systems are emerging at a rapid rate. Fewer and fewer libraries are islands unto themselves. Through interlibrary loan, the concept of each library being its community's window on the world or node in a global information network becomes more universally true with each passing day.

The College or University Community

Some colleges and universities are located in small places some distance from a metropolis. This situation gives the public librarian another educated user group in addition to the permanent residents, a wider variety of cultural opportunities, and increased numbers of potential opportunities for cooperation with other groups.

The Company Town

Some small communities, even remotely located ones, are populated almost exclusively by people who work in one industry and, sometimes, for one company. Occasionally a federal government installation provides most of the population. A public library in such a town may be unofficially governed, as is the entire town, by company officials and policies. There may be a paternalistic relationship between company managers and employees; conversely, unions may be strong, even militant. Administering a public library in such a community may offer less flexibility and more administrative challenge than may be found in the more diversified small community. Yet, in such a homogeneous atmosphere, the library's mission may well be to provide a wide range of opportunities in counterpoint. Such a mission could be stimulating to all concerned.

The Market Town

Many rural communities still exist chiefly as a market and meeting place for surrounding farmers and their employees and families. This picture continues to shift as agriculture changes from a small to a large business enterprise and as most small communities seek some industrial balance for their economy. Such a community's library is more likely to be a county library, especially if the same community doubles as county seat and market town. Here, problems of serving a scattered population are paramount. Modern farming is highly mechanized and requires fewer people than older methods. Thus, one is confronted with many acres, perhaps much livestock, but few people except in the central community that provides services and facilities to the farming population. Such communities may be somewhat conservative and will, of course, share the special interests and concerns of agriculture. The county agricultural extension service, including its homemaker services, will address many of the information needs of the community. The librarian should know the extension agents and their resources and should establish connections with them. Children of farm families are frequently bused for miles to their schools and have less time away from school than city children. All these differences must be taken into account in providing library service to a market town and its surrounding rural area.

These examples of specific small communities are just that: examples. Each community is unique in its needs and attributes, which is one reason that the Public Library Association moved away from designated standards and toward the process of routine and ongoing planning.

The Changing Marketplace

While in the late 1970s and early 1980s, librarians were faced with declining numbers of choices for employment, the 1990s presented an entirely different picture, and the outlook for the beginning of the twenty-first century is bright indeed. The ratio between available jobs and personnel to fill those jobs is largely either in balance or weighted in the applicant's favor, particularly if an aspiring librarian has the flexibility to seek employment in multiple localities. Further, the small public library presents a work setting that is both nurturing and challenging, as small libraries become part of systems and other networks, offering wider opportunities for service.

Some small libraries are seeking an administrator; others are adding new staff to an expanding library situation.

Qualifying for these different positions will vary from state to state. A few states require certification of public library directors; in other states, library boards require such certification of all library personnel. Where certification exists, such as in the state of Wisconsin, it is commonly tied to the size of the population served. Educational requirements may ask for a high school diploma (in the smallest communities) plus library training; at the other end of the continuum, the largest libraries mandate a master's degree from a library and information studies program accredited by the American Library Association.

The library as a part of the information industry offers employment to individuals with diverse educational backgrounds. Study in the liberal arts and sciences forms the foundation for librarianship. Further, the small public library is in a special position to benefit from the talents of individuals at different stages in their lifelong educational preparation.

Marketing/Planning: The Keystone

Developing a marketing and planning process for the services in a small library continues to be the most challenging of administrative assignments. Even with the focus appropriately on the customer, fiscal constraints may not sustain a budget of sufficient size and scope to meet identified community needs. This can be the case even when the community is providing reasonably good support on a per capita basis. It is a chicken/egg situation, and frequently customer need and demand must be documented and effectively presented to funding authorities before additional resources can be secured.

Every librarian who comes to a library with a small or insufficient budget is faced with the problem of reconciling theory with reality. The skill needed here is the willingness and ability to plan and to use concepts of balance and compromise to provide the best service that is realistically possible. It is also important to remember that compromises have been made and that appropriate goals must never be sacrificed to such reality, even though specific objectives might be temporarily constrained.

Thus the librarian must plan at several levels, beginning with a vision of the ideal service to the community, a vision that is based on careful and thorough community analysis and articulated through an appropriate statement of mission and service responses. Assistance with formulating statements of mission, roles, and service responses can be found in the *Planning and Role Setting for Public Libraries* manual, a product of the Public Library Development Project, and in *Planning for Results: A Public Library Transformation Process.*[1]

While the mission statement itself targets specific community-related aspects—such as target groups served, types of materials, relationships to provision of education, information, recreation, and culture—the *Planning and Role Setting* manual provides a list of suggested roles from which the librarian may select those most appropriate to the local community. These roles are summarized in figure 1.1. No more than two primary and two secondary roles should be selected. Such a selection by no means suggests that the public library does not perform all roles, at least in part. Rather, by limiting the options, the librarian is able to establish priorities and to focus existing resources to better meet identified community needs. Appendix B is an excellent example of how these concepts can be used in a planning process.

In 1998 the Public Library Association commissioned a revision of the *Planning and Role Setting* manual. Entitled *Planning for Results: A Public Library Transformation Process,* this revision expanded the original eight roles to a total of thirteen service responses. These service responses are summarized in figure 1.2. Although the service responses recast the original role statements in greater detail and broader scope, the approach of focusing resources on only a portion of the responses continues to be good advice. Certainly, all public libraries use all of the service responses at different times depending on customer need, but a targeted approach is preferable to expend scarce resources in the most effective manner.

In addition, it is necessary to plan with a vision in mind. While fiscal reality may be a temporary constraint, complacency is the enemy of all progress. In addition, the "ideal" may not be as unattainable as it first appears. Perhaps there is a way to reach the quality of service that the community should have. Unless this possibility is considered and all avenues explored, how can the librarian be sure? Even if the service contemplated in the vision is not possible this year or the next, it may come to fruition sooner than it would if no vision existed.

Beyond the vision and mission, with the corresponding decisions regarding roles and service responses, lies the pattern for making them happen. The planning process, with its long-range goals as targets, informs current decisions. Definite, attainable stages in the progress toward long-range

FIGURE 1.1

Public Library Roles

Role	Description
Community Activities Center	The library is a central focus point for community activities, meetings, and services.
Community Information Center	The library is a clearinghouse for current information on community organizations, issues, and services.
Formal Education Support Center	The library assists students of all ages in meeting educational objectives established during their formal courses of study.
Independent Learning Center	The library supports individuals of all ages pursuing a sustained program of learning independent of any educational provider.
Popular Materials Center	The library features current, high-demand, high-interest materials in a variety of formats for persons of all ages.
Preschoolers' Door to Learning	The library encourages young children to develop an interest in reading and learning through services for children and for parents and children together.
Reference Library	The library actively provides timely, accurate, and useful information for community residents.
Research Center	The library assists scholars and researchers to conduct in-depth studies, investigate specific areas of knowledge, and create new knowledge.

ADAPTED FROM: Charles R. McClure and others, *Planning and Role Setting for Public Libraries: A Manual of Options and Procedures* (Chicago: American Library Assn., 1987), 28.

FIGURE 1.2

Public Library Service Responses

Service Response	Description
Basic Literacy	The library addresses the need to read and to perform other essential daily tasks.
Business and Career Information	The library addresses a need for information related to business, careers, work, entrepreneurship, personal finances, and obtaining employment.

Service Response	Description
Commons	The library addresses the need of people to meet and interact with others in their community and to participate in public discourse about community issues.
Community Referral	The library addresses the need for information related to services provided by community agencies and organizations.
Consumer Information	The library addresses the need for information that has an impact on the ability of community residents to make informed consumer decisions and to help them become more self-sufficient.
Cultural Awareness	The library helps satisfy the desire of community residents to gain an understanding of their own cultural heritage and the cultural heritage of others.
Current Topics and Titles	The library helps to fulfill community residents' appetite for information about popular cultural and social trends and their desire for satisfying recreational experiences.
Formal Learning Support	The library helps students who are enrolled in a formal program of education or who are pursuing their education through a program of home-schooling to attain their educational goals.
General Information	The library helps meet the need for information and answers to questions on a broad array of topics related to work, school, and personal life.
Government Information	The library helps satisfy the need for information about elected officials and governmental agencies that enables people to participate in the democratic process.
Information Literacy	The library helps address the need for skills related to finding, evaluating, and using information effectively.
Lifelong Learning	The library helps address the desire for self-directed personal growth and development opportunities.
Local History and Genealogy	The library addresses the desire of community residents to know and better understand personal or community heritage.

ADAPTED FROM: Ethel Himmel and William James Wilson, *Planning for Results: A Public Library Transformation Process* (Chicago: American Library Assn., 1998), 53–122.

goals can be set, formally cited in each operational one-year plan, and pride can be taken in the realization of these intermediate steps. The marketing elements of determining which products to offer, identifying what each product costs to produce (price), deciding how to distribute the products (place), and communicating how the library meets community needs (promotion) interact with the elements of planning effectively to connect the library's efforts to customer needs—with a final demonstration of mutual benefit. The community, trustees, and staff share in the excitement and pride of such accomplishments, and motivation to continue striving is enhanced.

In the following pages, many matters concerning library management are discussed, with special attention paid to the small public library. While commonly accepted principles and procedures are presented, remember that the focus of library service must always be on the customer. This focus governs all administrative decision making and keeps the librarian's attention looking outward into the community. Concepts of marketing, planning, and customer service are the engines that drive the chapters of the book forward.

This book will have achieved a large part of its purpose if the reader, who is assumed to be a novice librarian in a small public library, steers successfully between the twin shoals of moving in too rapidly and upsetting staff, community, and trustees with uncomprehended changes or decisions that are not customer-focused on the one extreme and allowing what is unacceptable in the existing situation to continue indefinitely for fear of upsetting people or creating problems. Emphasis is placed on community-centered goals and objectives, derived from a study of the community and its information needs. (See chapter 2.) Such a study concentrates on the community served, involving the community, staff, and director in a project in which they all learn together. The community learns more about the library and what the library can do and become; the librarian and staff learn more about the community—its characteristics and needs. The total group, working together, learns to know and respect its members and the commitment that they share.

Thoughts for the New Millennium

Am I convinced of my library's importance to my community?
Do I fully understand the concept of my library as my community's window to the world of global information?

Does my state require certification of public library directors? If yes, am I certified at the highest level appropriate for my library's size? If no, do I have a personal plan for continuing my education so that I can be as competent as possible?

How do I define *professional*? Do I assume that the term is tied to a degree, or can I view it as an attitude of service?

Does my library operate within a routine and systematic planning process? If not, what steps can I take to initiate such a process?

Have I incorporated marketing strategies into my planning efforts?

Note

1. Charles R. McClure and others, *Planning and Role Setting for Public Libraries: A Manual of Options and Procedures* (Chicago: American Library Assn., 1987); Ethel Himmel and William James Wilson, *Planning for Results: A Public Library Transformation Process* (Chicago: American Library Assn., 1998).

2 Library Governance

A community is more than a group of persons and institutions situated in one geographical locality. It is also organized by its citizen members into a governmental unit with officials that have delegated powers and with laws or ordinances regulating its public business. The local community is part of a hierarchy of legally constituted government structures that extends to the federal government itself and, in today's world, into a global society and marketplace.

Today, the influential political figures at the national level cleave very closely to the notion of federalism, that is, an amalgam of locally independent states that have contributed a portion of their autonomy to a national authority through the mechanism of representative government. In fact, while this nation is commonly portrayed as a democracy, it is a representative republic rather than a true democracy; citizens elect legislators to govern on their behalf instead of participating directly in every issue. Historically, however, the vested power of the states has always been a closely guarded tenet, and this concept has filtered downward to the local level from which it originated. Consequently, local governments jealously guard their jurisdiction from state and federal encroachment. This proprietary stance is compromised, however, by funding structures and the desire to secure dollars from state and national governments—largess that brings with it attendant strings upon how that money is spent. In addition, state and national legislators are variously influential, and their political power is closely tied to length of service, membership on key committees, and networks of people and favors exchanged.

Therefore, there are segments of public business reserved to the community, to the township, to the county, to the state, and to the federal government—in other words, to each layer of the governmental onion. As a part of public business, the public library is necessarily involved at various levels with the several governments that affect its own local jurisdiction. Further, as a public agency of that jurisdiction, the library has its own prescribed internal government as well.

◯ As a public official, the library administrator must be familiar with laws and regulations—those of the library itself, the local government, the state, and the nation—and with the political process. At each level, legal and administrative matters concern even the smallest public library. To function as an effective public official and, especially, to accomplish the plans developed after a study of the community, the library administrator must have a knowledge of the governmental framework through which plans must be implemented.

The Library's Legal Basis

The governance of the public library, like all governance, rests on laws, regulations, and customs. Normally, libraries are set up in accordance with state legislation of the enabling type; that is, it is permissive, rather than mandatory, law. While the legislation does not require the establishment of libraries, it lays down conditions for their operation where they exist. State library laws vary considerably in the amount of detail included, and some of the language of governance can be found in administrative codes as well as in statutes. Language can commonly be found that addresses such areas as a general declaration of policy, the public library's reporting structure, general duties of those in authority at the state level, certificates and standards, public library systems and their governance, state aid, distribution of materials through a state network, circulation records policy, composition of library boards, tax structures, and funding for schools (if appropriate).

Frequently, local ordinances and regulations supplement the state law. These are generally put in place by the local funding authority (for example, a city council or county board). Such legalities may spell out in detail the way the library is governed locally, but they must be consistent with state legislation. In addition, federal legislation regarding libraries is increasing in scope and importance. Such legislation governs the number and types of grants available from federal sources, but the federal role does not super-sede the primary legislation that occurs at the state level. It is the state law that permits library establishment, provides for library finance, and lays down rules about local library governance.

The librarian must be aware not only of the law itself—including leg-islation and administrative codes operating at the state level, federal legis-lation, and local ordinances and regulations—but also of interpretation and the different levels at which interpretation may occur:

1. the interpretation of a local legal officer is binding on a library un-less superseded by . . .
2. the interpretation of the legal officer of the state, handed down in an official opinion, is binding unless superseded by . . .
3. the decision of a court in an actual case is binding unless super-seded by . . .
4. the decision of a higher court; or the later decision of a court at the same level presenting a different interpretation that has equal weight but not necessarily more; or new legislation.

Custom, or administrative practice, has almost the force of law in many localities when it is not in conflict with an actual statute, ordinance, opinion, or decision. Therefore, it is of utmost importance that the librarian and trustees of any public library be familiar with the law in all its various aspects. The law indicates not only what must and must not be done but also what may be done. Frequently, acquaintance with the law and local government procedures will open up new possibilities for action by the li-brarian. For example, legislation passed to enable public schools or a pub-lic hospital to accomplish some objective (such as opening or closing a new unit, or fund-raising) may be general enough to apply to the library and thus enable the library to function in a way formerly impossible. From an-other perspective, it is not unusual for legislation to be passed without complementary funding authorization; it is imperative that library support-ers not only follow the progress of legislation but also continue with their lobbying efforts until sufficient funding levels have been ensured. There are also instances in which legislation that appears to be progressive and desirable on paper becomes empty words because no "teeth" have been written into the law to ensure compliance. The local legal officer can be a valuable source of information and advice to library supporters; it is a com-plex pursuit, but well worth the effort.

State library agencies, which keep informed on state legislation affecting libraries, are able to advise the local librarian of pertinent provisions. State agencies as a rule also publish convenient compilations of the state library laws, and state library consultants are familiar with the ways in which the law is interpreted throughout the state. These resources are invaluable to the librarian, and ongoing routine communication patterns should be established and fully utilized.

Although not holding any official legal capacity, state library associations can be very useful in terms of educating library staff in political matters and organizing or assisting with lobbying efforts. Many such associations have legislative hot-line networks that are designed to use a grassroots approach toward influencing state legislation.

Working with Local Officials

The library will have both official and more informal relationships with local government. These relationships may be close or somewhat distant. The library itself may be governed by a board of trustees that has vested legal powers; in another configuration, the library may be a department of the municipality, with a board of trustees that is advisory rather than legally responsible. In the former situation, the library may be viewed by municipal officials as not very much a part of local government, since policymaking is the responsibility of the board of trustees. While this sounds like a negative scenario (and can be seen as such in some communities), there is much to be said for the autonomy of an operational board because issues of access and intellectual freedom are not subject to the whims of political fancy.

In the latter instance, where the library is a department of the municipality, the librarian may be regarded as a department chair and a real part of local government. This, too, has its positives and negatives: The library may be viewed as a central player within the municipal organizational structure, but it is also subject to the political and economic winds that blow.

In either model, but more commonly with the legally accountable board, there may be difficulties in the division of responsibility between the lay board and the paid administrator. While the state government is responsible for the major laws under which a library operates, the state ordinarily will not involve itself in the library's daily operations unless:

the library receives some state funds, either directly or through a co-operative or system of which it is a part;

the library receives federal funds administered at the state level;

the library initiates requests for assistance from the state library agency; or

there is vested in the state some supervisory or regulatory authority—for example, a law certifying public librarians—that is administered by some agency of state government.

While the library usually operates under a special law and may have an administrative structure differing from that of other local services, it is still very much a part of local government. Like other public agencies, it is supported primarily by local taxes. To a greater or lesser degree, the library follows the local pattern in such matters as financial accountability, personnel procedures, purchasing, and budget presentation. Because local conditions will vary, it is important for the librarian and the trustees to know their particular situation thoroughly.

Where there is a good, businesslike local government structure, it is to the advantage of the library to avail itself of the knowledge and skill of local officials. For example, the local purchasing officer may have made comparative studies of computers that will be useful to the library, or the finance officer may be able to give the board or staff member in charge of the library's fiscal accounts suggestions for keeping the accounts more effectively. A cordial working relationship should be maintained in the many matters in which the library's business brings board or librarian into contact with other local officials.

The Permutations of a Library Board

The library board, depending upon local and state laws and regulations, will relate differently to the library from community to community and from state to state. In some communities, the library board is a legally constituted body, accountable to the citizens for both finances and good management. In other communities, the library is governed directly by local officials, just as are other major services (such as fire, police, public works, and so on). Where there is a city manager, there may be a tendency to change lay operational boards into advisory bodies; the manager works directly with the various department heads, of whom the librarian is one. In some ways, the librarian has more independence in this latter model; in others, less. In yet other localities, the library is officially designated as a city department but has a legally responsible library board that is authorized by state statute.

Each system has advantages and disadvantages, and it is up to the librarian to build upon the available strengths and to develop a satisfactory relationship with the players. Time and patience may be needed to achieve the mutual understanding that makes for good teamwork, regardless of the legal structure and the legally responsible individuals.

Working as a Department Head with an Advisory Library Board

In situations where the library is an agency of local government, city or county, and governed by the normal regulations and ordinances of the jurisdiction, local government assumes many of the responsibilities. The library's staff members are automatically city or county employees, subject to the salary scale, classification plan, employment regulations, and personnel rules of the jurisdiction. Purchasing and payment of bills may be handled by the central purchasing department, so the library does not have much responsibility in this regard. Checks may not even be issued by the library but by the central authority. This centralization need not mean that the library does not have a good deal of freedom in selection of staff and purchases, within the regulations. When the budget has been approved by the central authority, the administrator and board may have a good deal of discretionary power. However, economies of scale in central purchasing, legal requirements as to bids, and other regulations adopted in the public interest by the central government will apply to the library and thus restrict the authority of the trustees.

When the librarian serves as a department head under a city manager or other official, the librarian becomes a full-fledged member of the official family and is not set apart by a special status that makes the library an exception. In this relationship, the librarian

attends department head meetings;

normally uses the services of the jurisdiction's personnel officer, purchasing department, finance officer, and accounting department;

is in official touch with other agency heads, thus gaining a fuller
understanding of the jurisdiction's operation and needs as they
relate to the total community as well as having regular channels
of communication with the other agencies with which the library
may work;

has access on a regular basis not only to the knowledge of other officials but also to the equipment and facilities of local government,
which may include computer time, a government telephone line,
or fax services.

In an organizational structure in which the library operates as a department of the municipality, personnel matters are typically centralized;
this arrangement presents its own set of advantages and limitations. In this
situation, personnel administration and policy are not solely the responsibility of the librarian and board. A special officer, often a person with
professional training in personnel administration, is in charge of overall
personnel work for the entire jurisdiction, including the library. Sometimes
there is a centralized personnel board or commission. Such centralization
almost always occurs where there is civil service, and it is found increasingly in parts of the country where the city manager or county executive
system is the pattern. Many small jurisdictions have adopted this system
or have copied some of its methods, and librarians need to be familiar with
it where applicable.

The personnel officer (or committee) normally sets up a classification
and pay plan for the entire jurisdiction. All library positions will thus be
classified by this officer, and all salaries will be determined in the personnel office. The issue of comparable worth is being debated in a number of
states. *Comparable worth* may be loosely defined as the concept that positions requiring similar educational background or training and having
similar duties and responsibilities should be compensated at similar rates of
pay. Thus, an argument can be made that the library director's salary should
be on a level with those of other municipal department heads, that library
clerical personnel should be paid the same wage as clerical personnel performing similar functions in other municipal units, and so forth.[1]

The personnel officer will also review reclassifications requested by the
library, prepare job specifications, and set up procedures for employing new
staff members. Under this system, librarian and board cannot make pro-
motions or raise salaries at will, nor can they independently create new

positions. All requests for changes must be carefully justified and will be granted or denied on the basis of their validity as related to the total personnel structure of the municipality and available monetary resources. Any changes must be justified; if adequately documented and tied clearly to both the library's plan and the related program budget, they have a reasonable probability of success. Obviously, there is a close coordination between the personnel officer's decisions and the budget, and any budget request involving a significant staff change normally requires approval.

The help of trained and experienced personnel officials can be of great value to the librarian, but the existence of these officials does not relieve the library of all personnel responsibilities. Learning how to work with a personnel officer may be challenging for a librarian whose previous experience has included more autonomy in personnel matters or for a librarian whose government has recently set up its first personnel office. It would be easy to make one of two mistakes: either to resist the new system without attempting to understand it or to abdicate to the personnel office all responsibilities in the field. Either approach can be damaging to the library in both the short and long term; it is essential that the library administrator learn to work cooperatively with whatever system is legally in place.

It is important to remember that the personnel officer is a specialist in personnel and the librarian is a specialist in librarianship. Both specialists need to work together to provide the most effective use of the library's largest budget item: personnel. Typically comprising between 60 and 80 percent of the budget, the library's human resources are an important investment. The personnel officer and the librarian need to cooperate in classifying positions, preparing job specifications, and working on salary schedules. To understand the principles underlying the work of the personnel officer, the librarian needs to "speak the language" and to make clear the library's program and needs as well as being competent in librarianship.

A librarian with these skills will find a capable personnel officer an ally in many situations. Personnel officers understand the need for special training if the librarian can demonstrate that a position requires it; they are aware of the importance of salary-step increases, fringe benefits, and in-service training programs. If the opinion of the personnel officer supports the assertions of the librarian and board that library staff is underpaid, or that extra compensation is needed in special circumstances, then such a statement by an objective expert may carry extra weight. Thus, while there may be some disappointments, delays, or frustrations in dealing with a centralized personnel office, there are also potential rewards for the librarian who takes the trouble to understand and cooperate with a personnel officer.

This, of course, is one model. In many localities, personnel matters are completely under the control of the librarian and the board. In many ways, the librarian faces special and more-complex challenges when the entire weight of personnel decision making is centered in the library. If so, the librarian is well-advised to extend competence in personnel administration to beyond "speaking the language," and continuing education can be a valuable ally. (For a more detailed discussion of personnel administration, see chapter 7.)

In summary, therefore, the scenario where the library is an official municipal department presents distinct opportunities and potential limitations. If, however, the librarian has the legal responsibility to work in concert with a library board that is ultimately responsible for library operations, these advantages and limitations are not negated. Rather, the librarian is faced with a balancing act, attempting to gain and nurture credibility as a municipal officer while relating successfully to a legally constituted board of trustees. While this dual role may certainly be a challenge, it is a challenge worth mastering.

Working with an Operational Library Board

To be legally constituted, each public library board must be appointed in conformity with the state law. The law not only defines how trustees are appointed or elected but also how many trustees shall serve, when they are appointed/elected, the length of terms of office, and the representation of educators and members of governing bodies on the library board.[2] Where state law does not address all of these areas, it is wise to incorporate them into official bylaws.

Some laws are so worded that, if taken literally, they would require the board to lend the books, take inventory, and perform other daily library tasks. Board members usually understand that these duties are to be delegated, but other duties that the librarian may claim as professional responsibilities may be inadvertently assumed by the board to be a part of its prerogative. In general terms, the board is responsible for policy; it charts the direction for the library and approves necessary policies. Procedures for implementing those policies are developed and managed by the librarian. (See chapter 5.) Occasionally, a municipality may seek to invoke tenets of home rule in an attempt to exert additional control over library operations. The functions of the board, therefore, cannot always be determined by recourse to law books; other considerations enter the picture, and there is variation among public libraries in the United States in this regard.

Help in defining the board's functions may be found in two ways: by looking at the historic rationale of a board (why does a library have a board?) and by considering the legal and jurisdictional position of the library itself. The term *trustee* gives one clue to the historic function. Early public libraries were, in many cases, founded as a result of large endowments, or at least the libraries received such funds fairly regularly. The trustees in such libraries may have been created as a result of a donor's will or the terms of a gift. The trustees' function was the same as that of a bank acting as trustee of an estate: to safeguard and invest the funds and to ensure that they were properly used. Some libraries are still in the position of having large sums of money to manage in this fashion, and this fact affects not only the function but also the makeup of the board. In other communities, the library was originally founded by a club or association and may for some time have served only the founding body's members for a fee. Vestiges of this historical situation may be found in the laws of some states, which permit such association libraries and require that the boards be appointed from the association's ranks.

However, while historical record may be informing, in practice the library board and the library administrator must create a working relationship in which the separation of powers is defined and clearly understood. In general terms, the operational library board has three primary areas of responsibility:

- hiring the library director
- making policy
- financial oversight and approval of the budget

Within these three broad areas, much confusion can occur about the responsibilities of the librarian and the board. Excursions into the other's "territory" can result in a difficult working relationship and decreased effectiveness. The following guidelines summarize the lines of responsibility:

1. The board hires and fires and evaluates the library director; all other personnel management of both paid and unpaid staff is the responsibility of the director.

2. Statements of policy may be recommended or written by the library director; adopting such policy is the purview of the board.
3. The director normally develops the budget in conjunction with representatives of the board; approval of the budget is a board responsibility.

More detailed distinctions between the duties of the trustees and the library director may be found in figure 2.1.

Selection of Board Members

Library boards are usually made up of laypersons rather than professional library personnel. As laypersons, expert in their own individual areas of performance, board members must receive orientation and ongoing continuing education if they are to be knowledgeable in library matters.

Regardless of the historic, logical, or legal basis for its existence, a library board is intended to represent the people of the community; therefore, a board's composition should reflect the constituents that it serves. Election of trustees is one approach to achieving this reflection, and some communities do use this method. However, the majority of operational boards are appointed, their members selected by a mayor, county executive, or local legislative body. The danger here is that the appointment may be a semipolitical one, made to repay some hard-working political helper regardless of that person's suitability for board membership. Inclusion of specific term lengths in the board's bylaws can be useful in limiting the effects of political influence.

The purpose of representation is to ensure that the views of the various segments of the community are heard and considered, including both library users and nonusers (for every nonuser is a potential library customer). Gender, age, occupation, and ethnic heritage are all important considerations. Ideally, the board should be made up of people who represent the views of their own segments of the community and are prepared to listen to and take into account the needs of the community as a whole. A proactive library board will seek to reach the presently unserved through special services designed to meet their identified needs. It is unfortunate when a board becomes a battleground for antagonisms arising from political, social, or other interest groups. It is also less productive when the board is too homogeneous, for the necessary diversity in backgrounds and

FIGURE 2.1

Division of Responsibilities between Trustees
and Library Director

Board	Library Director
Hire	*Hire/supervise*
A competent and qualified library director	All other library staff
Review	*Prepare/recommend*
The library's organizational structure	The Library's organizational structure
Annual budget	Annual budget
Monthly financial statements; pay bills	Monthly financial statements and bills
Develop (with librarian) and approve	*Prepare/recommend/implement*
Written policies	Written policies
Short- and long-range plans	Short- and long-range plans
Wage classifications	Work load and work flow patterns
Annual budget including exploration of funding sources	Annual budget
Contracts for services and their negotiation	Draft contracts
Capital improvement plans	Analyses and recommendations for improvements
Public relations program	Public relations opportunities
Comprehensive risk management policy	Necessary insurance coverages and purchases
Know/explore	*Know/provide information on*
Local, state, and federal laws	Local, state, and federal laws
Service of the system and state library agency	Services of the system and state library agency
Alternative funding sources	Alternative funding sources
New developments in librarianship	New developments in librarianship
Attend	*Attend*
All board meetings	All board meetings
Professional meetings and workshops (especially those for trustees)	Professional meetings and workshops
Community activities	Community activities
Report	*Report*
Regularly to governing officials and public	Regularly to the board, governing officials, and general public

ADAPTED FROM: *Wisconsin Public Library Trustee Handbook* (Madison: Wisconsin Dept. of Public Instruction, 1989), 15–17.

opinions will not be present. While such diversity may produce some confrontational situations, having a broadly based membership on the board is highly desirable.

Although the library administrator may not have any responsibilities for the method of board selection, in many cases advice is solicited, and the librarian may have the opportunity to make helpful suggestions. It is possible to write qualifications for board members into the bylaws; this may help to ensure good appointments. The librarian might also suggest to the appointing body (or have the board itself suggest) that open hearings be held at which persons wishing to be considered for the board would be interviewed by the appointing body and the existing board. Interested and qualified individuals may also be encouraged to contact the appointing authority and express a desire to be appointed.

Interest in the community, its people, and its future is a natural qualification for membership on the board, but it is only one criterion. Willingness to work and attend meetings is more important than a prestigious name. Leading citizens may make excellent board members; however, they may sometimes have too many other commitments. When this is the case, influential citizens may be asked to serve on an advisory committee to the board—a commitment that entails no meetings but establishes important connections for the library. While the librarian does not appoint board members, it is both advantageous and appropriate to suggest good candidates—citizens with a highly developed service ethic who will work for stronger, more customer-centered library services—and then lobby for those candidates.

Board size is normally set by law. Too large a group is unwieldy in transacting business and, where its size cannot be changed, must be divided into working committees to function satisfactorily. The committee approach is often adopted in any event, as small groups of three to five can be very effective and can report back to the full board. Tradition decrees that the board contain an uneven number of members to avoid tie votes. Some states regulate the number of consecutive terms a member may serve, and almost all provide for overlapping terms for continuity. The purpose of these provisions is clear: an effort to combine experience with new blood and fresh viewpoints. As mentioned earlier, if the law does not make such provisions, the board itself may do so in its own bylaws. Some boards have chosen to operate without bylaws; this is definitely not recommended and may lead to serious problems.

Meetings of the Library Board

State library law may designate the frequency of library board meetings; in other instances, this frequency may be decided locally. Periodic meetings are necessary to conduct business and pay bills. Prior to each official board meeting, the library administrator and the president of the board should work together to prepare the agenda, the minutes of the previous meeting, the financial report, and any supplementary materials; these materials should be distributed to each board member in advance of the meeting. Including a timely and relevant periodical article with these materials can be an effective strategy to help board members learn more about library matters and the entire information industry.

Board meetings are the time and the place for explanations, presentations, and questions. They are always open to the public, except when personnel matters are under discussion, and are subject to open meeting laws. In some localities, meetings are presented live or videotaped on a local community cable station. Staff members, both paid and unpaid (volunteers), can be invited to make presentations about their special areas of expertise and should be encouraged to attend board meetings as their schedules permit. Elected officials, library system representatives, and other specialists (for example, architects or insurance personnel) can be invited to make informal presentations about areas of concern to the library board.

Board Members as Public Officials

The library's legal and jurisdictional status strongly affects the functions of the board. In some states, it is common to find library districts that are completely self-governing; some are empowered with taxing authority. The trustees of such a library constitute the only legal authority under which the library operates. They are, for purposes of that library, the government. Their authority, except as restricted by the law, is enormous. In this situation, there is a good deal to be said for an elected board. Where appointment is the rule, it is especially important that the trustees be selected with care and, among other representational considerations, with a view toward their legal and financial knowledge as well as administrative experience. (Note: This is good advice for selecting trustees in any situation.)

In other communities, where the board is considered advisory to a library that functions as a municipal department (as discussed previously), the legal responsibilities are significantly reduced. Yet, even in this structure, the board does have a public persona and can still represent customer constituencies. In addition, the expertise of individual board members remains a valuable resource for the library's management.

Regardless of its official status and functions, a library board is a public body responsible for a portion of public business. Its meetings should be planned and should follow a formal agenda. Minutes should be kept, especially detailed ones in the case of important decisions. A board is itself a legal body—that is, its authority lies in its functioning as a group; individual members do not possess official authority. This is a fact that the library administrator needs to remember, especially in situations with a board whose individual members tend to give orders or to act informally as individuals rather than formally as a group.

In a small community, where personal acquaintance is common and a first-name basis is almost always the rule, it may be more difficult to strike the right note and to develop the appropriate librarian-trustee relationship. Furthermore, prior experiences of both the librarian and the board may color expectations and perceptions of areas of responsibility. Appropriate changes in the relationship can be successfully effected by an able librarian and civic-minded trustees without loss of goodwill on either side. When the librarian and trustees cooperate for the development of the library and agree on fundamental objectives and principles, working together can be a satisfying experience.

Strategies to Enhance Library Governance

Many strategies can be employed to enhance library governance and subsequent effectiveness in the community. Two such strategies are construction of the program budget and selective dissemination of information (SDI).

Program Budget

Although discussed in detail in chapter 6, it is important to note here that the development of the budget is a crucial element in working effectively with local officials. Although many municipalities require a line-item format for budgetary submissions, the construction of a program budget is a necessary prerequisite for any budget hearing—and is part of every planning process. If the library's budget is developed so that every direct and indirect cost is directly tagged to a library product (such as a service or program), then the budget is readily explainable to local officials. In fact, budget "defense" becomes budget "explanation," and the librarian's and library board's arguments are more easily understood by the lay officials of the community who hold the responsibility for budget oversight and approval. These arguments are enhanced if the board requests (and receives) monthly performance reports devolved from the program budget and also from the results statistics gathered from implementing the process presented in *Output Measures for Public Libraries.*[3]

Selective Dissemination of Information

Selective dissemination of information is a tool of incredible impact that can dramatically influence the opinion makers of the community. Developed in special libraries and the corporate sector, SDI has been effectively used to connect library customers with information resources that can help solve problems. In some instances, this has resulted in significant cost savings for the organization. However, SDI has been only occasionally adopted by public libraries, even though the outcome of such preemptive service has the potential to be significant.

Briefly stated, SDI includes the following steps:

Identify the power in the community and how it flows. Power may result from positions held, personal charisma, association with other powerful individuals (for example, being their spouse or confidant), or the ability to influence others.

Once the powerful individuals in the community have been identified, discover what issues—on both professional and personal levels—are currently important in their lives. These issues may be related to their work, hobbies, families, civic responsibilities, etc.

Seek out citations and current materials related to these issues—and then deliver this material to them before they ask.

This proactive identification and delivery of materials immediately relevant to the needs of community leaders establishes the library as a key resource and an agency that produces personal benefit. When the library becomes essential to the quality of life of these trendsetters, the community opinion of the library changes from the former paradigm of "that nice building on Main Street that has recreational reading and children's programs" to a new paradigm of the library as an effective information resource that is central to community life and prosperity. Because of these new perceptions, individuals who wield significant influence locally are invaluable allies as the library develops its marketing and planning strategies and seeks to become the information center of the community.

Taking the Long View

In today's world, print and audiovisual materials, radio and television, computers, and other technologies make information available in unheard-of quantities. Access to this information is more and more complex, and the majority of citizens cannot afford their own paths to comprehensive access. The public library serves the community as a window to the world of information—a more important community resource than ever before.

As a lifeline to poor families or the elderly living on fixed incomes, as a supplementary resource to media-rich households, as a mediator in the bewildering world of new information technologies, and as a backup resource to business information centers, the public library is an economic bargain to the local community. Recognizing that the public library is a continuing educational resource that is available to each individual throughout his or her lifetime, the small amount of funding support that the library receives, as compared with the time and cost of K–12 education, truly makes the library the "best deal in town." Further, even a small increase in this support level could provide citizens with a host of additional benefits and opportunities. The major challenge for library trustees is to understand the relevant circumstances of their communities and to translate this understanding into the guidance of a dynamic library program appropriate for today's world.[4]

In summary, then, a metaphor may state in simple terms what complex reality finds difficult to express: Library governance provides the stage; the municipality deserves a creative and vibrant performance and must provide adequate resources for that to happen; the trustees create and play an exciting musical score; the librarian serves as both conductor and choreographer, coordinating all the dancers in a pattern of intricate steps. Let the dancing begin.

Thoughts for the New Millennium

Do I fully understand how my library is legally constituted? Whom can I ask for further clarification?

What is the nature of my relationship with my state library agency? Am I aware of what the agency can do for my library and for me? Do I ask for help when I need it?

Am I a member of my state library association? If yes, have I become an active participant, volunteering for committees and running for office? If no, do I realize how important this membership would be to my professional growth?

What type of structure governs my library board? Are there term limits? Are there bylaws? How are board members selected? When I create the agendas for meetings, do I take the opportunity to include a recent library-related article to help the board's understanding of the profession?

How could SDI enhance my library's effectiveness?

Notes

1. Additional information concerning salaries can be found in the *American Library Association Salary Survey* (summarized periodically in *American Libraries*) and in the annual *Library Journal* issue that examines salary trends for new library school graduates.
2. *Wisconsin Public Library Trustee Handbook* (Madison: Wisconsin Dept. of Public Instruction, 1989), 14.
3. *Output Measures for Public Libraries: A Manual of Standardized Procedures.* 1st and 2d eds. (Chicago: American Library Assn., 1982, 1987).
4. Robert Wedgeworth, "The Trustee in Today's World," in *The Library Trustee,* ed. Virginia G. Young (Chicago: American Library Assn., 1988), 7.

3

Studying the Community and Developing a Plan

T he word *small* is a comparative one, implying the existence of something larger and perhaps more complex. In the case of libraries, it suggests a smaller community, collection, staff, and building than would be found in larger public library situations. Inevitably, assumptions related to size are made that imply that a larger library has the capability to provide services, or degrees of service, that are beyond the scope of the smaller library. "Small," therefore, is often viewed in terms of limitations. This is a relative conclusion that implies that larger is better. Nothing could be farther from the truth.

While it is obviously true that a smaller budget will allow for less resources, it is also true that a lesser degree of bureaucracy may also be present. Such an environment can often nurture increased creativity, with a chance to more rapidly "make things happen." Consequently, while quantity of resources may be limited, quality and innovation need not be; rather, some opportunities may be enhanced.

The issue of limitations is of serious concern to libraries of any size, but it is definitely an important matter for the consideration of the board and the administrator of the small library. It can be addressed only by asking What shall this particular library try to do and to be? These major questions must be answered before many more-specific ones (such as what kinds of materials shall we buy, or what qualifications shall we seek in our staff) can be answered adequately. Why do we need a library? What should it accomplish? In what ways is our community different—and better—because the library is there?

Certainly, it is true that all libraries face these questions, but when resources are small or constrained, responses become even more meaningful. This chapter will focus on the importance of the marketing/planning process in the small library situation, with emphasis on assessing community needs as the prerequisite to decision making. Figure 3.1 can be used as a graphic illustration of the cyclical nature of the overall process.

The Planning Team

When consideration of studying the community and developing a plan becomes a serious possibility, the prospect is likely to seem overwhelming. After all, the human resources of a small library may well include the librarian, possible (but not guaranteed) part-time staff, and the library board.

FIGURE 3.1

The Planning Process

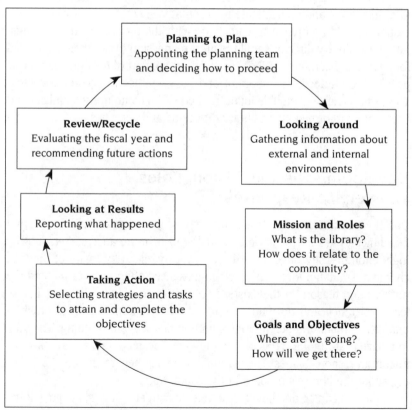

ADAPTED FROM: *Wisconsin Public Library Standards* (Madison: Wisconsin Dept. of Public Instruction, 1987), 8.

How can such a small group undertake such a major project and still keep the library open?

The answer to this very important question can be found in the creation of a planning team. A planning team would have a diverse membership, including the following groups: library staff, library board, library director, and, most important, representatives from specific target markets such as the media, local schools, small businesses, human service agencies, youth groups, churches, senior citizens, and so forth. The exact composition will depend upon the library's community and the target markets that can be identified. The team may swell to rather large proportions when delegates from all these groups are invited; the actual work will need to be done by subcommittees of three to five individuals.

On another level, it can be very useful to create an advisory group that consists of the powerful members of the community: the mayor, CEOs of local industries and media, state representatives, etc. These powerful individuals should be invited to participate with the promise of no meetings; rather, the library director should request permission to call them as needed for advice and comment. When no meetings are part of the agreement, few people—no matter how important and busy—refuse to become involved. This strategy elicits valuable input from powerful community members and keeps them informed about library directions and activities.

Developing Mission, Vision, Roles, and Service Responses

Questions concerning why the library exists in a community do not sound like difficult ones for the librarian and library board to answer. Yet, surprisingly enough, they have never been seriously asked by many of those in charge of small libraries. Librarians and trustees often take for granted the purpose and reason for the existence of the library. They follow the line of least resistance and do what has formerly been done, or what other libraries in similar and neighboring communities seem to be doing. They fail to realize that in taking this course they are sidestepping one of their most important responsibilities. The planning team can help to enlarge the thinking about the library's purpose in the community.

Libraries can do and be many things, to a greater or lesser degree. If the small library cannot do and be everything that is possible in the large metropolitan area library, how does it decide which of the functions it will not fulfill? The fact that a library is small does not make the search for a purpose easier. In some ways, it is harder for a small operation to determine its reason for being; a great deal of selectivity is required, calling for a special effort to choose wisely. But in order to choose, two kinds of information are needed:

What are the normal functions of public libraries and levels of service from which a choice is to be made?

What are the characteristics and needs of this particular community that will assist in determining appropriate library services?

Chapter 1 presented the original list of potential roles and a list of revised service responses, both developed by the Public Library Association (PLA). From these lists (or other locally important roles), the roles or service responses most applicable to the library's particular community can be selected. These determinations should be made in the light of the library's mission—relative to audience, materials, and service parameters—and vision of where the library should be going. Priorities must be established because, particularly in times of fiscal constraint, the library cannot be all things to all people (much as the traditional service ethic might suggest).

Mission and Vision

Both mission and vision are essential to determining service parameters, yet they offer very different lenses through which to view the relationship between the library and the community. The mission statement looks at today, at what is presently in place based upon the best possible information and preferably upon the data derived from a recent community analysis. It places the library in the context of its community and clearly states the customers to be served, the library's philosophy of service, and the scope of the collection and products offered to the community.

Vision, on the other hand, focuses on tomorrow. The vision statement outlines the scope of the library's hopes and dreams for meeting community needs—and what it will take to make those dreams a reality. Therefore, in many ways, the vision is a natural extension of the mission, and the two statements work together to chart a course into the future.

Roles and Service Responses

The evolution from the original eight roles developed by PLA (see chapter 1) into thirteen service responses was rooted in the changing characteristics of technology and communities. The service responses are published in a two-volume work, *Planning for Results: A Public Library Transformation Process.*[1] The twin concepts of results and transformation are clear indicators of the direction that public libraries are heading in the new century. Accountability is a major concern of funding authorities today, and there is great emphasis on measurable outcomes, impacts, and results. In addition, the viable public library that truly seeks to become competitive in a changing marketplace must, indeed, "transform" itself to perform effectively in this new environment. In a time of constrained resources, libraries must assess performance in the context of identified community needs, directing resources to core essential services and recognizing that a library cannot reasonably be all things to all people, as much as staff might wish to do so.

However, on a brighter note, today's smaller library is in a more fortunate position than its predecessor of a few decades ago. It need not completely discard any legitimate service nor fail to meet any reasonable information need. It can, increasingly, offer a wide range of materials and services to its community through membership in a library system or other cooperative group such as a statewide network. Technology has enabled resource sharing to become faster, easier, and less expensive. The choice to be made locally, therefore, is not which services to offer but which to offer on site, in direct service to users; which to offer in collaboration with another library or agency; and which to refer to an appropriate source. It is easier to choose when one knows that the services and information that the library will not offer directly can be given indirectly through cooperation or referral—either of the customer to another library or source or of the request itself (in which case, the needed material or answer comes back to the local library for the customer's convenience).

In summary, then, today's information environment is such—through developments in both technology and the social fabric—that the public library in the tiniest town can reliably claim to be that community's window to the world of information and a node on the global information network. This is no idle claim; it is happy reality in today's world.

Reconsidering Service from a Marketing Perspective

The modern public library has moved beyond the simple purpose of attempting to satisfy its "natural" customers—those people who seek it out regularly and, in a number of user studies, have been characterized as tending to be younger adults, better educated, and working in the professions or business. The library that has assumed, in an earlier state of innocence, that its purpose is accomplished by serving and pleasing this group of regular users has been challenged by a sterner professional mandate reminding it that it is a public institution and that it must make an effort to identify the needs of the entire community, and this effort includes engaging in outreach efforts and cooperative activities with local agencies. The importance of effective, proactive management has been clearly stated: "The challenge of change, the pressure for accountability and the emergence of the 'enterprise' culture all emphasize the fact that library services need to be proactive rather than passive; and thus need to be positively and effectively managed."[2] This emphasis on accountability produces a number of consequences:

1. It makes a study of the community absolutely necessary.
2. It requires a library to reconsider its priorities and to redistribute its resources to most effectively meet the needs of the community.
3. It requires a library to provide not only what people ask for but also to consider what they might use if more resources were directed to identified community needs. Since the public-at-large does not as a rule know as much about library materials and services as the library staff, the latter must be proactive in providing and suggesting, not merely passive in responding to requests.
4. It requires a library to consider not only different needs but also different methods of meeting them—different locations, levels of materials and services, media, and ways of delivering information.
5. It requires a library to devise or utilize new relationships it may not yet have attained, such as an increased use of referral—to other community agencies, to individuals who may have special information they are willing to share, and especially to other libraries through formal cooperation. This type of expanded service is made possible to many smaller libraries through their membership in library systems or consortia.
6. It also requires a library to rethink and step up its publicity efforts, aiming at identified target markets and communicating the benefits that library services provide.

To summarize, the modern conception of a public library will require many small libraries to transform themselves. Merely reflecting a community is no longer enough, although a community's known wants and needs will, of course, be the baseline for library operations. However, in today's economic pinch and taxpayer squeeze, the library must project itself as a valuable needed local service—a service that provides documented benefits (results) to the community. As stated earlier, the community must be different—and better—because the library is there. If the community is not different and better—or if it perceives that the library has no beneficial impact—it may decide that it can do without the library.

Identifying the community's wants and needs is the first step in designing a strategic marketing plan that aims to create benefits for customers. This step is known as a "marketing audit."

Conducting a Marketing Audit

The term *marketing audit* is a broad umbrella that arches over two interlocking concepts: community study (external environment) and agency assessment (internal environment). Both environments must be considered when conducting an audit: a snapshot in time of "what is."

Even the community study can be subdivided into macro and micro external environments. The macroenvironment must be acknowledged and considered, but it comprises the larger world patterns upon which the small public library can have little effect. However, since this macroenvironment can have a definite impact on the library, particularly in terms of economics and available technologies, the administrator must at all times be knowledgeable and aware of current events and anticipated trends. It is rather like sailing: the person at the helm must have knowledge of how winds behave, the capabilities of the boat, the direction desired, and so forth; whether the winds are mild or of hurricane velocity is beyond the sailor's scope of control, but a skillful hand can adjust to whatever conditions present themselves.

The microenvironment is an altogether different story. The microenvironment incorporates the immediate community and includes present needs and potential trends. This portion of the external environment is of most immediate concern to the library, and both its characteristics and anticipated changes can be influenced by the library. It is the library's first responsibility, and the study of this community is a primary component of true accountability.

The Structure of a Marketing Audit

The first step in a marketing audit, forming a planning team, was discussed previously. The remaining four steps provide a useful framework for designing an effective audit:

> *Determine what elements will be covered.* Aspects to be considered include the desired depth of coverage, resources available (fiscal, human, physical, time), and expectations of the planning team and staff.
>
> *Develop procedures for collecting data and monitoring the process.*
>
> *Collect and analyze the data.* Locate available secondary sources (what has already been collected by others) and then design a mechanism for gathering primary data (original data) to fill in the gaps in what is known.
>
> *Prepare reports and presentations of the results.* Develop both written and verbal presentations, incorporating executive summaries and graphics.[3]

Figure 3.2 shows how to go about a marketing audit. Discussion of this structure can inform the thinking of the planning team and the staff, allowing the planning/marketing process to move forward with everyone on the "same page."

Figure 3.2

Steps in a Marketing Audit

1. Form a planning team. Invite representatives from target community groups—such as small businesses, education, chamber of commerce, village/town/county board, churches, media, social services agencies, youth groups, etc.—to join with members of the library board and staff to serve on such a team. Divide into task forces to gather various types of data.

2. Gather as much data about the community as possible from secondary sources; learn from what others have already done.

3. Examine the library's own records and statistics to put together a profile of strengths and limitations.

4. Determine what data still needs to be assembled; decide which strategy (interview, survey, focus group, public hearing, etc.) would be best to use in the community.

5. Keep the community involved and informed at every point in the process.

Studying the Community

Members of different service professions study their communities for different purposes. The health department is interested in diseases, the conditions that cause them, facilities for treatment, and measures of prevention. The recreation department studies concentrations of population and age distribution and transportation facilities to identify appropriate recreation and park activities for various community groups and to place them in strategic and convenient locations.

The library's community study is also related to its function and is a necessary preliminary step, as well as an ongoing necessity, to its proper performance. The library is, in one sense, a multipurpose agency; in another, its function is focused—the direct provision of information. *Information* in this context includes not only specific facts but also the means of self-education and the broadening of horizons.

The library studies the community (the micro external environment), therefore, chiefly to learn its information needs. At the beginning of a community study, it is neither necessary nor desirable to identify those needs that the library will emphasize—such priority decisions are best made after all the data are collected. The library's search is for information needs of all kinds, wherever they may occur, with no preconceptions to cloud the results.

There will, of course, be data that are presently recognized as library concerns—and that have already been collected by other agencies or groups. Included here are demographic data concerning educational level, household income, occupation, and gender distribution. This "secondary" data should be gathered before any "primary" methods are used. (Primary data includes what has not been collected elsewhere; methods to gather such data include such strategies as in-person or telephone interviews, mail surveys, and focus groups. These methods are discussed in more detail later in this chapter.)

Examples of secondary data that should be available locally include

age levels and groups How many children? young adults? older people? members of racial and ethnic groups? non-English-speaking people?

education How many citizens with college or graduate degrees? other educational levels? How many are attending special classes for additional education or retooling? What is the literacy level of the community?

economic facts What are the occupational patterns—industries, small businesses, farms? What are the numbers of skilled and unskilled workers and their professions?

schools and colleges What educational facilities exist, including specialized, vocational, and remedial institutions, both public and private?

community habits What are the sizes and types of homes? What are popular recreations and interests?

cultural opportunities Are there regular concerts, theaters, lectures, and amateur groups?

civic interests and problems What are the patterns of community growth? needs for expanded facilities? matters of public concern?

religious institutions How many? What denominations? How large? How many have weekday group meetings, discussion groups, and children's summer programs?

clubs and organizations Are there service clubs? special interest and hobby groups? book and current affairs discussion and action groups? civic groups? senior citizen or neighborhood clubs? scout troops and other youth groups?

institutions Are there hospitals? health and welfare institutions?

The sources that may be available locally to provide this data include

U.S. census, especially tract or district records (gathered every ten years, and now available in electronic form)

school records

local chamber of commerce or equivalent

planning department of the community, county, or region

agricultural sources (Grange, Farm Bureau, farm and home extension agents)

published directories of businesses, industries, and national organizations with local units

files of local organizations (Many libraries keep their own card or computer files of community organizations and officers or contacts. This is a useful and desirable practice.)

newspapers, especially local and regional, that give details of meetings, projects, and new organizations

personal interviews with representatives of organizations, institutions, and businesses (These have an added value in making friends for the library and creating an opportunity to talk about its services.)

When looking at other community institutions and organizations, the library study should not seek only to learn their information needs. Such local groups often provide additional help to the library in its search for a focus for its services:

In and of themselves, they are evidences of community interest and concern.

They may have information about the community that they will share with the library. For example, the kinds of information about the community that a recreation department has already gathered for its own use has been previously noted.

Some may be in touch with other special groups in the community and be able to cooperate with the library in reaching such groups. For example, a nursing home will not only know some of the interests and information needs of its patients but may be able to work out with the library a convenient way of serving them.

They may already be providing for a special information need. That fact is of importance to the study in that an identified need may already be met. The library may avoid duplication of service by meeting this customer need through referral. The library's responsibility is somewhat lightened if a part of the community's needs is served elsewhere. In most cases, such community resources are very interested in cooperation rather than duplication and welcome referrals from the public library.

The organizations and institutions are likely to possess useful expertise. Even if they are not able to accept any or all possible referrals, they may be willing to give information over the telephone to a librarian who calls on behalf of a customer. On occasion, they may also be willing to give the library the benefit of their expertise in evaluation of specialized materials and in speaking or acting as reactors at library meetings.

When conducting the study, individuals as well as groups and organizations may be identified for future relationships:

potential users of existing services who are not aware of the library's holdings and functions

potential users of interlibrary loan services—people with unusual needs who do not realize that the library can help obtain special resources

people interested in helping the library as volunteers in special services that may be instituted as a result of the study—such as taking books to the homebound

individuals with specialized knowledge who may become human information resources

people who may be interested in forming, or joining, a Friends of the Library group. (Friends of the Library are organized in many communities, large and small. Activities include such activities as support at budget time, data collection, and fund-raising efforts.)

Some community information needs are commonly reflected in every public library: supplementary requirements of students of all ages; information about home, garden, children, pets, household finance, family relationships, entertainment, parties, etiquette problems, weddings, showers, and games; current fads and fashions in hobbies; continuing interests in decoration, do-it-yourself projects, and vacation destinations; and popular reading and plays, music, and sports. These topics are common across communities, but they will also have local applications that are community-specific. In addition, religious organizations, scouting groups, clubs, and other organizations may have information needs that have not been previously brought to the library. The community study should not assume the library's knowledge on any of these topics or interest groups but ensure that the library's information about its community is complete and up-to-date.

One major aspect of adult life creates information needs that the library may not have accepted as part of its mission—the community's occupational life. While the work of the home is generally provided for, paid employment's information needs may not be met. In the community study, it is important to include a knowledge of the occupations represented locally, and the information needed as a result of these occupations. Such information occurs at different levels: The beginner needs basic training in the details of the job; the supervisor needs information about human relations and training skills; top management needs a variety of specialized information not only about management itself but also about markets, technological developments, and the like. The small business needs similar information at a level appropriate to its needs. All these inquiries should be included in the study, even if the library has not previously operated in this arena.

The staff of most small libraries maintain, with some justification, that they have all they can manage in dealing with the expressed needs that present themselves at a library desk. Modern professional thinking, however, encourages a new line of thought. During a community study, it is necessary to identify information needs that are unexpressed, perhaps not even consciously known, and also to make clear what citizens have a right to expect from the library. While, at this stage, the library may not as yet have accepted a responsibility to attempt to respond to unexpressed needs, they must be taken into account and their importance as library responsibilities assessed along with that of other, better known and more familiar concerns.

There are several reasons why certain information needs do not find expression, and especially why they do not present themselves at a library desk:

The very need may preclude its recognition: While some people "know that they know not," others "know not that they know not."

The problem may lie in the library or the public's perception of the library. Needs may not be brought there because people are not aware of the library's resources and connections—or what they have a right to expect. Or perhaps the library is not prepared to help because it has not as yet accepted a particular area of need as its responsibility.

This whole area of identifying and taking into account unexpressed needs is a broad one, and sometimes meets with reluctance. In addition to the natural complaint of a small library's staff that it has all it can do to handle the needs that do arise, there is the question whether it is, indeed, the library's business to try to help people with needs they don't even know they have! Expressed this way, the idea sounds presumptuous. In reality, however, most libraries regularly enter this arena. When a display is put up in the library on a topic of local concern, a national election, or a subject of international importance, is not the library staff, in effect, calling the customers' attention to something that is desirable for them to know about and that they might not have thought of on their own initiative? This type of unobtrusive "suggestion" that a customer might need information is similar in purpose and method to displays in stores that remind people of what they might need but may have temporarily forgotten.

The community study, then, should go beyond the simple identification of topics and areas that consciously concern the community. For example, musical groups and performances provide evidence of one of the community's interests, a source of an information need. If the community lacks such groups, the library's community study should note this lack so that, when the total picture is studied, the question of whether the library ought to make an effort to provide a means of addressing this gap can be raised.

The study will search not only for areas of need by subject but also for variations in ability to use information. An information need is not satisfied until the response is understood by the individual with the need. In practical terms, this means that a customer with a literacy problem will not benefit from complicated instructions for repairing the car, a homebound individual will not be able to physically come to the library, or a customer with limited vision will find printed material relatively unusable but will gladly welcome audio works. These illustrations point out that there are barriers that prevent people from easy access to information—barriers that the community study must identify so that library operations and materials can be adjusted to meet the needs of the population.

Methods of Collecting Primary Data

Once secondary data has been secured and the planning team determines that there are still questions about the community that have not been addressed, it is time to collect primary data. The key to effectiveness is a clear understanding of what the planning team needs to know; extraneous questions about what might be interesting to know only serve to lengthen the survey or interview. Possible elements for questions include

- demographic information
- perceptions of library effectiveness
- usage rate of the library
- reasons for nonuse

- audiovisual equipment presently owned or slated for purchase
- preferred formats and learning styles
- ideas for products and services

Conducting some type of survey is a common method of securing primary data. Sampling methodology is generally used to establish an N (number to be surveyed) of manageable size. Information on how to select a sample, plus tables of random numbers to use as a baseline, can be found in books on elementary statistics. Local expertise from teachers of mathematics or statistics can be utilized by the team. Types of surveys include telephone surveys and mail surveys. Face-to-face interactions are also frequently used as mechanisms for gathering community information. These interactions include interviews, focus groups, and community meetings. It can be useful to combine methods to develop a more comprehensive profile of the community. The local situation and available resources should determine which methods to use.

TELEPHONE SURVEY

Telephone surveys are very popular and involve telephoning a sample of the citizens in the community. The telephone book can be the source of the sample, but this will disfranchise all individuals with unlisted numbers. A local college or university research lab can provide a computer-generated listing of telephone numbers to avoid this problem. A survey document (or interview schedule) needs to be developed, preferably with the assistance of someone trained in questionnaire design. Local schools, colleges, and businesses may be sources of such expertise. Volunteers can be used to staff telephones during a telephone survey, but they need to be carefully trained so that each respondent is asked the same questions in the same way. An advantage of telephone questioning over the mail survey is the opportunity that respondents have to add comments during the conversation with the interviewer. In addition, one strategy for good public relations is a simple question on the part of the interviewer: "Is this a good time to call, or shall we reschedule a call for a later time?"

MAIL SURVEY

The questions in a mail survey tend to be more formally phrased than those presented in other survey formats because there is no opportunity to ask the respondent for clarification. Mail surveys also require a larger sample (N) because the response percentage of this method tends to be quite low. It is absolutely necessary to include a stamped, self-addressed envelope to improve upon this lower response rate.

INTERVIEW

In-person interviews can take place in a variety of settings, such as in the library with library users or out in the community (door-to-door, at the grocery store, etc.). Interviews are very staff/volunteer-intensive, but they also provide unique benefits. For example, attitudes and perceptions may surface that would not have been picked up in a survey. Like those of a telephone or mail survey, interview questions need to be standardized and asked of everyone to provide comparable data.

FOCUS GROUP

A focus group can be viewed as an expansion of the interview. Individuals with some shared characteristic(s) are invited to participate, and under the leadership of a trained interviewer, the questions proceed from the general to the very specific.

COMMUNITY MEETING

Calling a community meeting is probably the least productive means of gathering data. In general terms, the audience for the meeting consists of citizens with vested interests, and the full range of community needs is unlikely to emerge.

Looking Inward

Once the external environment has been analyzed and current and potential trends identified on both micro and macro levels, it is time to turn the audit's spotlight on the library itself. What is the library presently like? Who are the customer groups? What programs and services are offered? What is the size of the budget? of the collection? What outreach or communication efforts are made to extend services into the community? The library's own records and statistics are a treasure of information and must be mined to paint the library's profile. The library's present strengths and limitations must be identified to determine what resources are available to meet identified needs and what resources must be secured.

Doing a SWOT Analysis

One very effective way to structure an examination of the library's internal environment is the SWOT analysis. The acronym stands for strengths, weaknesses, opportunities, and threats. (See figure 3.3.) There are at least two procedures for doing a SWOT analysis:

> After gathering all the available data concerning the library's profile, the planning team places flip chart paper on a wall, one sheet for each category. In discussion, the team members identify elements for each of the four categories, and one person writes these elements on the appropriate sheets.

> After gathering the data, the team members come together and independently use adhesive notes to jot down individual elements. The notes are stuck up on a wall under the *S, W, O,* and *T* categories. Notes can be rearranged and recategorized during the following team discussion.

The major difference between the two methods is that one is done as a "committee of the whole" during discussion and the other is an individual determination that is followed by full-team discussion. The SWOT analysis serves as a comprehensive and very graphic depiction of the library's current status.

FIGURE 3.3

Example of a SWOT Analysis

Strengths	Weaknesses	Opportunities	Threats
Quality of staff	Size of budget	Bond issue for new building	Bond issue doesn't pass
Community support	Lack of space	Conduct community analysis	Potential municipal budget cut
Volunteers	Lack of staff	Begin planning process	Time needed to conduct study
Size of collection	Some outdated materials in collection	Buy new formats	Insufficient funds for new formats
Commitment of library board			

The Study Is Over . . . Now What?

Now that the data gathering is finished and analysis of the results has yielded useful information, it is time for the administrator, the board, and the planning team to step back, reflect on the process of studying the community, and determine how the library best fits into the local environment. This reflection should include such elements as

recognition that the modern library's role has changed and, especially, that the small library can, through referral, offer a wide variety of materials and services

recognition that the library's present customers do not include all segments of the community

acknowledgment that the present collection and staff may not be appropriate to meeting community needs

willingness to consider a change of focus, in both customers and services, to identify unmet needs, formulate clearer objectives, and make the library a more positive community influence

acknowledgment that study of the community—its makeup, interests, occupations, information needs, educational levels, barriers to information access, organizations, and institutions—must be an ongoing process (repeated in a major way every five years or whenever major change occurs in either the external or internal environment)

Through the community study, the library has identified information needs already met or partially met by the library. In addition, outside information sources through referral should have been located. Finally, the study may have suggested unmet needs for information and possible unexpressed needs.

After careful study of the results of the community analysis, the next step is the selection of those needs that the library will attempt to address locally. For each selected need, an analysis of existing resources in the library, including staff skills, may suggest possible goals and objectives, such as more materials, different formats, materials at different levels of difficulty, public programs and meetings, service to groups, service outside the library, staff development, or better lines of communication.

For each identified gap in service, a portion of the library's short- or long-range plan should be developed with goals and objectives that will provide the necessary service. Another possible remedy may be through referral to another community agency or to a library system. This solution requires that the community be made aware of the library's ability to obtain what is not available locally, that the library board and director take whatever steps are necessary to ensure that the library has all connections that will help it to make referrals, and that the staff consider the service of referral as important as direct service.

Creating Goals and Objectives

Goals and objectives become the practical response to what has been learned in the marketing audit. They can be written quickly, or they may take a good deal of time. The process can include much or minimal library review and discussion. The planning team should consider how much time would be needed and how much time is available for the level of effort desired. Since planning is a human activity, it deals in possibilities, contingencies, and change. Effective planning is flexible and adaptable, and choosing a level of effort is one of the most significant ways in which the planning process can be adapted to a particular library's needs, purposes, and resources.[4]

Goals are broadly written statements of intent; they are painted with a "broad brush" so that they can serve the library over a longer span of time. A goal has been defined as "a broad or general statement of desired or intended accomplishment. Its scope is broad and unspecific, and it is usually long-term in nature (two to five years). . . . The statement of goals simply allows a view of the forest instead of the trees."[5]

In all goal-setting exercises, it is imperative that emerging trends be identified so that reasonable and possible goals may be written. As stated earlier, local planning agencies and businesses can be wonderful resources for this type of information. The process of securing such data is valuable in itself, for to foster the necessary "ownership" in planning that will ensure successful implementation, a wide spectrum of individuals need to be involved. Asking for necessary and helpful data is one way to begin nurturing that sense of ownership. Of course, paid and unpaid staff and representatives of different customer groups must also be directly involved as planning proceeds.

Once organizational goals have been developed, it is time to write measurable objectives that will organize the library's resources in the most effective way so that the library moves toward achieving its goals. Since these goals have been written in more general prose, objectives must be specific and measurable. Stated in terms of an expected outcome and written in clear language, objectives are more focused than goals. Well-written objectives are

consistent with the library's goals and other objectives

specific in terms of tasks, results, time, and responsibility

measurable so that ongoing evaluation can easily determine when the objective has been attained

time-specific, stating when the objective is due to be accomplished

responsibility-specific, stating who is responsible for seeing that the work described in the objective has been accomplished

short-term

tied to expenditure of the library's resources

clear, with language that is precise, verifiable, and understandable

designed around action verbs that imply improvement or movement (i.e., "apply, begin, construct, develop, improve, etc.")[6]

In addition, it can be useful to construct parallel sets of objectives addressing each goal, thus placing the library in a proactive, well-thought-out position in the event of change. Sets of objectives should be created that correspond to the following questions:

- What if conditions (economic, societal, political, etc.) remain the same as they are today?
- What if conditions change markedly in a positive direction?
- What if conditions change markedly in a negative direction?[7]

Figure 3.4 illustrates how this approach to goals and objectives can be put into practical, outline form. Set A reflects little environmental impact; B reflects a negative environmental impact; C reflects a positive environmental impact. When objectives are constructed in this flexible, future-oriented way, they become tools that relate closely to changing environments.

After the three sets of objectives have been developed for each goal statement, the next logical step is the formation of specific tasks or action strategies for each objective, the sum of which results in the accomplishment of

FIGURE 3.4

Example of Three Sets of Objectives

GOAL 1: To Provide Internet Workstations for In-library Use	
Objective Set A	1. Purchase three computer workstations for in-library use by fall 200X
	2. Develop a "welcome Internet" party by fall 200X
	3. Develop an Internet literacy program by December 200X
Objective Set B	1. Contact Rotary, Kiwanis, etc., to solicit donation of monies or equipment by fall 200X
	2. Communicate with citizens, indicating benefits of contributing their older computer equipment to the library by fall 200X
	3. Develop a "welcome Internet/thank you" party by fall 200X
	4. Develop an Internet literacy program by December 200X
Objective Set C	1. Purchase six computer workstations for in-library use by fall 200X
	2. Purchase/license assorted software by fall 200X
	3. Develop a "welcome Internet" party by fall 200X
	4. Develop an Internet literacy program by December 200X

the objective. These action strategies that "make it all happen," like the objectives they support, are also written in measurable terms. An important ingredient is the responsibility designation that identifies the person(s) responsible for seeing that each action is accomplished. When actions are written in this manner, it is easy to assess whether and when each action is finished or how close it is to the targeted completion time. Figure 3.5 illustrates how action strategies relate to objective set A from figure 3.4.

Monitoring the Process

The development of goals and objectives can be a staff- and time-intensive activity. Without conscious attention to "staying on track" as the process

FIGURE 3.5

Action Strategies Supporting Objective Set A

Objective	Action Strategies
1. Purchase three computer workstations for in-library use by fall 200X	a. Develop equipment specifications by April 200X [Responsibility: director]
	b. Send out RFPs to vendors by May 200X [Responsibility: director]
	c. Review proposals by June 200X [Responsibility: director, board]
	d. Notify successful vendor and order equipment by July 1, 200X [Responsibility: director]
2. Develop a "welcome Internet" party by fall 200X	a. Appoint party-planning team by June 200X [Responsibility: director]
	b. Raise funds for party by July 200X [Responsibility: party team]
	c. Plan the party by August 200X [Responsibility: party team]
	d. Give the party in October 200X [Responsibility: party team]
3. Develop an Internet literacy program by December 200X	a. Appoint literacy team by July 200X [Responsibility: director]
	b. Plan the Internet literacy training program by September 200X [Responsibility: literacy team]
	c. Produce the training by December 200X [Responsibility: literacy team]

evolves, direction may become misguided or even lost. The planning team needs to carry as part of its charge the responsibility for ongoing monitoring of its efforts so that work remains on target. Questions that may be of use to the planning team include

Are current measurement techniques adequately monitoring the rate of progress toward the objective? Is more data needed?

Is the time line still on target, or is it behind or ahead of schedule? Are changes in the plan being documented as it evolves? Are the expectations of progress still realistic?

Should additional or different strategies be developed?

Are costs running close to original estimates? If not, are other objectives being affected?

Is the objective becoming unrealistic due to new information? Should it be modified or eliminated?

Should new objectives be developed to better achieve particular goals?

Is the objective still relevant to the library's defined role? Have any environmental factors changed?

Is the development of new objectives or goals indicated to meet changing needs?

Should the priority ranking among goals and objectives be revised?[8]

These questions will lead the planning team into discussions and ultimately into decisions regarding the process and its progress. The time and responsibility lines written into each objective and action strategy will make it easy to do the final evaluation. The final evaluation will ask questions such as, "How successful was it?" "Should we do it again?" "What should we do differently?" The next chapter continues this discussion and focuses directly upon a marketing approach to implementing the planning process.

Thoughts for the New Millennium

Do I understand how important a routine planning process is to effective library operations?

Have I appointed a planning team, composed of both staff and customers/stakeholders, to lead the planning effort?

Does my library have both mission and vision statements? Have they been approved by the board?

Have roles and/or service responses been selected to help set priorities of service?

Do I understand that the marketing audit involves analysis both of the community and of the library's assets and limitations? How can I limit the study to a scale that is appropriate to the resources that I have available? What type of data collection would be most reasonable in our community?

Am I willing to take the time to create three parallel sets of objectives? Do I understand how doing so can help me relate to changing circumstances?

Notes

1. Ethel Himmel and William James Wilson, *Planning for Results: A Public Library Transformation Process* (Chicago: American Library Assn., 1998).

2. Bob McKee, *Planning Library Service* (London: Clive Bingley, 1989), 11.

3. Darlene E. Weingand, *Managing Today's Public Library: Blueprint for Change* (Englewood, Colo.: Libraries Unlimited, 1994), 22–3.

4. Charles R. McClure and others, *Planning and Role Setting for Public Libraries: A Manual of Options and Procedures* (Chicago: American Library Assn., 1987), 49.

5. Ching-chih Chen, *Zero-Base Budgeting in Library Management: A Manual for Librarians* (Phoenix, Ariz.: Oryx, 1980), 24.

6. Darlene E. Weingand, *Marketing/Planning Library and Information Services,* 2d ed. (Englewood, Colo.: Libraries Unlimited, 1999), 63.

7. Ibid., 53.

8. Ibid., 130.

4 From Objectives to Customer Service through Marketing

Customer service is the final intent and result of all the library's products—no matter how small the library. While this ultimate output may be temporarily obscured by the day-to-day problems of budget, schedules, and crises, everything done in and for the public library should ultimately contribute to identifying and meeting community needs. Budgeting must be conceived in terms of service—how to best meet the community needs through the resources available. Materials selection, cataloging and classification, building plans—all these operations are designed with service to the community in mind. Certainly, all planning and all administration should be consciously centered on the library's customers. The community study not only focuses attention on this ultimate mission but also provides information that will enable the library to effectively relate its products directly to identified community needs.

What Are the Library's Products?

The public library is a nonprofit organization and, as such, does not offer products specifically for sale (although some libraries do charge fees for such products as duplicate rental collections, audiovisual equipment, and extended online searches). Rather, the products that the library develops are service-oriented and are supported by the finite amount of resources allocated on an annual basis. The range of possible products should evolve from the information gleaned from the marketing audit and, therefore, be designed to meet identified community needs in the most effective way possible.

Philip Kotler, in his *Marketing for Nonprofit Organizations,* has configured the concept of product in terms of three primary definitions:

1. *product mix*—the set of all product lines and items that a particular organization makes available to consumers
2. *product line*—a group of products within a product mix that are closely related, either because they function in a similar manner, are made available to the same customers, or are marketed through the same types of outlets
3. *product item*—a distinct unit within a product line that is distinguishable by size, appearance, price, or some other attribute[1]

For example, a typical public library will have product lines consisting of collection, services, and programs. Some may add one or more product lines, such as a café or a gift shop. The sum of these product lines is termed the *product mix.* Within each product line are numerous product items, such as those illustrated in figure 4.1.

Even in times of declining resources, the librarian has control of this marketing mix and can make adjustments. The following possibilities illustrate this control (but do not reflect any recommendations):

The length of the product mix can be increased beyond the basic product lines of collection, services, and programs by adding a

FIGURE 4.1

The Product Mix

Product Lines	Product Items
Collection	Books, periodicals, films, phonodiscs, audiocassettes, CDs, videos, DVDs, pamphlets, art prints, tools, toys
Services	Circulation, interlibrary loan, reference, homebound access, Internet access
Programs	Story hours, literacy tutoring, tax assistance, art and garden shows, puppet shows, book and video discussion groups
Gift shop	Jewelry, bookmarks, book bags, T-shirts with library logo
Internet café	Internet access, coffee, tea, juices, pastries

food service or a gift shop; it can be decreased by temporarily discontinuing a product line.

The width of the product lines can be increased by adding another format, such as digital disks; it can be decreased by discontinuing a format, such as 8mm films.

The depth of the product items in the collection can be increased by enlarging the numbers within each item (i.e., enlarge a video collection from 50 to 75 titles); the depth can be reduced by an extensive weeding project that results in fewer books, tapes, etc.[2]

These examples of expansion and contraction illustrate the inherent complexity, interrelationships, and fluidity of the simple term: *product.*

How are the library's products determined? What decisions need to be made to develop the most appropriate products? The foundation, once again, is the marketing audit. No decision making can be considered reasonable and realistic, much less effective, without a careful assessment of the internal and external environments in which the library must operate. If the foundation is the marketing audit, then the guiding light is a focus on the library's mission and vision, as codified in its goals and objectives. Focus is the light that illuminates the deliberations of the planning team from the initial discussion of mission, through the setting of goals and objectives, through product design and implementation, and into the creation of promotional strategies. When the planning team is able to focus on the data from the marketing audit and the desired role(s) and image to be projected, then the product design effort is likely to remain on track.

Price: Determining the Cost of Products

Price can be defined as the cost to produce a product. In the profit sector, cost factors are calculated, a profit margin is added, and a price for the goods or services is set based upon those calculations. For nonprofit agencies such as the public library, an inverse approach must be applied: The budget is the known quantity, and all possible products must compete for a share of those funds. In both profit and nonprofit organizations, the cost factors are similar; only the decision-making process differs.

A direct relationship exists between cost factors and the budgeting process. Many municipalities require that a library submit the budget in a line-item format: separate lines for personnel, equipment, materials, and so forth. Even in this situation, it is definitely to the library's advantage if the librarian also creates a program (or product) budget. In a program budget, the costs for each of the library's product items is determined individually, including both direct costs (those personnel, supplies, and other expenses that can be directly attributed to the specific product) and indirect costs. The program budget totals can be directly plugged into the line-item format. For example, once determined, the sum of personnel costs for each of the library's products provides the "personnel" line for the line-item budget. This compilation of product-specific sums can be calculated for each category in the line-item budget. Figure 4.2 illustrates this relationship.

While direct costs can be readily identified and applied to the developing program budget, indirect costs are more difficult to nail down. Indirect costs include the library's expenses for permanent personnel, heating/lighting, rent, utilities, equipment, and so forth. One formula that may be used in an attempt to allocate indirect costs is a calculation based on staff time. Although a "quick and dirty" method, a calculation of how staff use their time can be useful in apportioning indirect costs. To properly ascertain how paid employees spend their time, a time log constructed according to product lines and/or items is used. The data is collected over a sample period of days and weeks that represent typical library staff activity. Every fifteen minutes an observer or the staff member marks the products to which the staff member is presently giving attention. (See figure 4.3 and further discussion in

FIGURE 4.2

The Relationship between a Program Budget and a Line-Item Budget

Line-Item Budget Categories	Program A	Program B	Program C	Totals (to be plugged into Line-Item Format)
Personnel	$10,000	$5,000	$5,000	$20,000
Equipment	3,500	3,000	2,000	8,500
Supplies	1,000	2,500	1,500	5,000
Materials	8,000	7,000	3,000	18,000
Indirect costs	2,000	2,500	2,500	7,000

FIGURE 4.3

Example of a Time Log

Product Lines	Hours Worked (in 15-Minute Segments)												Total
	Hour 1				Hour 2				Hour 3				
Collection	✓		✓	✓	✓								1 hr.
Services		✓							✓	✓			¾ hr.
Programs					✓	✓	✓						¾ hr.
Gift shop													
Internet café											✓	✓	½ hr.

chapter 6.) At the conclusion of the data collection, percentages of staff time vis-à-vis each product are determined. These percentages can then be applied to each indirect cost area and the results used as indirect cost figures for each product item.[3]

Once the cost for each product is determined, decision making can proceed with cost/benefit ratios in mind. High cost products that have low demand generally produce minimal benefits. Conversely, high cost products in high demand may generate considerable benefit and should be carefully analyzed. On the other end of the spectrum, a low cost product with low demand is also worth a careful look because of its low cost to produce. The flip side here is the low cost product with high demand—an obvious "winner." These considerations cannot even be attempted unless costs have been calculated for each existing and potential product, and the setting of product priorities requires this information. Figure 4.4 illustrates the relationship between cost and demand.

Setting Priorities

Chapter 3 listed points to consider following the marketing audit. The actual determination of objectives for any given year (in the operational plan, in support of the long-range plan) should be based on the facts obtained through studying the community but will also involve making choices. All desirable products cannot be implemented at once. Priorities can be identified with the help of the following criteria:

FIGURE 4.4

The Relationship between Cost and Demand

High Cost/High Demand	High Cost/Low Demand
Products for which there is a significant demand and that are expensive to produce	Products for which there is not much demand and that are expensive to produce
Requires a decision	*Target for phase-out*
Low Cost/High Demand	**Low Cost/Low Demand**
Products for which there is a significant demand and that are relatively inexpensive to produce	Products for which there is not much demand and that also are inexpensive to produce
Definitely retain	*Requires a decision*

A need exists that is appropriate for the library to address but it has not yet been met.

A need is within the power of the library to meet directly without extraordinary cost and without requiring so great an expenditure of time and resources that the rest of the library's service will be thrown seriously out of balance.

Some of the resources (interested staff, some materials) are already at hand. If early success can be facilitated, the staff will be encouraged and the community impressed—adding psychological credibility to more difficult endeavors that may be added to the library's product lines at a later time.

Spadework for a product has already been accomplished during the marketing audit, such as identification of a target market and institutions/agencies with expressed interest.

Priority, as used in this chapter, refers to both new and present products designed to meet information needs that the library has identified. These needs may be completely new or those that have not as yet been satisfied. The intent is to merge new products into the total range of products that comprise the normal service pattern or product mix. Each new product must be weighed against products presently being offered. Although it is a difficult exercise for most libraries, all products must be continually analyzed—and those products that have outlived their usefulness should be decreased or discontinued. Figure 4.4, "The Relationship between Cost and Demand," can be helpful when assessing the effectiveness of products; each present and potential product should be assigned to one of the four quadrants. Priority setting can be a challenging activity, but with identified community needs as a guide, the challenge is well worth the effort.

The following case studies illustrate the process of applying marketing principles to specific target markets. The key to understanding any target market is an awareness that service is an individual matter, and that the characteristics of a group cannot be applied across the board. These examples are only two of many target market priorities that a library may consider. They illustrate, however, some of the ways a library can implement a product priority once it is established.

CASE STUDIES

A. Target Market: Older Adults

Older residents have been located through the community study; community agencies and institutions have responded with interest to our questions and indicated a desire to cooperate. Potential volunteers have also been identified and are interested in responding to this need.

We might begin the product development process by considering the senior group as two target markets—those able to come to the library and those to whom service would have to be taken.

The first group is served to some degree by traditional library service, but the community study has highlighted additional and unique needs for this customer group. However, only a portion of older adults is served by traditional service patterns, and any information that predates the community study typically portrays a common denominator. We should not forget that the individuals who do not fit into the common profile, and whose needs may therefore differ, may not wish to use our services. In the senior years, this group may include such persons as a retired professor, the foreign-born spouse of a former armed services member, or an older—but still performing—musician. Some of the identified needs will have to be met through cooperation with other community agencies; others will be satisfied by services and materials given at the library.

Submarket #1: Mobile Older Adults

PRODUCT DESIGN

If we determine that our first-priority effort with older citizens will be to improve service to those able to physically come to the library, then we must first pay attention to the characteristics common to this age group: a wish for comfort, convenient hours, sociability, a slower pace of interaction, and a friendly atmosphere. Some elderly customers will want large-print materials or books on tape. Others will want older books of a type read in earlier days. Daytime film or video programs are often popular, and materials are often available from a film circuit or a library system. We can plan some group activities especially for this age group, but all activities need not segregate them from other customers as long as we keep in mind the unique needs of older adults. We could also waive fines for senior citizens.

Submarket #2: Nonmobile Older Adults

PRODUCT DESIGN

We may place serving nonmobile older adults as a secondary priority and design products that use volunteers to provide materials and deposit collection services to the homebound.

Institutionalized people or people served by regular programs of another organization are known to other professionals who can provide information and help. If we serve these customers regularly, for example, through a visit to a nursing home once every two weeks, they become known as individuals, and we can more easily identify their needs and wishes. We could place small deposits of materials at off-site locations; these should reflect customer tastes and be changed at regular intervals.

The cumulative effect in such service is far superior if we can have the same person served regularly by the same library staff member (paid or unpaid). The training of unpaid volunteer staff will take some of the time of our regular staff members.

PLACE/DISTRIBUTION

The designed products will not reach our target customers unless we include appropriate distribution and communication channels as part of our overall design. Distribution will be as important a component in our overall product as the specific service itself.

Physical facilities and issues of access will be important considerations for mobile older adults. Even for this physically fit group, effective distribution may include moving materials to locations more convenient to everyday life patterns, such as to shopping malls or social centers, or even providing electronic access.

Distribution to homebound customers may be limited by the availability of volunteers or cooperative arrangements with institutional facilities. However, electronic or mail access may be workable with this group.

PROMOTION/COMMUNICATION

Promotion may be distributed through agencies already in touch with members of these target markets, but we must make an effort, as well, to reach those not served by those agencies. Follow-up publicity from the community study will provide an excellent opportunity for stories in the general newspapers or for radio or television interviews. This publicity should stress not only group-type activities but also our services and materials. We can print or duplicate promotional literature for posting or pickup at churches, supermarkets, banks, and medical offices (where older adults regularly visit). The key here is to use a channel for communication.

EVALUATION

Evaluation is a two-part activity: (1) monitoring the product design and documenting progress and decision making, and (2) assessing whether the objectives have been realized and analyzing the outcomes in terms of excellence and benefits. We can make measurement of outcomes both objective and subjective, including participant counts, interviews, and observation.

For our services to nonmobile adults, actual circulation counts are not usually practical and, if attempted, are likely to be unreliable; therefore, personal visits are more effective and can be much more easily evaluated.

B. Target Market: Small Businesses

Specialized service extended by larger libraries to small businesses calls for expensive reference tools and journals and is thus beyond our budget. However, there are some useful and appreciated services that can be undertaken for this important element of our community.

Our community study has identified our local major companies and small businesses. If our study has not adequately identified the specific needs of these firms and their employees, finding out may take a little detective work, especially if the proprietors and managers are not accustomed to turning to us for information. When patronizing these businesses as customers, our staff (especially the employee who has the responsibility for this new service) should become alert to possible information needs.

PRODUCT DESIGN

Some subjects of interest will be obvious and within the scope of what we can reasonably provide: information on merchandise display, personnel supervision, some tax regulations, strategies for effective management, and budgeting and fiscal control.

Most small businesses will use the directories of manufacturers and distributors if they know that they are here; they will call to inquire about the manufacturer of a product with a given trade name if they realize that we can supply this information. If our budget does not permit purchase of these directories, we can seek last year's edition from larger libraries in our area.

The large manufacturing plant in town has a personnel manager who can inform us of internal training programs for employees or areas in which our materials might help individuals prepare for promotion.

To provide this product, part of a staff member's time must be devoted to business service. We must give attention to preliminary community work, development of the business collection, provision of reference service (including telephone reference), training other staff in the use of special business materials, and publicizing the service. Our library system may have a specialist on board who can advise and assist. In addition, through the system, we can access business magazines, indexes, and directories that are beyond our budget.

PLACE/DISTRIBUTION

This outreach will take time and effort initially, but it can move forward as a regular library product without too much special effort once our staff is familiar with the service and it is used and accepted by the business community. Distribution strategies should include SDI, the provision of timely and targeted information to meet identified needs before the request is even made. In other words, if we know that business A is struggling with personnel problems, we can gather and provide various materials on successful personnel practices.

PROMOTION/COMMUNICATION

Communication with this target market must take place on the customer's own "turf." Library staff should belong to organizations such as the chamber of commerce and Rotary and should regularly attend the meetings. In addition, staff should develop personal contacts with small-business employees—this can make the difference between so-so service and truly effective service.

EVALUATION

Checks of circulation of business titles, use of business journals, telephone calls from firms, and in-person reference questions in the field can be valuable indicators of success.

The chief points for those involved with product design to remember include:

1. Do not attempt too ambitious a program that will collapse under its own weight.

2. Do not attempt to implement all the top priority objectives and attendant products at once.
3. Plan ahead, giving attention to publicizing the product where potential customers can be reached and trying to evaluate results—but without overburdening or irritating customers.
4. As a product succeeds, continue it as a normal activity and move on to other priority objectives and products to which extra time and effort may be devoted. For example, volunteers or a cooperating agency or club might take over a service, enabling the service to require only minimal supervision.
5. Give a product ample time to catch on. The public is not as aware of changes as the library staff—it may take longer than expected for word to reach the target group.
6. However, if after a genuine effort and adequate trial period, results are minimal, do not continue to expend time and money on an effort that is not working. Try to find out why not, and correct the situation. Use more and better publicity, or move on to another, more hopeful priority, unless this effort is so important that it must be continued even with meager results. If this is the case, perhaps expectations were too high and need to be made more realistic.

Levels of Service

There is no reason to suppose that the identification of new needs and priorities will cause the library to cease serving its existing customers, and it is a mistake if outreach to new customers decreases services to faithful and frequent customers. The challenge is to relate all priorities to a corresponding level of service. The phrase *levels of service* refers to both priorities and the amount of effort required. In case study A, service to less mobile older adults, although a secondary priority in the example, may well have demanded a higher level of effort initially until it was well in place. In very general terms, the following definitions of service levels can be used:

Level 1 is a minimum level of service, such as the availability of the library for browsing and checking out materials.

Level 2 is a moderate level of service, often termed "normal," in which library services are available to those who seek them out.

Level 3 is a higher level, in which library outreach is weighed in equal measure with in-house use.

Level 4 is still higher, as library personnel become actively involved in local community affairs, serving on committees and boards and seeking out information needs.

Level 5 is the highest level, in which advocacy is standard practice, as library personnel not only engage in referral but also in follow-up to ensure that the need has been met.

Level 5+ is an expanded level, generally available only in large libraries, in which in-depth service that involves large quantities of time is offered on a cost-recovery basis.

Levels of service can be regarded as a continuum, and, hopefully, librarians' aspirations will seek to move ever closer to the level 5 end of that continuum. However, at all levels the quality and depth of service depends on the amount of staff involvement in the effort to make materials useful to the customer. Even at the lowest level—where materials are provided, shelved, and listed and where the customer selects and finds his or her own choices and makes use of the staff only for the mechanics of circulation— the staff is realistically involved beyond the circulation function: Behind the appearance of the materials are the selection, ordering, cataloging, and preparation needed to make materials available. Some library customers prefer such minimum service; they want to do their own searching and make their own selections, even when additional service is available. For the benefit of these independent customers, the library must make sure that the collection is well organized so that self-service will be successful.

How far the library will go in levels of service depends on its objectives and on its resources, especially its staff. Some of the staff activities that can be plugged into the various levels of service include

helping customers find specific materials

teaching customers to use the catalog and simple reference sources

advising customers on current selections

looking up factual information for customers

assisting customers with selections on a long-range, planned basis

preparing lists of selected materials from which customers can make their own choices

engaging in more- or less-complex searches for information or material on a subject

preparing individual learning courses or complex bibliographies

The first four staff activities listed will surely continue to be given to all customers. The only conceivable difference in service to the customers may relate to what is available. For example, if priority objectives have reduced somewhat the ability to purchase a variety of popular materials, the following suggestions may help the situation:

more paperback copies of popular titles

more leasing of popular materials, thus supplying copies during periods of popularity without having to keep them (This practice also reduces time spent on withdrawals and physical preparation. Too much of the budget, however, should not go to leased collection supplements.)

long-term loans of popular materials from the system to the local library or through a swap arrangement with other system members

The more-specialized types of levels of service listed may not be requested frequently (perhaps because customers are not aware of the possibility) and need not necessarily be regarded as too time-consuming. For example, the time spent on the preparation of lists of materials may ultimately result in reduced time spent on individual service in the case of a general list of popular reading or on a topic of current interest (e.g., genealogy). A list can also, of course, be made especially for the use of a target market. The makeup of a community will determine how much self-service customers can be expected to prefer. A well-educated customer, familiar with the arrangement of the library, may not normally need much help in selecting materials, although reference service may be required. On the other hand, children will need more help, and a segment of the community less familiar with the library may well require additional attention.

The value and quality of service will depend on the collection and, more specifically, on the staff's knowledge of the library's resources. To give good advisory service or to give good reference and information service, a staff member must be familiar with the library's holdings. The staff member must also know how to ascertain a customer's tastes and interests and how to make professional knowledge available to the customer in a way that will be both accepted and welcome.

While this discussion has thus far centered on activities occurring within library walls, increasing types of service are being extended out into the community, including informing the community of the library's resources via newspaper, radio, television, and other media

discussing materials and services at community meetings

setting up displays at meetings

leading or assisting discussion or reading groups

offering programs in which library books, videos, or recordings are used, either directly or indirectly

either independently or as cosponsor with one or more community organizations, offering lectures, panels, and other meetings on topics of local, national, or international interest and concern

offering SDI service, particularly to funders and opinion leaders

Some of these services may take place in the library; others take the resources of the library out into the community. All are truly library service if the library is trying to fulfill its role as its community's information center. For each priority service, as well as for each objective accepted as relevant to the current year, the library must consider the segment of the community to be reached, its characteristics and needs, and then determine the best way to provide the type of information needed. All formats and delivery systems should be part of the consideration process.

In some cases, when the resources of the library are taken into the community (as to a meeting as part of a display), it can be good public relations to have a means by which circulation can take place on the spot. In this situation, interested people, library materials, and a library staff member are all together—although not inside the library building. Much can be accomplished, in terms of access and convenience, if the materials can be put into customers' hands immediately.

Public Relations as a Service Function

Although the promotion/communication function was mentioned earlier, the "umbrella" of public relations—the library's relations with its publics—deserves special mention. Making known the library's resources is an important part of service. The community that provides a library building, a library staff, and a collection of materials has no library service unless building, materials, and staff are *used.* If the library simply exists, to be used by those who seek it out, and makes no effort to tell the citizens about the facilities they own and the services and benefits to which they are entitled, the community's investment is not being used to the fullest.

Occasionally, public officials are dubious about any attempt to publicize library service, since it is a public resource. They may feel that it is not ethical for public servants to spend public money in the effort to increase the use of their own services. Basically this reaction arises from uncertainty about the importance of the public library's function—in actuality and in the community's estimation. No one questions the necessity of stimulating—in fact, requiring—the full use of public schools. Health services are normally publicized widely, with the full approval of all. Is it not an indication that the library is not felt to be essential, that library service is thought of as a luxury when the obligation of the library to encourage the fullest possible use of its resources is brought into question?

If the library is faced with official disapproval of publicity, its first public relations job is with the officials themselves. To succeed here, the librarian must make sure that the library is giving a type of service that entitles the library to be thought of as essential. Next comes the challenge of clarifying in the minds of officials the library's true mission and role(s). Ways of working toward this goal include the following:

Emphasize in the budget presentation the mission, roles, goals, and objectives of the library. Highlight the priorities of service relative to the documentation of community needs. Make benefits and results the keystone of this presentation.

Offer invitations to officials to visit the library. When they can observe people using the library's services, it is much more impressive than any number of statistics. Some libraries organize monthly breakfasts (or other activities) for local community leaders to foster communication and visibility.

Offer and give library service (especially SDI) to the officials in connection with their work needs as well as personal interests. If a stakeholder believes that the library is personally essential, it is far more likely that positive political votes and support will follow.

Emphasize the informational and educational aspects of library use in the annual report; present it so that it is attractive, interesting, and easy to read. Include photos, humor, and graphics to create a more "user friendly" document. Here, again, focus on benefits and results to effectively present the library's case.

A library that has developed community-centered objectives will probably make changes in the direction of its promotional activities. While continuing, on a modest basis, general publicity about the library's services, the library will also develop a promotional component for each of its products and thus aim directly at the part of the community that it wishes to reach. If the library must sacrifice some aspect of its current publicity work, the effort least likely to reach out to the community is that of elaborate in-house displays. While such displays clearly can stimulate potential interests in seasonal materials, they should continue to be highlighted but be prepared simply, without requiring inappropriate amounts of staff time. Instead, the setting of new priorities may make it urgently necessary to reach the target population(s) through the media and other methods most likely to be noticed by those markets. Radio, special newspapers, religious institutions, clubs and lodges, unions, medical offices, grocery stores, and other potential promotional sites will naturally serve as channels through which the library's message can best reach the target audience(s).

The baseline for public relations, however, rests in people-to-people interaction. A friendly smile, a willing attitude, a desire to "go the extra mile"—these are resources beyond price.

Staff Attitudes toward Service

In developing and expanding the library's range of products and services, the librarian needs the wholehearted support and cooperation of the staff. Staff attitudes, as well as the service pattern, may need to be broadened. Staff members who have been accustomed to giving limited service may need the new sense of excitement and challenge that comes from trying to find, somewhere in the collection, the exact piece of information a customer needs. Becoming more fully acquainted with the collection, learning to talk with the customer to tactfully learn about needs and reading ability (the reference interview), reaching out into the community to give service, presenting library-sponsored programs, offering to obtain for the customer what is not available locally, and being an advocate for the customer in a referral situation—these aspects of library service may seem strange to some staff members if their experiences have not prepared them to take so active a role in providing service. Staff meetings, staff participation in planning and carrying out the objectives, the librarian's genuine enthusiasm, and the response of the public to the library's expanded service will help to kindle a matching spark in the staff, without whom the expanded program cannot succeed.

A staff accustomed to considerable busywork may honestly question the expansion of service on the grounds that there is no time for additional activities. The librarian owes it to the staff to arrange time for new responsibilities and not to assume too readily that time would be found if the staff were really interested. It is better to enlist the cooperation of the staff in gaining the necessary time through work simplification, use of labor-saving devices and equipment, and examination of routines for possible elimination of some duties. During this period of self-study, the librarian should stress the library's basic objectives against which each aspect of the work will be measured for its contribution. For the staff, the result of the joint effort toward efficiency and effectiveness will be a better understanding of goals and priorities, as well as improved work methods. For the librarian, there may well be a deeper appreciation of the actual work accomplished by the staff, a better understanding of the time required even by simplified routines, and a more realistic assessment of the time available for the new range of products. Finally, as stated earlier, there is no substitute for cheerful and helpful staff, and any measures that can be taken to foster a sense of team play and customer-centered service will earn many public relations dividends for the library and its objectives.

Thoughts for the New Millennium

What products does my library offer to my community? Are these the most appropriate products? How do we know? Do they meet identified community needs? Should other products be considered?

Do I know how much each product costs to provide? Am I including both direct and indirect costs?

Have I assigned each product to one of the four cost/demand categories? Are there products that should be phased out?

Would the concept of "levels of service" be useful in my library? Would additional customer groups be served? How would I implement such a strategy?

What outreach efforts are presently in place? To which groups of customers? What are ideas for other outreach activities?

How can my library's relationship with the community be improved? What strategies can I try to make the library more important in the lives of stakeholders?

Are the library's objectives written in language that is customer- and community-centered? If not, how can they be rephrased?

What attitudes are being expressed by my paid and unpaid staff? By me? How could/should these attitudes be improved?

Notes

1. Philip Kotler, *Marketing for Nonprofit Organizations,* 2d ed. (Englewood Cliffs, N.J.: Prentice-Hall, 1982), 289.
2. Darlene E. Weingand, *Marketing/Planning Library and Information Services* (Englewood, Colo.: Libraries Unlimited, 1999), 86-7.
3. Further explanation and a sample time log can be found in Weingand, *Marketing/Planning Library and Information Services,* 108.

5 Policies

Policies are those statements, regardless of length, that articulate the library's position on matters of philosophy and operations. Policies differ from objectives and from rules and procedures. *Objectives* are measurable statements of intent that, when completed, move the library closer to one of its goals; *rules and procedures* are those detailed operations that implement the intent of policy statements. While policies may be written by the library administrator, who is generally a source of informed recommendation for new or changed policies that grow out of day-to-day administration and constant contact with the public, policies must be approved by the library board. Even when that body acts solely in an advisory capacity, it is commonly consulted before major policy decisions are made.

Library board members should consider carefully each policy before it is adopted and recorded; once adopted, a policy should have the support of the entire board, the librarian, and the staff. It is the board's moral obligation to stand behind the librarian in carrying out policies. If the relevant written policy can be cited, reactive decisions can be avoided and crises are much less likely to occur. Policy making is essentially the making of decisions that fall between the planning process and day-to-day rules and regulations. Since policies are decisions made to implement plans, policy should follow, not precede, planning.

Thoughtfully developed, formally adopted written policies are essential to effective library operations. Reviewed annually and revised as necessary, they are guidelines that assist the library in fulfilling the roles/service responses selected for meeting the needs of the community. Many library boards create a loose-leaf policy manual that can be easily revised and updated.

The contents of this manual are categorized and numbered (e.g., Section 2: Personnel; Policy 2.1: Annual performance review). As each policy is adopted or revised, it should be dated so that trustees are always aware of the last date of review, and if necessary, the board can go back to the relevant set of board meeting minutes to review the previous discussion.[1]

Sometimes, there is confusion as to the difference between policies and related rules and procedures. In general terms, policies are broadly written statements that set the parameters for service; procedures and rules are specifics that spell out in detail how a policy will be carried out. (See figure 5.1.)

FIGURE 5.1 Sample Policy Sets

A. Service Outlets			
Goal	**Policies**	**Rules**	**Procedures**
To offer library service to the entire community at convenient locations	1. Some type of service outlet will be available within a half-hour's drive of every resident.	1. Bookmobiles will serve outlying areas more than thirty miles from another service outlet.	1. Concentric circles indicating miles will be drawn on a map of the service area.
	2. No bookmobile stops will be made within a half-hour's drive of the main library so that more people living at a distance may have bookmobile service.	2. Bookmobiles will remain at each stop for a total of two hours.	2. During good weather, bookmobile doors shall remain open.

B. Meeting Room Use			
Goal	**Policies**	**Rules**	**Procedures**
To make the library's meeting facilities available to the entire community free of charge whenever possible	1. Any organization willing to abide by the library's rules may book the library's meeting room for a meeting, on a first-come, first-served basis.	1. The library's own meetings, both for staff and the public, will be given priority in meeting room booking.	1. Maintain a booking system.

B. Meeting Room Use (continued)

Goal	Policies	Rules	Procedures
	2. All meetings must be open to the public.	2. If a meeting lasts beyond the library's normal closing time, necessitating overtime for the custodian, a fee will be charged.	2. Implement fee schedules.
	3. For free use of the facility, no collection may be taken or admission charged; if charges are made, the organization must pay the appropriate fee according to the library's fee schedule.	3. Rooms must be left neat; kitchen facilities, if used, must be cleaned.	3. Enforce a penalty system for noncompliance

C. Holidays

Goals	Policies	Rules	Procedures
1. To make library service available to the community at convenient times	1. The library will be closed on New Year's Day, Memorial Day, July 4, Labor Day, Veteran's Day, Thanksgiving, and Christmas.	1. Staff will share holiday duty.	1. A rotating schedule for staff duty on holidays will be established at each library location.
2. To seek and employ competent staff members, and to endeavor to retain those who prove effective	2. The library will be open on certain minor holidays; staff on duty on such holidays will be given compensatory time.	2. Compensatory time will be taken when the staff member can be spared.	2. Application for compensatory time shall be at least 24 hours in advance.

In these examples, the mix of policies, procedures, and rules is called a "policy set" that is articulated relative to the library's goals. (Policy set A in figure 5.1 applies only to those small libraries that serve a large geographic area.)

Policy sets should be viewed more as guidelines than as statements engraved in stone. Frontline staff need to be empowered to make on-the-spot decisions regarding policies, rules, and procedures in the light of customer circumstances.

Policies, then, need to be accompanied by appropriate rules and procedures to ensure that the policies are executed. Policy development is the focus of this chapter; rules and procedures are developed locally in the process of implementing policies. Some areas in which policies are necessary, or at least advisable, are

qualifications of the director and the method of searching for one

charges for service: fines, fees

outlets and hours of service

contracts with other libraries; system membership

personnel policies, including language concerning equal employment, affirmative action, qualifications, paid and unpaid leaves, salaries and benefits, hiring and termination

materials selection

services to specialized groups

services to nonresidents

meeting room use

public relations and publicity

payment for continuing education, conferences, memberships in associations

Policies should be written and clearly stated. Since they serve as public relations tools, policies should provide a firm foundation for the administration of the library and should support the relationship of the staff with the public. Policies should be readily available so that they are clearly understood, both internally by staff and externally by customers. Except where details are necessary, such as hours open and salary ranges, library policies should be expressed in broad terms and must rest upon the legal basis of laws applicable to the operation of the library.[2]

Changes in Policy

Policies are made and implemented by rules and procedures to carry out the library's goals and objectives. Lengths of loans, for example, are related to the size and nature of a library's collection. A small, struggling library in the collection-building stage may have to shorten loan time and restrict the number of loans made so everyone has reasonable access to the library's materials. Similarly, if staff time for a special service must be limited, this policy is made only so that the staff may serve everyone more equitably. A danger of proliferation of policies and of the rules and procedures that implement them is the development of a reputation as an overly rigid library. It is easy to give an impression of repressiveness to the public at large when, as it appears to customers, the library is constantly saying no.

Three precautions may help the library avoid this unfortunate reputation. First, the staff must not only *know* the policies but also the *reasons for them.* With this knowledge as a foundation, the staff must also take sufficient time to explain clearly (and consistently) why *Who's Who* may not be borrowed for a week for a research project, or why the fourth grade teacher may not take all the books on dinosaurs for six weeks, or why the company compiling a mailing list must use the city directory in the library.

Second, *exceptions* to rules and regulations may (and must) be made when a genuine reason exists and an unfortunate precedent is not likely to be established. For example, in a small community a responsible customer, known to the staff, who asks to take the atlas late in the evening and promises to return it early the next morning may be given permission—with the understanding that the book will indeed appear at opening time. However, "responsible" and "known to the staff" should not be interpreted as meaning an elite or favored clientele. Another example: If a policy about the display of local artists' works in the library requires that a jury of experts from a museum pass on the quality of the work, an exception could certainly be made in the case of art by developmentally disabled children or senior citizens that is presented as a group by a local human service agency. The key point to remember is that policies are guidelines and are not engraved on stone tablets. Where exceptions genuinely exist, such as the forgiveness of overdue fines because the customer had been ill, good public relations mandates that good judgment be exercised.

Third, and most important, policies and the accompanying rules and procedures should be *reviewed periodically.* Outdated policies may be enforced by a staff that had no part in creating them and has no idea why they were ever made. Sometimes there is still a good reason for a policy, procedure, or rule; in that case, review reaffirms the existing document(s). But, in many cases, the need for the policy will have disappeared. "Only two new books per customer" may no longer make sense now that the library's budget has improved or now that the library is using a rental service to supplement its new books.

Policy Making

Actual preparation of policy statements will probably begin with the administrator or library staff. Although a trustee or a citizen may initiate the process, it is more common that a matter needing a policy decision will be known first to the library staff. In some cases, it may be discussed in a staff meeting, and staff agreement is reached; in other situations, the library administrator may be the initiator. The next step is preparation of a tentative policy statement for board approval. If the matter is one of major importance and some complexity, such as a policy for Internet use, the board should give the administrator time to explain the reasons behind the recommendations and also allow time for full discussion. More than one meeting, or even a special meeting, may be required for really significant policy decisions.

When a citizen or trustee initiates a policy discussion and the board reaches agreement on the need for such a policy, the actual drafting of the statement is usually turned over to the librarian, who brings a draft to a later meeting for final approval. Sometimes a policy, even a very important one, can be adequately recorded in the minutes of the board meeting. Every such decision, however, should be officially recorded in some fashion. Approved longer policy statements should be filed as addenda to the minutes of the meetings at which they were officially adopted. Policy matters discussed but not approved should also be recorded.

The formulation of written policies has great value in clarifying issues and, if properly used, permits a good deal of delegation of authority. The library director may, within formulated policies, go ahead on programs without constantly checking with the board for approval. Similarly, the staff member who has been given responsibility for a particular aspect of service will not find it necessary to defer to the director for so many decisions. Thus, policy statements save time at the supervisory level and develop desirable levels of self-confidence, autonomy, and empowerment throughout the staff. In addition, they enable the staff to give the public a good impression of knowledge, consistency, and efficiency.

Before establishing policies, the board has an obligation to become acquainted with good library practice. The librarian is the chief source of information, but a good librarian will also welcome and stimulate the trustees' desire to learn more about libraries, to visit neighboring libraries (particularly in communities of comparable size and type), to read library literature, and especially to join national and state trustee associations and attend their meetings. In planning for library development, the trustees represent the community. This representation involves accountability in its broadest interpretation. The charge to trustees includes an assurance of efficient operations and fiscal responsibility; however, the ultimate measure is to make sure that the community has the best library service it can reasonably be expected to support—and one that is based upon the identification of community needs.

Today's library differs so much from the libraries that most trustees experienced in their growing-up years and is so much more complex that trustees find their work more varied and difficult than they may have expected. Doing their "homework," therefore, becomes increasingly important. Again, distributing one or more current articles from library literature along with the agenda for each board meeting can be a useful strategy for the continuing education of library trustees.

Establishing Specific Policies

This section focuses on some of the major areas in which policy is commonly required. Some additional areas are more conveniently covered in chapters devoted to related topics.

Materials Selection

One of the most important policy decisions is the one that gives direction to the development of the library's collection. The small library especially, since it must be selective in its use of limited resources, needs a policy that will provide helpful parameters. Librarians, and often trustees as well, will be faced with many questions and not a few pressures: Why do we not have more new books? More mysteries? The books I read as a child? The newest videos? Access to the Internet? One customer may be scandalized by a new novel or video; another will demand the latest racy rental video. The gourmet cook, the genealogy enthusiast, and the stamp collector will all want more than is available on their hobbies; the citizen concerned about disarmament or legislative redistricting, the teacher sending classes for material on science projects, and the advocate for environmental issues will all expect the library to produce material in quantity or depth.

The library that tries to meet these diverse demands without a policy for materials selection is often at a loss. No policy will take the place of an adequate budget in providing a comprehensive collection, but a carefully constructed policy will help the librarian spend wisely what money there is. The policy should ensure the continuous growth of the collection in accordance with the library's defined roles and goals and cover the following points:[3]

purpose and scope of the collection (adult and children's)

Who are the audiences? What will be collected? In what depth? How wide a range of materials? What formats? Will the collection complement/supplement the public schools? Are there cooperative arrangements with other libraries?

types of materials to be purchased, including formats

This is an amplification of the first point, with specific reference to genre, hardcover vs. paperback materials, percentage of materials in each identified format, reference versus circulating, etc.

staff responsibility for selection; use of professional selection tools

Who has responsibility for different areas of selection? What selection tools will be used as resource materials?

basis and method of withdrawing and disposing of materials

Provide a listing of criteria for withdrawing materials, including poor condition, outdated content, superseded works, identified inaccuracies, etc. Provide specific details of methods for handling weeded materials, such as library materials sales open to the public, sale to remainder shops, donation to such sites as a senior citizen facility, or outright trash disposal.

acceptance of gift materials

> Identify any limitations on acceptance of gift materials. Gift materials will usually be accepted with the understanding that the same selection standards will be applied to gift materials as to those purchased, that staff will have discretion in judging what gift materials will actually be added to the collection, and that final disposition of the gift(s) is to be left to the library.

affirmations of intellectual freedom, including the Library Bill of Rights and Freedom to Read Statement

> Include a discussion of the importance of first amendment freedoms and the library's adherence to these principles and the documents to support the policy statement.

referral to a procedure for handling citizen complaints about materials

> Although such a procedure is frequently interpreted in terms of dealing with complaints about materials that are made on grounds of unacceptable content, it should also be a procedure for expressing and resolving public complaints about needed and unneeded items.

The materials selection policy establishes parameters and guidelines for collection acquisition and management. It provides protection for the library's right to select and maintain a collection of materials that represent a wide range of viewpoints and that correlate with diverse learning styles. This protection supports the tenets of intellectual freedom and is the library's staunchest support when challenges occur. While materials selection policies vary a great deal in inclusiveness from library to library, attention is usually given to considerations such as the following eight questions.

1. How much weight should be given to public demand?

Some libraries can only be described as "demand-oriented"—an emphasis defended on the ground that the taxpayer who pays the piper has the right to call the tune. Clarification is needed in the definition of *demand*. Librarians and trustees who plan a policy are right in giving serious thought to the legitimate place of demand in selection. However, is a library meeting its responsibility when it buys enough copies of a best-selling popular novel or the latest "hot" video to meet the expressed current demand—if by doing so it fails to purchase an important reference book, a periodical that will give its readers a deeper insight into world problems, compact discs to reflect the community's purchase of different audio equipment, or other materials that will meet an unexpressed but nonetheless real long-range demand?

As an example, it has been demonstrated historically that great writing finds its audience through the ages, while the briefly popular work reaches its audience for the relatively short period of its popularity. In the long run, more people may read the great work, even though its audience at any one time will be smaller than that of the writing that speaks only to its day. This distinction, translated into terms of practical library procedure, is helpful. Of course, the library cannot buy only great works that will last for generations; it must have books that are important for today as well. The crystal ball has not yet been invented that can identify what materials will have historical longevity. However, a best-selling video or book may last for a very short time and, after a year or two, the duplicate copies bought to meet a short-term demand may be lonely testaments to fickle popularity. The loss of the substantial amount of information that would have been available through the not-purchased materials must be also taken into account as the library walks the tightrope of materials selection.

There are strategies, however, to accommodate perceived temporary demand without totally committing the budget to this end. One such strategy is the lease plan, which enables a library to lease a certain number of popular materials for a year and return them at the end of that year, when the demand has lessened. Another strategy involves creating a complementary rental collection from which duplicate copies of popular materials that are already available through normal reserve procedures can be rented for a week for a nominal charge. This latter mechanism is generally self-supporting and can be a real benefit to those customers who are willing to pay a small fee to avoid a lengthy wait.

Another set of selection criteria may be concerned more with the quality of the materials selected than with the group who will use them. Will some standard of excellence be applied in selection, or will anything that is requested be purchased? There is a view that materials acquired should meet high standards of quality in content and format; emphasis is placed on authoritativeness, factual accuracy, effective expression, significance of subject, sincerity of purpose, and responsibility of opinion. Acquisition of materials that failed to meet these standards would be resisted, regardless of the demand. However, an opposing view holds that the library should not hesitate to purchase a mediocre item that will be used in preference to a superior item that would not. Two libraries of similar size and environment may be very different institutions in terms of philosophy of selection choices and services.[4]

2. Should the library aim for a well-rounded collection?

The term *well-rounded collection* sounds impressive. Many a librarian who conscientiously strives to acquire, in reasonably balanced numbers, the materials in all fields listed in the standard materials selection media feels that he or she is doing the best possible job as a selector. However, another view can be proposed that supports the concept of a community-centered library: Collections that are rich in some fields and sparse (not devoid) in others represent the interests of the community. This type of collection development is on firm ground if the choices are based on a community study and supplemented by a sensitive and documented awareness of changes in public interest. With majority needs addressed, minority needs can be met through system membership, interlibrary loan, contracts among libraries with different collection strengths, and use of statewide resources.

3. What balance should there be between fiction and nonfiction? Between print and audiovisual media?

As there are many subject areas in nonfiction in both print and audiovisual media, the library will ordinarily need to devote a considerably larger proportion of the budget to nonfiction, especially in view of the higher prices of many of these materials. To lay down a hard-and-fast rule or percentage in the policy statement is not usually advisable (or even possible), but the principle of maintaining the nonfiction collection at a comparatively high level should be included. In the past, when libraries were primarily print collections, the percentage of fiction in the average small library's adult collection ranged from about 30 to 40 percent; the larger the total collection, the larger the proportion of nonfiction, as a rule.

However, today's library, with its multiplicity of formats, is in a period of fluidity, and it is difficult to assign percentages. The key to appropriate balance is analysis of the community study data concerning demographic characteristics, information needs, owned or to-be-purchased audiovisual equipment, and preferred learning styles. (Note: The identification of preferred learning styles will also uncover some of the needs of learning-disabled individuals for whom print materials are unusable but who have as legitimate a claim on library services as traditional print-oriented users.) One useful yardstick, however, may still be applied: If 90 percent or more of a library's collection is print resources, a careful reassessment of the community may be warranted to ascertain whether a larger budgetary commitment should be directed to audiovisual formats.

4. How much depth should there be in subject collections?

As the small library cannot ordinarily supply a collection that is well developed in all subject areas, it must contain less on some subjects and more on others. How far can or should it go in providing materials on those subjects it wishes to emphasize (based on the community study)? Are there any subjects for which an attempt to approach full coverage is justified? One such subject would be local history. Anything written about the local community, and much written about the surrounding region and even the state, is normally collected by the local public library. (An obvious rationale is: Who else will do it?) It is often necessary to acquire local materials laboriously and through unusual sources. Official minutes of the municipality, local history (print, oral, and visual), and other unique materials that are community-generated should automatically be part of the library's collection. Even when space is a problem, some solution—even off-site storage—should be worked out with the municipality.

Other special interests of the community, whatever they may be, are usually represented in some depth: agriculture, lumbering, fishing, or other local industry, for example. A local study group, a dramatic or musical organization, or a hobby club interested in local pursuits—geography, rock collecting, hunting, or mountain climbing—will mean that the library needs a fuller collection in the field(s) concerned. Topics of this sort are identified through the community study.

In addition to these fairly obvious emphases, the librarian will do well to keep in mind the needs of the intellectually curious citizens. For this type of customer, the library needs materials that stretch the "muscles of the mind." No collection, however small, should be geared solely to the average intellect. Many citizens will delight in the effort to meet the challenge of more-demanding materials and will come back eagerly for others.

For the same reason, the library should not purchase only the works of tried and true authors, musicians, and filmmakers—a temptation easy to yield to when the budget is small. The small library admittedly cannot make a wide selection of the work of new poets, novelists, dramatists, musicians, and photographers, but it should make a conscious effort to add some new works in each category. In selecting the best products of young and vigorous talents, even though those talents are not yet fully developed or recognized, the library helps to preserve its own vitality.

5. How many materials for different customer groups?

Some libraries attempt to spell out in detail in their policy statement the proportion of the budget to be set aside for materials for children, young adults, or adults; for education, recreation, or information customers; for farmers, small-business people, or independent learners; and so forth. A tentative division is needed, but it should usually be the result of annual planning based on community analysis rather than embodied in a semi-permanent document such as a materials selection policy. The policy statement is one of principle; although it should be subject to periodic review and revised as necessary, it should be general enough and flexible enough to stand for some time, and a statement that needs revision too frequently can scarcely be dignified with the name of "policy." Because the needs of customer groups may change with circumstances and with time—for example, the development of school library service, a change in the demographics of the community from primarily young families to older adults, or the influx of new business or industry to the community—it is usually not wise to include an estimate of exact budget proportions for any one group in the policy statement.

In any apportionment, changes in the local situation must be taken into account and, in any given year, adjustment of the proportions may be necessary to meet unanticipated materials needs for a particular customer group. In addition, the librarian is advised to consider projected as well as current use patterns when making the tentative annual division of funds. If, for example, children now use the library heavily and adults do not, the librarian should not necessarily assign a larger segment of the total budget to children's materials. To do so would be to accept and intensify an already unsatisfactory situation: Less money for adult materials will mean a less-adequate collection, which, in turn, would lead to even less adult use—a downward spiraling pattern. Further, the community analysis process should be used to investigate where adults in the community are presently getting their information: Important intelligence for effective library planning.

Such data results will also address another example, in which citizens presently use the library primarily for print materials with a recreational emphasis. The librarian's investigation of where these customers are seeking information can help to develop strategies that will identify and respond to those information needs rather than happily continue to focus on recreational reading. Finally, if videos (or any new format) were to be added to the collection, it is likely that an entirely new customer group would begin to use the library.

6. What is the library's stand on controversial materials?

Every selection policy statement must include the library's stand on controversial materials. It should affirm the principles of intellectual freedom as represented in the Library Bill of Rights (see appendix A), though it need not be confined to that topic. Although the small library, because of its limited collection size, cannot be expected to have materials representing every shade of opinion on every issue that may be considered controversial, it does have a clear obligation to try to have the best statements it can find of the positions fairly commonly held on issues of importance. It must be impartial in providing campaign biographies of presidential candidates, for example, and in offering material on the various sides of major issues of national or local consequence. This can be a problem for the library in a community in which most citizens have a deep emotional investment in one side of an issue; however, the library's responsibility vis-à-vis the principles of intellectual freedom is clear and needs to be clearly reflected in the selection policy.

Impartiality cannot always mean numerical equality, as materials are not always available in equal numbers. It may be necessary to search for well-defined statements of a position, but impartial representation is essential whether or not numerical equality is possible. The fact that material on current issues quickly becomes dated creates another problem. Pamphlets and periodical articles can often provide better coverage than longer works, which are somewhat out of date even on publication day if they deal with rapidly changing situations.

Other materials that may be controversial are items (in any format) that refer explicitly to sex or violence or that contain language that some people consider unacceptable. Some citizens find such materials offensive, and some believe them to be dangerous for others (although not necessarily for themselves). Some librarians share these beliefs and cautiously avoid such purchases—a form of precensorship that is ethically inconsistent with tenets of intellectual freedom. In considering potential purchases that may be viewed with disfavor, the librarian must distinguish between items created primarily for the sake of sensation and the work of serious authors/musicians/filmmakers who have something to say and use shock value as an artistic mechanism.

There is a variation among generations in their attitudes toward topics and expressions that were taboo in earlier times. By and large, the younger generations are more accustomed to free discussion of all sorts of topics and to the use of words that make their elders shudder. However, this is a huge generalization, and taste in literature, music, and art cannot be definitively linked to specific age groups. Since the library serves all its citizens, it must assess and attempt to satisfy the needs of a spectrum of customers. Materials exhibiting both conservative mores and franker attitudes are worthy candidates for inclusion in the collection; quality of the work can be a useful yardstick in making these difficult decisions.

7. How should gift materials be handled?

While day-to-day handling of gift materials will be delegated to the staff, there are policy implications for the board to consider.

Public relations aspects Donors tend to take for granted that their gifts will be added to the library and tend to demand explanations if this does not occur. However, not all gifts are appropriate, either in terms of content or physical condition; further, adding a gift entails a certain amount of processing expense. The policy statement should contain a clear indication of the library's right to dispose of gift materials it cannot use.

Special handling requests Donors of gift collections and of memorial gifts may ask that their donations be given special treatment—a glass case, for example. From the library's viewpoint, such special treatment may create problems of location and use. It separates gift materials from others on the same subject and thus reduces their usefulness as a working part of the library's collection. Even beautiful and expensive memorial gifts should be accessible; otherwise, the library cannot afford to house them. Many libraries identify memorial gifts by means of a special bookplate that names both the donor and the person in whose memory the material is given.

Criteria for gift acceptance Normally, items that do not meet the criteria for purchase will not be accepted as gifts. There will be occasional exceptions to this general rule, as in the case of expensive items that the library would like to own but cannot purchase because of their cost. At times, however, a valuable and unusual collection from a hobbyist or scholar might be of more use in another library; when such a gift is offered, the local library should make every effort to find a more appropriate recipient for the donor.

Special viewpoints in gift materials Sincere proponents of various causes or beliefs may offer the library quantities of materials espousing their special viewpoints. The library can use only a small proportion of such material. The policy statement must reiterate the library's need for balance regarding matters of opinion and the resulting need to add only representative statements rather than many items on any side of an issue.

The materials selection policy statement, or a summary of its contents, is often printed or duplicated and kept at service desks for distribution to would-be donors. Sensitive donors will see that a refusal represents a general policy and not merely a negative response to individual offerings, a fact that makes it easier for the person at the desk to deal with the situation and steer any queries or complaints to the director.

In addition, it is most important that the statement make clear the library's appreciation of gifts that it can use and their contribution to the community. None of the donor problems previously noted should overshadow this note of thanks. Some language recognizing the good intentions of those offering gifts that cannot be accepted is also a worthy addition to procedure statements.

8. How should the library dispose of unneeded materials?

Disposing of withdrawn materials poses problems of a practical nature and occasionally creates a difficult public relations situation. The presence of apparently useful library books in a public dump or awaiting destruction at an incinerator has given many a librarian a bad time with indignant officials and taxpayers. The first step toward solution of the problem is investigation of the materials' legal status. Library materials are public property and, as such, may be subject to special regulations. Second, the board must understand the need to weed and to include language in the materials selection policy that recognizes the importance of weeding and of the orderly disposition of materials that are no longer useful.

All materials that are removed from the collection should be clearly marked to show that they have been withdrawn from the library. Such materials may be sold, given away, or discarded. If selling is a legal possibility, the library may have periodic bargain sales at which the public may obtain materials at a modest cost, usually a fixed per-piece price regardless of the original cost. A Friends of the Library group is frequently the organizer of such periodic sales, and the proceeds are either returned to the library's coffers or kept in the Friends' control until a decision is made at a later date to purchase equipment or materials, sponsor staff development, finance a community study, and so forth. Other disposal alternatives include selling weeded materials to used-book, record, or video dealers; giving still-usable materials to a hospital or other charitable institution with the understanding that the recipient may dispose of them in any appropriate way; or giving requested books to a state library agency or libraries abroad.

The library that is a system member may also be able to share usable discards with other members. The small community's library frequently has materials that have served their purpose locally and that may be new to a neighboring library. Through the system, such discards can be accumulated in a central stockpile from which any member may select what is desired. Thus, the library, while ensuring that its own usable discards are put to good use, may also obtain a return in kind.

Regardless of the method(s) of disposal tried first, there may still be some materials that must be destroyed. Any public criticism of such destruction may be lessened if the librarian can explain that they are the residue left after the disposition of usable discards for reuse.

Hours of Service

Determining adequate and reasonable hours of service is a challenge in any size community. Since service is its business, the library should be open when service is needed. Yet the costs of long hours are high: There are expenditures for staff and utilities, and there are personnel issues affecting recruitment, retention, and morale of staff.

The small-business owner faces a similar, though not identical, problem: The cost of keeping a store open for the occasional customer is not affordable, and careful determination must be made of customer use patterns. The library, as a public service agency, does not look at its schedule in terms of profit and loss, but the librarian can and should attempt to develop a schedule that serves the total public best, given the library's resources of money and staff. If the staff serving the heavy public demand during rush periods is inadequate because some personnel have been shifted to hours when relatively few use the library, total service suffers; many customers may be unserved or poorly served so that a few may be served at their convenience.

Time checks of circulation and library use and study of community habits and leisure time will help the librarian make the appropriate decision regarding hours of service. The library should be open, and adequately staffed, long enough to be available to everyone in the community at convenient times. This includes those individuals who might work nonstandard shifts at a local manufacturing plant or hospital. If there is insufficient staff, more should be sought. This is where demonstration of mutual benefit is critical to the future of the library in the community.

In a one-person library, the librarian and whatever unpaid staff (volunteers) or student pages are available constitute the entire library staff. In this situation, hours of service are likely to be very limited, and creativity needs to be used to provide adequate service. A scenario could be written where the library *system* agrees to provide round-the-clock service, with member libraries open at assigned periods throughout all twenty-four hours. Another model could be operated by the state library agency with an "after hours" telephone number that can be called when local libraries are not open. Yet another local option could be access via cable television, computer, or telephone connections. Even in the tiniest town, police and fire protection (often volunteer) is available at any time through an on-call arrangement; the local library staff, too, could wear pagers or be available through some other communication pattern or device. If, indeed, the library is to be considered as essential to community well-being as those other services, limited hours of service cannot be considered.

Fines and Fees

The charging of fines for overdue materials is so much an accepted part of library tradition that it is usually taken for granted. A few libraries, however, have reported successful results in charging no fines at all. Librarians who believe in the no-fine philosophy contend that customers who want to keep materials overdue may develop a sense of obligation to return items on time when there is no penalty, whereas those same customers may feel completely within their rights to keep overdue materials as long as they are willing to pay the necessary fines. In addition, there is a real public relations advantage to the library that subscribes to a no-fine policy.

Librarians and municipal officials are not in agreement as to the chief purpose of fines. Is it to ensure the prompt return of materials, to penalize thoughtless and selfish users, to provide additional revenue, or to defray the costs of overdue procedures? Most librarians would concur in the opinion that the prompt return of materials is the major objective; if this is true, the system of fines should be judged primarily on the basis of its effectiveness in influencing customers to get materials back to the library on time. In some libraries, the policy of fines may actually prevent the return of materials and may cut down the use of the library. Amnesty, or forgiveness, days, as practiced in a number of communities, show that while many people are afraid to return materials that are long overdue, they will use this special opportunity to do so. Newspaper stories occasionally tell of books returned after many years, and reporters seem to take pleasure in computing the astronomical fines that have accrued. Readers of the stories often do not know that most libraries' maximum fine amount is quite modest.

Whether to charge fines, how much to charge, and whether to differentiate in the case of children, senior citizens, or type of material (such as paperbacks) are decisions that should be made on the basis of experience in a particular community. Like other library decisions, policies on fines should be made deliberately and not by default because it has always been done or because other libraries in the area charge fines. Before any decision is made, the library should determine the cost incurred in the fine-collection process; both direct (postage, staff time, and record keeping) and indirect (customer goodwill or the lack thereof) costs should be considered.

Even libraries that have eliminated fines expect readers to pay for lost materials. It is wise to have clear language in the policy stating what criteria are used to determine the amount to be paid. Most public libraries use the list price rather than the discount price when charging replacement cost for lost materials to compensate in some measure for the costs of processing; in some cases, an additional processing charge is included. Losses due to such misfortunes as fires and floods are usually absorbed. Common sense also rules out such rigid practices as charging fines and materials costs to the estates of deceased customers. Front line staff should be empowered to make on-the-spot decisions concerning the collection of fines;

if a customer has been delinquent because of extenuating circumstances, such as a hospital stay, staff should feel comfortable in removing the fine charge from the customer's record.

It is most important that all library users be treated justly under policy guidelines. Nothing creates more indignation than the suspicion that unwarranted favoritism has been shown to some or that a rule that has been strictly interpreted by one staff member might have been less strictly interpreted by another. It follows, therefore, that the rules should be written out so that they can be applied consistently. However, flexibility to respond to individual circumstances is good practice.

Another type of fee common in the past was the fee for use of the library by a nonresident of the community. When a locality taxes itself for its library, it rightly seeks some kind of payment to meet the cost of serving those from outside the community who do not contribute to the tax. State and federal aid has to some extent modified this practice, as it frequently provides funds for cooperation among libraries. In such cases, the local library is still being paid (although perhaps in services rather than dollars) for its service to nonresidents, just as the other libraries concerned are being paid for serving the small library's users who take advantage of the lowered barriers. In some situations, neighboring communities or members of systems compile circulation and reference use statistics several times each year to establish formulas to be used to calculate reciprocity fees. The concept of a statewide library card surfaces from time to time and may well be an indication of things to come.

The controversy regarding fees for costly or labor-intensive services may become an increasingly visible issue in the small library. Problems of cost have driven some libraries of various sizes to consider fees for long reference searches and for the use of online information retrieval systems. The relationship between what a library can reasonably provide and customer need for more in-depth service poses significant issues for the library. However, the reality of appropriate scale should be considered, and services that extend beyond those that the library's tax base can support might indeed have a charge attached so that they may be available to the customer. This concept of levels of service would differentiate between tax-funded core services and services that go beyond that basic level. Policy language must clearly spell out exactly what services are related to each level.

Some libraries have also established fees for certain categories of materials, such as videos. These practices create ethical and philosophical issues for the librarian. In today's world, it is important for librarians to re-alize that libraries are not institutions devoted solely to the collection of print materials; audiovisual formats and computer access to information are legitimate and necessary library services and should be built into the normal library budget. In some states, there is a legal obligation to do so.

If customers want services that are not as yet available in the local li-brary, the library's connections with its neighbors or its statewide network may provide access to what is needed. This expanded access may, or may not, have a fee attached. In such cases, decisions about fees will be made elsewhere, and the immediate responsibility of the local library will be con-fined to communicating to the customer the availability of the service and the costs that may be incurred.

Special Services

Services to citizens with visual, auditory, or other sensory or physical im-pairments, as well as to those with learning disabilities, should be a part of every library's range of products. Consideration should be given to materi-als, access to information, and movement into and within the building. Federal law, through the Americans with Disabilities Act, requires that physically handicapped people be given access to public buildings, and every effort must be made to eliminate architectural barriers. Title I of the Library Services and Construction Act has been used in the past to make federal funds available to the states to provide library services to the physically handicapped, including the blind.[5] The Library of Congress Division for the Blind and Physically Handicapped provides books both in braille and on audiocassette to designated regional centers throughout the United States, and the librarian needs to be aware of how referrals should be made. The addition of audio materials to the library's collection will be welcome not only to the visually impaired but also to those individuals with learning disabilities that prevent their processing of print information. In addition, audio books are becoming increasingly popular with commuters, joggers, and those who want diversion while painting their living rooms.

Many libraries organize a homebound service that uses volunteers who select and deliver materials to individuals temporarily or permanently confined to their homes. In addition, collections that are placed in nursing homes, senior citizen centers, hospitals, and other institutions are rotated at intervals to provide a change of materials that can be most welcome.

Personnel Policies

The effective library board and director will develop and adopt personnel policies that clearly define the rights and responsibilities of all employees and that can be applied with consistency. Policy statements should be created concerning

employment practices, including affirmative action, equal opportunity, recruitment, selection, hiring, and job descriptions

personnel actions involving probation, performance review, tenure, promotion, reassignment, demotion, suspension or other disciplinary action, reinstatement, records, in-service training, layoffs, dismissal, and resignation

salary administration of salary schedules, pay-day dates, and deductions

employee benefits including health, life, and income continuation insurance; pension, vacation, and education benefits; and eligibility of part-time employees for benefits

work conditions including hours, scheduling, flexible time, job sharing, overtime, compensatory time

holidays that are observed

grievance procedures[6]

These personnel policies may be unique to the library or may be tied to the requirements of the municipality. In any event, it is the responsibility of the library board to ensure that such policies are in effect. Additional discussion of personnel matters will be found in chapter 7.

Finally, it must be remembered that policies determined by the library board set the parameters of the library's daily operation and its program over time; close correlation with the planning process is imperative if the policies are to be effective. The considered and creative establishment of effective library policy offers both challenge and opportunity in this time of rapid change. The use of political wisdom in implementing that policy can make the difference between a static or dynamic library environment.

Thoughts for the New Millennium

What policies are presently in place in my library? When were they last reviewed or revised? Is there a practice of reviewing policies annually?

What policy categories are not as yet written for my library? Is policy development given a high priority?

Is there a current collection-development policy? How are materials selection, different formats, challenged materials, gifts, and weeding handled?

Does the library have its own personnel policy? Is it correlated with the municipality's policy as appropriate?

Do all staff members feel empowered to make frontline decisions regarding exceptions to written policy? How can I make staff more comfortable with flexible application of policies?

Does my library charge fines? If yes, has the cost—including staff time and postage—been calculated to see if this practice is cost-effective?

Notes

1. *Wisconsin Public Library Trustee Handbook* (Madison: Wisconsin Dept. of Public Instruction, 1989), 37.
2. Virginia G. Young, "The Trustee as Policymaker," in her *The Library Trustee: A Practical Guidebook,* 4th ed. (Chicago: American Library Assn., 1988), 24.
3. *Wisconsin Public Library Trustee Handbook,* 37.
4. Jerry Pennington, "Collection Development," in *The How-to-Do-It Manual for Small Libraries,* ed. Bill Katz (New York: Neal-Schuman, 1988), 165.
5. Young, "Trustee as Policymaker," 27.
6. *Wisconsin Public Library Trustee Handbook,* 33.

6 Finance

One of the most challenging aspects of public library administration is effective fiscal management. Accountability is increasingly demanded by funding authorities. While true accountability involves far more than working effectively with the library's finances and funding and is rooted in identifying and responding to community needs, the management of monetary resources is an important component of administration and is the responsibility of both the library director and the library board. Finance in the public sector, of which the public library is an integral part, differs somewhat from fiscal management of a private organization, even one that is nonprofit. In most instances, the majority of funds that support the library are public monies derived from taxes and are thus subject to a variety of legal and administrative requirements that the library must observe while, at the same time, following the normal practices of a small business. There are some exceptions, however: Many small libraries can trace their origins to a woman's club or some other organization that started them with private funds, and some are still partially supported from such funds.

In today's economy, no source of revenue can be ignored, but there can be problems when the library has the reputation of association with a semi-philanthropic agency. A public library should receive most of its funds from tax sources, and communities with library budgets funded in large part from private sources or eked out by bake sales and book sales need to work to bring public support up to a functional and realistic level—a level that will pay for reasonable levels of staff, materials, utilities, building maintenance, and other necessary costs.

Once it is supported by public funds, the library is subject to laws and regulations that govern

- the source of the library's primary income, which may include the local municipality, township, county, state, and some locally distributed federal monies;
- the manner in which the budget is developed, presented, and justified;
- purchasing procedures;
- internal accounting and accountability; and
- to some extent, such matters as contracts, fees for services, and donations.

In some of these areas there has been, and continues to be, a good deal of change in recent years, resulting in inconsistencies in funding patterns. A library's primary income, particularly if it is derived from real estate property taxes, can be seriously affected as the fortunes of the community ebb and flow. Budgeting methods have also moved through different stages of development; while most municipalities still require a line-item presentation, many libraries have found program budgeting to be a necessary and more effective first step. (See "Preparing the Budget" later in this chapter.) In addition, some libraries have abandoned the traditional route of charging fines for overdue materials and have found that there has been little, if any, negative impact on library operations.

Yet, there has been a rethinking of the question of charging fees for selected services, sometimes prompted by the library itself and sometimes suggested by municipal officials. This rethinking has its roots in concern about the rising costs of all government services, in the desire to continue to provide needed and increasingly sophisticated services in a climate of fiscal constraint, and in recognition of new and more costly technologies. The concept of levels of service, introduced in chapter 5, has become attractive to many public libraries. To serve the needs of a diverse clientele, some libraries have identified the range of services that public taxes can support and have developed a fee structure for those services that are beyond that basic level. However, the strong philosophical tradition of "free" and equal access acts as a strong deterrent and the debate remains unresolved.[1]

Yesterday's library was a very local entity, and its tax support structure evolved quite naturally from the subscription libraries of the last century. Today's library, even if viewed in the community as a local product, is that community's window to the world of information and, as such, necessarily interacts with library systems, networks, and other multiport structures. The extensive and growing interlibrary loan mechanisms suggest that local funding may be yesterday's solution patched into a world that is quite different, and that a larger funding base, such as at the state—or even national—level, would be more appropriate as libraries become part of a more interdependent, global society. Yet, even state support may not be equitable if, as is often the case, funding formulas are tied to population served by the existing tax base, thus handicapping sparsely populated rural areas that have distance as an access concern and where nearby communities are outside the immediate taxing area. There is a real mandate for study of these issues and a commitment to flexibility of policies if order and fairness are to emerge from the present fiscal chaos.

Sources of Local Income

All public libraries receive most of their income from public funds, or they cannot be considered completely public libraries. Public money is derived ultimately from taxation, but the money can come from a variety of intermediate sources, such as the general fund, library taxes, or earmarked tax funds. There are other types of local public funding, but the three noted here probably pay for the vast majority of the public libraries in the United States. In some cases, a library's funding may be drawn from two of these funding patterns, or even all three.

Appropriation from the General Fund

Most public libraries receive funds from their jurisdiction (city, town, county, township, or other governmental structure), just as do other services of the central administration. The government's general fund is made up of revenues from a variety of sources, chiefly from taxes that are not earmarked for any particular service or activity. These may include taxes on real estate, sales, and income. General-fund libraries prepare an annual budget and present it to the local budget officer or committee, as do other locally funded units. Governmental approval of all the budgets follows a hearing for each unit that may well result in a cut or increase, and the total of these unit budgets results in the overall budget of the jurisdiction for the next fiscal year.

The local tax rate for real estate is set to bring in the bulk of the amount needed, along with estimates for the yields of other unallocated taxes. In this situation, the library competes with other local units for funds and must justify its requests to receive its allocation, but it may also receive an increase if a request is presented in a convincing fashion. Since the budget of the library is thus appropriated by elected officials, the goodwill of the voters is an important political tool. If the library has "done its homework"—analyzing the community, identifying customer needs, producing products/services/programs that will respond to those needs, and communicating those benefits to the customers—then it can have a powerful ally in voter support and goodwill.[2] If, however, the library is viewed by its community as an agreeable but expendable amenity, it will be among the first services to feel the blow when budgets must be cut. In many ways, the library's destiny is in the hands of the library staff and the degree to which the library has been developed into an essential service.

Library Tax

Many state library laws contain permissive legislation making it legal for any jurisdiction to levy a tax for the establishment and operation of a public library. In most cases, this type of tax is on real estate, and tax revenues are based upon taxpayer-voted levels of millage—for example, 1.5 mills or 4 mills—on the assessed valuation of the taxable property within the taxing unit (1 mill = $0.01 on each $1,000).[3] There is usually a limit placed on such library taxes, expressed in terms of mills. Historically, real estate taxes have brought in most local revenues, and even today—despite sales and income taxes—real estate taxes constitute the main source of local funds. Real estate owners, who have thus borne the burden of funding most of local government, are less and less interested in seeing property taxes increase. Where a referendum is required, the library is well advised to promote its case to the voters through active use of marketing and planning principles.

Most library taxes do not require a referendum (except for major building or remodeling projects) once the library is established. Local elected officials are empowered to levy the tax up to the limit indicated in the law. Only if there is a tax limit established for the real property tax as a whole, either at the state or local level, may a referendum be called, assuming that the limiting law permits this option for taxes beyond the designated limit.

In states where tax limits for library purposes were set some years ago, the income for the library may be relatively low, even at the top of the range, because of escalation in the general cost of living. Costs have tended to increase more than real estate assessment and tax yields. If the limit is more recent and higher, the library should not assume that it may request and receive the top millage as a matter of course. Local officials will determine how many mills of the permitted library tax will actually be levied. Here again, a carefully documented and justified annual budget request is necessary, and the support and goodwill of taxpayers is very influential. Many small communities and counties may have a habit of giving the library a certain number of mills below the limit without any real consideration of need or proposed expenditures. In other jurisdictions, the librarian and board may be informed of the amount to be expended without a hearing rather than being given an opportunity to present and defend a budget request. A new librarian in this situation will have a good deal of local tradition and inertia to overcome; proposals for change may be seen as a nuisance and "out of line" by some officials. The board, of course, is the first group to convince of the merits of breaking such fiscal habits.

Some libraries that receive all their income from a library tax based on real estate assessments are not so closely tied to a government jurisdiction. A separate library district created solely for the purpose of providing library service is the fiscal structure for many small and medium-sized public libraries in the United States. In this situation, the local government's role may be confined to appointing some or all members of the board, which is the sole governing body for the library. The board not only approves the budget in this case but may also have taxing power to raise the funds to supply the income needed. A tax limit is usually imposed by law in such situations, and it is common for library districts with taxing powers to have a referendum when they seek a major increase in the millage. Thus, while in nonreferendum years such libraries are a little more removed from the immediate influence of the taxpayer than those that receive their funds through elected officials, those libraries must depend directly on the voters when a major increase is sought.

Earmarked Tax Funds

In a few states and local jurisdictions the yield from one or more specific taxes is earmarked for library purposes. This earmarked tax may or may not be, and in fact usually is not, a tax on real estate. In some localities the proceeds of the dog tax form a major part of the library's budget. In Michigan, for many years, libraries received a large proportion of their income not from an earmarked tax but from the earmarking of penal fines for library purposes.

Earmarked funding has its advantages and disadvantages, but it creates a totally different situation with regard to the budget than do the other, more common methods. First, there is no logical connection between the tax structure and library service; the connection is purely arbitrary. Second, the amount of income to be received from this source for library purposes will be fixed. The library's budget request cannot bring about an increase in the amount the library will receive. (However, it is true that when several libraries compete for the yield of one earmarked tax, there will have to be a method for decision making, and budget requests will be reviewed by the body making the decision. The total amount is inelastic; the libraries are competing with one another, and no matter how great the need or convincing the argument, the total income from such a course cannot be exceeded.) It follows that in such cases the budget process tends to begin with an estimate of probable income rather than an assessment of genuine need.

Libraries receiving their funds from earmarked taxes have no need to compete for funding with other government services, a fact usually viewed as a considerable advantage. They have a degree of independence, fiscal and otherwise, from government authority, which tends to give their boards total legal responsibility, subject only to state law. They are normally remote from the influence of taxpayers as long as the power of the purse is not in taxpayers' hands. There is an advantage, in a sense, in the lack of dependence on a real estate tax, for it is this tax that local property owners find most burdensome and that they often take steps to moderate—by voting down requests for review in referenda, by voting out the officials who raise the budget and taxes, or by imposing legal limitations on millage or percentage of property value. The library whose income springs from another source may be less noticeable as a part of the taxpayer's burden, but this remoteness may result in a distancing from the customers to be served—a distinct disadvantage.

State and Federal Aid

In addition to local taxation, citizens pay sizable sums in taxes to their states and to the federal government. These two larger jurisdictions are, at the present time, making some financial contribution to library income.

What is done varies widely from state to state. In over half the states, some state money helps local libraries either directly or through grants to regional cooperatives or systems, which local libraries are encouraged to join. In some states, the amount of state assistance is fairly generous and may be used for a variety of purposes. Several states, for example, are legally empowered to assist financially in building libraries. When state aid goes directly to an individual library, the library is usually required to meet certain standards to be eligible, such as a minimum per capita local budget, employment of a professional or certified librarian, a certain number of hours of public service, and so forth. When state aid is given not directly to the local library but to the regional cooperative or system, the purpose is to ensure the benefits of economy of scale in the expenditure of state funds by serving a population large enough to justify the purchase of specialized materials and services. (More details on this type of cooperative and on economy of scale will be found in chapter 9.)

With the purchasing power of local taxes shrinking, public librarians have begun to look to state and federal governments for a larger proportion of operating costs, basing their arguments partly on the larger proportion of total taxes collected at these levels, partly on the importance of a well-informed citizenry as a matter of national and state policy, but most importantly on the reality that resource sharing among libraries plays a larger and larger role in today's world, blurring the lines of local jurisdictions in terms of customers served. With each local library as a node in a global information network, the argument for shared funding among many levels of government becomes stronger. It is important to investigate the budget cycle of each governmental level to understand the pattern of when to request, when to send documentation, and when to make formal presentations. Procedures must be known and followed carefully if the library seeks to interact effectively at these various levels.

Since many libraries receive most or all of their income from the local real estate tax—and since that tax is growing increasingly burdensome, to the extent that some voters are refusing to increase it and, in some cases, definitely limiting it—it becomes necessary for the local library to join the state's library agency and library association in efforts to gain or increase the state's participation in support of libraries. This includes becoming knowledgeable and developing a single voice regarding proposed library legislation and funding; sharing opinions concerning the use to be made of federal funds; and, on the local level, making sure its own operation is as effective and efficient as possible and that the value and benefits of library services to the quality of life are understood by both officials and taxpayers.

Areas that are sparsely populated or have less of an economic base are at a special disadvantage when forced to rely on local efforts to support their library services. Here, the real estate tax brings in a sum that may be inadequate for the library's needs, either on a per capita basis or in terms of overall funding. However, many states provide funds to library systems; these systems may be federated (local governance is retained by member libraries) or consolidated (local governance is merged into a centralized board governing the entire system area). Money from library systems, in filtering down to the local library, can take many forms: interlibrary loan, cooperative cataloging, a shared automation system, consulting support, and continuing education programming or funding support. Belonging to a library system can be particularly important for these libraries.

In some areas, there may be sizable groups of minority or certain ethnic populations for which special types of funding may be available. Some of these funds may be available for the library if the administrator and board are aware of them and make application. Aid in preparing proposals and applications for such monies may come from public officials and also from the state library agency. The state library agency should have information about possible sources of aid. In general, such programs are funded only during their early stages, and the local jurisdiction is expected to find continuing support if the programs are successful.

Special funds, such as those from the former federally funded Library Services and Construction Act (LSCA) and the present Library Services and Technology Act (LSTA) are often available upon demonstration of need. These funds are frequently channeled through the state library agency or the regional library system after being requested by the local library. Projects qualifying for LSCA funds were generally related to library buildings, for either new construction or remodeling; LSTA proposals must be related to technology and its applications. These federal monies help to defray the actual costs, but local funding is also frequently required.

Supplementary Funding

The word *funding* in this book has been used to refer to funding of any kind. While taxes provide primary funding for most public libraries, libraries are increasingly looking to supplementary funding to maintain quality services in times of fiscal retrenchment and to offer additional services. In this sense, funding can include gifts and donations, fundraising activities, and bequests. More and more libraries are establishing foundations as a central focus for securing supplemental funding. Further, it is wise to remember that funding can take the shape of cash, equipment, services, bonds, and property.

Public libraries are not among the major beneficiaries of private giving. Several factors have contributed to this situation:

Foremost, there is the perception that libraries, funded through tax support, are already adequately funded.

Many potential donors are unaware of the increasing pressure on library budgets.

Pressures on budgets result not only from inflation but also from social change, new technologies, increased leisure time, and an ever-increasing need and demand for continuing education.

It is only recently that libraries have become more assertive in making their needs known to the community and to potential donors.[4]

Gifts and Donations

Beyond the basic level of local funding, additional funds from gifts and fund-raising efforts are welcome. Groups such as the Friends of the Library, the chamber of commerce, and the American Association of University Women; service clubs such as Rotary and Kiwanis; and local businesses can do a great deal to provide money for special programs and activities that might otherwise be impossible. Support can be monetary or tangible, such as additional computer workstations (with a sign prominently displayed indicating the donor).

Every organization in a community has information needs and problems that need solving; the library should take an active role in identifying those needs and provide information and materials that will help in organizational problem solving and decision making. If the library is responsive to the information needs of such organizations, if library staff members serve on community committees and boards, and if efforts are made to interact with these groups in a proactive manner, then positive relationships are forged that provide support for the library, some of which may well be financial.

Fund-Raising Activities

While the board certainly has an overlapping and vested interest, the Friends of the Library is most often the group that spearheads fund-raising efforts. Organized as an advocate for library concerns, the Friends' membership consists of community members who are active supporters of the library. A Friends group offers many benefits to a library: It can organize volunteers, run book sales and other fund-raising activities, provide refreshments for library events, and assist in data gathering, just to list a few possibilities. Frequently formed from a core of volunteers, the Friends group has the potential for spreading out through the community, generating ongoing support for the library. While some administrators are confused about possible duplication of responsibilities between the Friends and the board, the primary areas of authority of these two groups are appropriately quite distinct: The Friends group, as organizationally separate from the library, provides a focus for private fund-raising activities that can be invaluable to library operations; the board, as the policymaking authority, oversees both official fund-raising, such as deferred-giving campaigns, and decision making. If no Friends group currently exists in a community, the librarian is well-advised to consider putting organizing strategies into motion. Organizations of Friends groups often exist at the state level, and a national group can be found in the American Library Association.

Fund-raising may sometimes be viewed by local funding authorities as a way to reduce public tax contributions to library operations. This perception must be rigorously challenged. Any supplemental funding that comes to the library should be viewed as exactly that: supplemental. There is no substitute for local funding support of the public library, and additional funds should be used to expand the scope of what the library can provide.

Bequests and Endowments

New to library fund-raising is active solicitation of what is now known as deferred giving. Some libraries are developing attractive brochures that provide information on library programs and put forward the suggestion that an endowment to the library can be an appropriate memorial. These brochures are distributed to estate planners, lawyers, and medical offices in the community and must be tactfully and tastefully designed to be effective. This method of seeking alternative funding builds on established community goodwill and can be used to best advantage by the library that has built up a relationship of perceived mutual benefit over time.

Corporations and Foundations

Grantsmanship is both an art and a skill. Successful grant writers acknowledge that there is a relationship between the total number of proposals written and the percentage of success, which indicates that practice does indeed increase one's chances. Decisions regarding which proposals to fund are usually based on the philosophy and attitudes of the funding agency. Doing one's "homework" by looking up potential corporations and foundations in publications of The Foundation Center, in *The Foundation Directory,* or on the Dialog database; discovering what types of projects have been recently funded; and identifying categories and priorities of corporate or foundation interest can lead to productive results.[5] The trustee, librarian, or volunteer charged with seeking funds from corporations or foundations should identify likely possibilities, contact an individual responsible for managing the resources of those organizations, and make inquiries regarding the appropriateness of the request for funds. Proposal formats and requirements vary and the fund seeker needs to inquire as to the proper presentation. While grantsmanship at this level has been more commonly practiced by larger libraries, there is no reason why the small public library cannot effectively prepare and submit a proposal, particularly if the corporation or foundation (or one of its subsidiaries) is in the local geographical area. It is important to remember, however, that the library administration should be careful to keep supplemental funding separate from the normal budget and to prevent these additional funds from being used (by the municipality) as a reason for reducing the "official" budget.

Preparing the Budget

One of the most important parts of library business in which the librarian and board work together is the preparation of the budget. A budget, like other aspects of library management, is made easier by careful planning.

The budget for each year supports the short-range or operational plan with price tags attached to the various items. If the librarian and trustees are agreed on goals and objectives and have together worked out both a short- and long-range plan for library development, then preparation of the budget becomes a matter of determining how much of the plan can be attempted in any particular year in light of current costs and local financial conditions. If the long-range plan has been approved in principle by the appropriating or taxing body or by planning officials and approved by the library board, preparing the budget and securing approval becomes even more straightforward.

Previous library budgets are excellent indicators for determining where the library has been. While the last two years are the most important, looking back for at least five years can be most instructive and reveal patterns and trends. Important questions to consider relate to the basis of support for the library: What are the tax sources, and how are they collected and distributed? Does the library have endowments and trusts, and how can they be used? Are there levies for library support? Are the levies voted by the general public, and when do they expire? Is there a capital improvement levy or bond issue that is funding improvements to the building?[6]

Long-range budget planning is one of the library administrator's most important duties. It is only too easy, under pressure of everyday tasks, to operate on a year-to-year basis budgetarily, taking advantage of opportunities when they arise and tightening the library belt when conditions are unfavorable. Similar difficulties occur with the planning process, as daily tasks absorb time that might have been devoted to planning. However, many librarians and boards have found that a careful, detailed, and imaginative plan for better library service, with clearly indicated stages for implementation from year to year, will be favorably received by both the community-at-large and by officials. (See chapter 3 and the sample short- and long-range plans in appendix B.)

A long-range plan should take into account whatever population projection and movement information is available from local and state sources; community advances in educational and other facilities; proposed major highways, thoroughfares, or industries; and potential revenue from state and federal sources. Where cooperative or system developments are anticipated, their implications, too, should be considered in the long-range plan. It is not usually possible to budget in detail on a long-range basis, but it is wise to estimate costs and to take into account the probable increases in salaries and the prices of major items involved. This is the *price* component of marketing: the identification of costs involved in providing the various products/services and an assessment of cost/demand for each product in order to set priorities of service. (The cost/demand relationship is illustrated in figure 4.4. Every product that the library offers to its community should be assigned to one of the four quadrants—which is not possible unless both cost and demand calculations have been made.)

Budget Formats

Most libraries operate on a line-item budget format, which indicates how much is available for salaries, how much for equipment, and so on. This type of budget can be extremely detailed or somewhat general and is typically the format required by municipalities for budgetary submissions and reporting. The line-item budget may list each position and the exact salary attached to it, or it may indicate only a lump sum for all salaries. Similarly, it may allocate a sum for total equipment, or it may specify a sum for a computer, another amount for a book truck, and so forth. Some of the divisions usually found in a line-item budget are salaries, capital outlay, and operating expenditures, although the exact terms used may vary. For the library, the first item covers actual salaries and sometimes fringe benefits for permanent staff. Capital outlay includes major expenditures such as construction, remodeling, a bookmobile, and furniture and equipment costing more than a predetermined sum (such as $500 or $1,000). Operating expenditures include supplies, utilities, insurance, services, and repairs, along with less expensive items of equipment or furniture.

Since the categories of the line-item budget are set up for all functions of the total government, including all units, they do not make special provision for one of the library's major budget items: materials. Some libraries simply add a line to the budget to cover materials; others must include them within the broader budget structure.

Libraries can be faced with a serious problem if materials are required to be budgeted in the capital outlay section, as legal requirements concerning competitive bidding, marks of ownership, and regular inventories may be activated. While the materials collection as a whole is the library's most important possession and represents a long-term public investment (hence the inclusion in the capital portion of the budget), individual materials are lost and withdrawn almost every day. Cumbersome procurement and accountability procedures are not feasible for a possession so fluid, and many libraries have found it advisable to include the materials budget under operating expenditures. If local regulations make it impossible to remove materials from the capital outlay section of the budget, the librarian should discuss with the appropriate officials methods of simplifying procedures as much as possible to meet the library's special needs. Perhaps determination of what is "capital" can be made on the basis of cost rather than long-term investment. In this scenario, a capital expense might be anything costing more than $500 or $1,000, for example, and everything under that figure would be attributable to an operating expense line. This solution would remove most library materials from being considered a capital item.

The Program Budget

Alternative types of budgeting increasingly adopted by governments at various levels include program budgeting (see figure 4.2 for a comparison between a program budget and a line-item budget), sometimes as a part of PPBS (planning, programming, budgeting systems) and zero-based budgeting (ZBB). In each, emphasis is not on the items requested (for example, a staff position or a piece of equipment) but on the products to be provided.

Library products, assigned to the categories of product lines and product items, were illustrated in Figure 4.1. The purpose of using a program budget that subdivides the overall line-item budget into minibudgets directly related to specific library products is to enable government fiscal officers to understand the services they are buying and the cost of each. (See figure 4.2.) In addition, this budget type can effectively offer a choice of level of service (discussed more fully later in this chapter). To continue service on any given program at the current level would incur one set of costs; to increase its benefits by 50 percent would add another set of costs; to carry it on at the very lowest possible level would involve another cost figure, with a consequent decrease in benefits. Figure 6.1, presented later in this chapter, introduces the concept of developing three budgets; this approach can be used for the overall line-item budget as well as for each individual product-based minibudget.

Small governments typically do not use an alternative to the line-item budget system as often as larger ones do, and when they do, they tend to simplify the details. However, it is to the library's advantage to prepare a program budget first with all direct and indirect costs identified. The advantages of constructing a program budget far outweigh the time involved in collecting data and determining direct and indirect costs.

Direct costs are those readily attributable to a specific activity, such as personnel, equipment, materials, and supplies procured solely for that activity. *Indirect costs* are not assignable to any one activity and are sometimes referred to as overhead; they may be divided into two major categories—indirect support services and indirect operating expenses. Support services may encompass administration, permanent staff, finance and bookkeeping, maintenance, acquisitions, cataloging, mending and bindery, and security and custodial services. Operating expenses cover utilities, telephone, insurance, equipment and supplies, furnishings, postage, rent, and depreciation.[7]

All costs of all types connected with each product—personnel, materials, equipment, supplies, etc.—must be calculated. If a library operates under a fully developed program budget, all activities—including those behind the scenes—are prorated among the different products and product lines. Utilities and other indirect costs can be assigned to the various products by using the following "shortcut" method:

1. Identify which products, categorized by product lines, the library provides to the community.
2. Develop a "sampling frame" of several days during several representative weeks during which data will be collected.
3. Create a time log that lists these products or product lines on a vertical axis and 15-minute time increments on a horizontal axis. (See figure 4.3.)
4. Have each staff member (even if there is only one) place a check mark each 15 minutes opposite the product or product line that is being worked on.
5. At the end of the data collection, add up the time spent on each product or product line, and calculate the percent of total work time spent on each product or product line.
6. Use these percentages to divide up indirect costs, and assign those costs to each product or product line represented in the program budget.

In addition, the cost benefit of each product can be calculated by weighing cost against demand and projected benefit. In other words, there are four possibilities for each product. (See figure 4.4.)

a. The product is in high demand, and the cost to provide it is also high.
b. The product is in low demand, and the cost to provide it is high.
c. The product is in high demand, and the cost to provide it is low.
d. The product is in low demand, and the cost to provide it is low.

With the first and the fourth results, a decision must be made according to anticipated benefit; a product that is in high demand, yet is costly, may or may not have a high priority in relation to other potential products. A product that is in low demand, yet costs little, may be worth providing simply because it uses minimal resources. Clearly, a product with low demand and high cost is on the list to cut. The ideal, of course, is a popular product with a low price tag.

Products can be positioned in priority order based upon the cost-demand conclusions. Once determinations are made so that each product is placed in one of the above a–d categories, a reasonable assessment and setting of priorities can be done.

The amounts calculated (i.e., personnel cost, equipment, etc.) for each product minibudget can be easily added together to construct the required line-item budget for submission to the municipality. In other words, all personnel costs from the various products are added together and the sum is entered after "personnel" in the line-item budget format.

The program budget is directly correlated with the operational plan—a powerful rationale for funding when presented at the budget hearing. As the budget is constructed, cross references should be made to specific goals and objectives in the short-range plan.

The philosophy behind the program budget is closely related to the planning process that the librarian and trustees will actually use. They determine what they hope to accomplish during the coming year, then consider how much the products will cost. The library asks for this sum, and it must explain what it expects to do with the money, why those products represented in the program budget are worth doing, how they fit into the total library picture and the community's needs, and sometimes why a particular item is superior to various alternatives. This is called *justification*. A justification for a computer software program, for example, follows.

It is estimated that this computer software program will reduce the clerical time in budget preparation and account keeping by 30 percent. This time will be used in analysis of internal and community statistics in connection with the study now under way (approved in the budget of fiscal 20–). At the end of the community study, and as a result of anticipated increased library use, it is expected that additional staff would be needed to keep service records. The clerical time saved through use of this computer program can then be devoted to this work, avoiding a request for additional clerical staff at that time.

Justifications should be brief and should, if possible, cite statistical reasons for a need. Where a drop in use or staff time spent is anticipated, it is wise to anticipate questions and show how released time would be used.

The Budget Hearing

In addition to the written justification, most library budgets are granted a hearing before a budget official or appropriating body. Most public libraries operate on a calendar fiscal year, or January through December. Practically speaking, although budget preparation is really a year-round activity, the budget figures are pulled together in final form for presentation at a budget hearing in October. The hearing offers an invaluable opportunity to explain the library's function, needs, and benefit to the municipal funders and to the community. Often the board president takes the lead in presenting the budget, with the librarian available to answer questions. Whatever the circumstances, this important interview is critical to the library's future, and it is essential that the person representing the library is knowledgeable, sure of the facts, and able to stay within the time constraints of the presentation.

If the budget calls for a greatly expanded program, with additional product items, for a library that has heretofore filled a modest role, a special effort in budget presentation is necessary. Such an effort should include

completion of a marketing audit, including analysis of the macro-environment, the community, and the library's operations

prior acceptance of a long-range plan, if this can be arranged, so that the officials recognize the budget as the first step toward agreed-upon improvements

full and freely expressed board approval and support of the program

evidence of citizen support expressed by written endorsements and by the presence and testimony of community leaders (For example, if the PTA has helped with the community study that has led to the submission of the new budget, it would be helpful if that organization were to present a resolution.)

presentation of a program budget in conjunction with the operational and long-range plans

brief and clearly written justifications, with meaningful comparisons, statistics, and graphics

realistic appraisal of the library's needs in relation to the total budget of the community

a continual emphasis on the identification of community needs and the library's response to these needs presented in terms of community benefits

There are cases where librarians simply forward the budget to the funding authorities; this is unacceptable. In every case, the budget presentation at a public hearing is an important part of the process, and every effort should be made to ensure that a presentation takes place. Once the budget is approved, work begins on the next year's budget—in conjunction with updating the long-range plan and constructing the next year's operational (short-range) plan. This tandem approach of budget and planning, with community and staff involvement, provides a sound basis for a successful budget presentation the following year.

An Entrepreneurial Approach: Three Budgets

There is another strategy that has been little used by public libraries of any size. This strategy is related to the argument expressed earlier recommending the development of three sets of objectives and actions (see chapter 3 and figures 3.4 and 3.5) that represent positive, negative, and little change in environmental impact. In keeping with and in support of this approach, it can be very powerful to also develop three budgets that address different fiscal realities. (See figure 6.1.) Note that if line items are required, program budget versions should also be submitted.

It can be emotionally draining for a librarian to cope with sudden fiscal problems. If a budget version has been created during a period of calm that wrestles with functioning under fewer resources, better decision making can result. At the other end of the budget continuum, a "blue sky"

FIGURE 6.1 | Developing Three Budgets

Budget A Little economic change	A realistic fiscal projection The budget actually submitted to the funding authority
Budget B Negative economic impact	A response to a potential and sudden economic downturn or required budget cut Allows the librarian to think through what might be done if the economic climate actually worsens A calm and rational consideration of possibilities, best done before the high emotions of true fiscal calamity emerge May never actually "see the light of day"
Budget C Positive economic impact	The "blue sky" budget A very effective educational and political tool Addresses lack of understanding by many funders and much of the community concerning what the public library can do for them Addresses lack of public knowledge of what even a small increase could buy in terms of community benefit Should be submitted at the same time as budget A, with full justification of the recommendations for expanded services

budget that creates a more optimum fiscal situation for the library can be very powerful politically. Funders and citizens often have a very limited understanding of what the library can actually contribute to the community's quality of life—and to their personal lives. Objectives, actions, and supporting budgetary information that provide a window into the possibilities of library service can not only enhance the library's operations but can actually educate those in power to more clearly perceive the library's potential and the benefits to the community that could result.

Purchasing

Usually, the library must follow definite regulations regarding public sector purchasing. These have as their purposes assuring all legitimate vendors or contractors an opportunity to share in public business; obtaining the required product or service at the lowest cost, thus making best use of public money; and avoiding business transactions that might be suspect, such as conflict of interest, favoring firms that have made campaign contributions, and so forth. The more-complex regulations apply chiefly to sizable expenditures, since no money would be saved if extra paperwork were required to save a few pennies on every minor purchase.

Bidding is the main means by which public sector business is allocated. Most libraries, as part of a larger jurisdiction, will follow the regulations that are in place. In some, the local purchasing agent or department will take care of the details of all purchasing, including the bidding procedure. Careful attention should be given to the criteria to be included in requests for proposals. If incomplete or inadequate information is included, a low bid may be received that cannot do the job that is required. Further, bids should be carefully analyzed to assess whether the vendor/contractor can actually deliver what is promised. Much unhappiness has occurred within the parameters of the bidding process when either instructions or bidder promises have proceeded without sufficient thought and analysis.

As previously noted, one difficulty that the library may face occurs if its collection must be considered as a unit and listed in the budget under capital outlay. Another problem may arise if, for example, a local official wishes to offer the library's annual book or periodical contract to the lowest bidder among the jobbers. Discount alone does not identify the best vendor in such cases, and it is incumbent on the library to develop specifications that will ensure that the service received will not require paperwork that is so excessive that it will overbalance any savings in cost.

Specifications are necessary for many items on which bids are required. When the items are standard, the purchasing officer will know what to specify, but if an item is a special library need, it is the library's responsibility to make the requirements known. Even if a particular vendor's product is known to be good, bidding procedure requirements prohibit sending the order direct; however, the librarian and purchasing officer can identify the characteristics of the product that make it superior to its rivals, characteristics that may save the library money in the long run. For example, library materials and equipment must be durable and of good quality to withstand heavy use. Considerations such as size, weight, desired configuration, color, energy consumption, electrical requirements, finishes, mechanical operation, types of material, speed of operation, and delivery dates must be considered and spelled out in detail. When equipment such as an automation system is under consideration, specific language needs to be included concerning performance, successful passing of certain "benchmark" tests (actual running of the equipment under various conditions of use intensity, with attention to speed of response), and examination of similar equipment in libraries of like size. All identified characteristics are then included in the specifications. Any bidder whose offer fails to meet the specifications is disqualified. On completion of the order, any product or service that is below the standards set can be considered unacceptable, and the contractor or vendor can be required to make good on the deficiency.

Accountability

Accountability has emerged as a mandate in both public and private sectors. One of the definitions of accountability relates to the judicious use of budgeted funds. Every public employee who expends public funds has always been held accountable for them. This has meant that financial records are kept and audits held to ensure that the funds have been spent only for appropriate and authorized purposes, that there has been no misappropriation of funds, and that there have been no improper practices, such as conflict of interest in contracts or purchases. As a public official, the librarian is responsible for the expenditure and safeguarding of public money. Funds should be spent as wisely as possible; records should be in order, and all money must be accounted for. Any appearance of laxity should be scrupulously avoided.

For small, everyday expenditures, it is helpful to have a petty cash fund that may be used as needed. Occasional emergencies arise in which small items, such as display materials or paperbacks, may be needed in a hurry and for which a cash purchase would be the most expedient. When petty cash is used, obtain a receipt if possible; in any case, keep a record of the expenditure, with date, purpose, and supplier. The petty cash fund is usually kept small and replenished when it runs low to avoid its use for items that could be ordered and billed in the normal way.

Count cash receipts daily and keep the cash in a safe place until it can be deposited. Safeguard postage stamps and supplies; keep only enough for normal current needs, and make them immediately accessible to everyone. While such a careful policy may seem overstrict to the staff, and even a reflection on their honesty, it is in reality a protection. Waste, carelessness, or personal use of publicly owned property, however minor, can create a most unfortunate impression on the taxpaying public. It is wise to lean over backward to avoid creating even the appearance of such practices.

Today, the term *accountability* has taken on a broader meaning. Public servants who receive public funds are expected not only to be honest and careful but also to produce results with the money entrusted to them. These results must be measurable so officials and citizens will be able to see precisely what their money has bought for them. The measurable results can be achieved if the library has developed measurable objectives and keeps data related to output measures. Accounting reports that track the results of output measures and monitor the progress of the goals and objectives that have been set during the planning process identify how the library is meeting the needs of the community; these data can be inserted into monthly and annual reports. Evaluation of results is the final stage in a planning process in which objectives and actions have been designed to state what will be accomplished, by when, and within whose responsibility. Coupled with a program budget, this process clearly defines projected outcomes, and evaluation of these outcomes is straightforward.

However, while quantitative reporting has its very important place, qualitative or anecdotal reporting can also be very valuable. For example, many interesting and meaningful stories are related at the circulation desk. These stories need to be communicated to funders and citizens as examples of the library's impact on human lives. Consequently, use of the library can be described not only in terms of materials use but also in terms of more effective workers and businesses, more attractive homes and gardens, healthier residents, and citizens better informed on matters of community interest and importance. Anecdotal information, couched in human interest terms, can be an eye-opener to the board itself, and it almost always gives officials and the public at large a better picture of what the library means to its community. Even simple statistics, if reported in human terms, become more meaningful. (See figure 6.2.)

Yet this type of accountability is still the tip of the iceberg. Accountability, in its truest sense, encompasses both financial stewardship and measurable results. In the context of the identification of community information needs and the library's response to these needs, results are best communicated through an awareness of mutual benefit. This is the partnership model that is given substance and direction through the planning

FIGURE 6.2

Interpreting and Communicating Statistics

Simple Statistics	In Human Terms
Annual library circulation: 10,000 items	Population served: 1,000 Library tax impact per household: $15 Per capita annual circulation: 10 items Average cost of item: $30 Total value per capita: $300

process, with the community and the library regarded as partners in pursuit of mutual benefit; the public library's ultimate accountability is to successfully serve as the information center of its community and the enhancer of the quality of life.

Thoughts for the New Millennium

Do I always present my library's budget at a budget hearing? Does my board president accompany me to the hearing—and even present the budget?

Have I tried writing grant proposals? Have I put together a brochure about deferred giving? Have I looked for other types of supplementary funding? Do my funders understand that such funding does not substitute for publicly funded support?

Does my library have a Friends group?

What does my library's annual report look like? Does it consist of columns and columns of numbers? What stories could I include to bring the library's contribution to the community alive?

How can I provide statistics to reflect benefits to each citizen?

What budget format am I using? If required to submit a line-item budget, am I willing to take the time to create a program budget?

Developing three budgets may be entrepreneurial, but it also takes time. Am I enough of a risk-taker to experiment with this approach?

Notes

1. The word *free* is in quotation marks to emphasize the fact that public libraries are *not* free of cost, as they are supported by public tax monies, but they are free in terms of equal access to all citizens.

2. The terms *product, services,* and *program* can be used interchangeably: *product* is a marketing term identifying what the library produces for the use of its customers; *services* is a generic term describing what the library offers—services as opposed to a physical product. *Program* came in use in budgeting circles before marketing language (i.e., product) became part of the library's vocabulary. Therefore, while *program* is used in this text in discussions of budget, *product* is the operant term in all other cases.

3. Jane Robbins-Carter, "Finance: Introduction," in her *Public Librarianship: A Reader* (Littleton, Colo.: Libraries Unlimited, 1982), 329.

4. Ann E. Prentice, "Gifts, Grants, and Bequests," *The Library Trustee: A Practical Guidebook,* 4th ed., ed. Virginia Young (Chicago: American Library Assn., 1988), 73.

5. The Foundation Center, *The Foundation Directory* (New York: The Center, 2000). Available from the Foundation Center, 29 Fifth Ave./16th St., New York, NY 10003-3076, (212) 620-4230 or (800) 424-9836, fax: (212) 807-3677, on-line: http://fdncenter.org.

6. Alan Hall, "Budget Preparation," in *The How-to-Do-It Manual for Small Libraries,* ed. Bill Katz (New York: Neal-Schuman, 1988), 84.

7. Philip Rosenberg, *Cost Finding for Public Libraries: A Manager's Handbook* (Chicago: American Library Assn., 1985), 5.

Personnel
Administration

Experience tells us that the bulk of any public library's budget, typically from 60 to 80 percent, is directed toward staff cost, namely salaries and related benefits. An economic commitment of this magnitude makes it reasonable for one to approach the topic of personnel management with a heightened awareness of the importance of staff to the library—on both human and economic levels. Further, as the competition within the information industry increases and the volume of available information grows geometrically, it is the library's staff that become the "competitive edge," standing as an intermediary between customers and the information that they seek. Therefore, staff knowledge and competence is the best measure of accountability for the library, large or small.

Like other aspects of library management, decisions regarding personnel must reflect the community served. The community study will provide guidance regarding many personnel considerations, including staff selection, numbers and specialty areas, and the nature and distribution of tasks. The library that serves a college community may need to provide different specialties and skills than does the library that serves an industrial town or a rural area; bedroom communities and towns with a high percentage of retired persons or young children will also have unique requirements.

A staff profile that is relevant to community needs can be as important as—or more important than—other library services, and this concept should be kept in mind when personnel decisions are made. The staff profile includes types of positions, such as Librarian I, Clerical I, and so forth (with appropriately written job descriptions); the number of positions of each type;

and attributes of successful candidates. There needs to be a match between the staff that are available and the implementation of short- and long-range plans that are based on community needs. Admittedly, it is true that the ideal staffing situation must be tempered by the reality of what persons are available to be hired, but, as in other management decisions, the goals must always be kept in mind to inform the decision-making process.

However, there are general principles of personnel work that are applicable regardless of individual community needs. Organization of work, classification of positions and salaries, delegation of responsibility and authority, coaching and performance review, and development of training opportunities are aspects of personnel management that have much in common everywhere. Therefore, if the library director and trustees are unfamiliar with personnel practices, there is much to learn from the literatures of both personnel management and library and information studies. Every library, regardless of staff size, needs to adopt or adapt standard personnel principles to ensure the proper balance between the needs of the library for capable, efficient, approachable, and constantly improving employees and the needs of the staff for competitive salaries, good working conditions, job satisfaction, variety of work, and opportunities for professional growth. It should be noted, however, that today's worker no longer is satisfied with job attributes that are focused primarily on salary and working conditions (although they certainly are important); meaningful work and "making a difference" are high values.

In the small public library, the staff is generally a close-knit group. The formalities that may exist in a larger library would be absurd in a small one. The staff members will work as a team; there will be a general knowledge on the part of everyone of the personal concerns of everyone else. To some degree, informality will extend to relationships with library users. All this friendly give-and-take is natural and inevitable and can enhance the library's interaction with the community. The atmosphere of friendliness that it generates adds to the staff's enjoyment of work and to the public's pleasure when using the library.

However, all good things need to occur in moderation, and the work of the library must take precedence. If informality gets out of hand, if schedule changes and special privileges are recklessly granted, if friendship reaches the stage where the authority of the librarian is weakened, then the library itself is also weakened. A businesslike as well as friendly environment is necessary, and it is the library director's responsibility to establish, through both direction and example, the appropriate balance between efficiency and cordiality.

One method of achieving such a balance is a careful assignment of duties and responsibilities. On a small staff, there must be flexibility and interchangeability, yet the primary responsibility for each piece of work must be given to a single individual. Just as on a ball team each member has one specific position to cover, so on the small library team each person should have the lead responsibility for a particular area or areas. This is best accomplished through clearly written job descriptions for each staff member. The fact that in a one-person library all work duties are the primary responsibility of a single individual, with possible delegation to volunteers or student assistants, does *not* negate the need for a detailed job description and an annual reassessment of that document during the performance review, particularly as changes occur.

Further, there is a need for the development of policies regarding schedules, time off, and other personnel aspects to facilitate the right tone for operations. Friendliness and informality can then exist within established guidelines, and the library staff will gain in community respect as well as in job satisfaction.

Personnel Policies

The creation of formal policies provides the necessary framework for consistency in personnel practice. The following points are important inclusions in a personnel policy:

1. a description of each job in the library, degree of responsibility, educational and other qualifications required, special abilities or skills required, and the salary scale attached to the job
2. a regular salary scale, giving minimum and maximum salary or wages, amount of increments, period between increments, etc.
3. provision for probationary appointments, with length of time specified
4. a statement concerning working conditions—adequate heat, light, rest rooms, etc.
5. an outline of what constitutes a regular work week, with specified number of hours
6. a statement concerning number and length of work breaks

7. a listing of Social Security and fringe benefits, coordinated (as appropriate) with those available to other public employees—that is, hospitalization, other insurance, pension plans, workers' compensation coverage, vacation and other leaves (paid or unpaid), sick leave, holidays, etc.
8. a statement concerning appeals and other protection against unfair discharge or demotion
9. a statement regarding attendance at library meetings—who attends, whether time off with pay or travel expenses are awarded
10. a statement concerning opportunities for further training and whether paid time or paid fees are provided
11. language concerning termination of employment, whether voluntary or involuntary, including amount of notice required and a stipulation that resignations should be in writing; guidelines for disciplinary actions and coaching
12. provision for hiring substitute staff when needed
13. a statement on responsibility of the librarian for administration of the library and one on the responsibility of trustees for making library policy
14. a statement describing the content and frequency of performance review[1]

Once these guidelines are codified into a comprehensive personnel policy, the other aspects of personnel management can be put effectively into place.

Personnel Functions

Many functions are performed within the overall umbrella term "personnel management." Some of the primary functions are discussed in the following sections.

Hiring and Interviewing

Before staff can be recruited, both position and job descriptions need to be written; if they already exist, they need to be reviewed and updated to meet current library needs and expectations. There are real differences between a position description and a job description. While this differentiation may be more relevant to a larger library, it is necessary to note the unique characteristics of each. The *position description* focuses on a classification, such as Librarian I or Library Clerk I, regardless of who holds that position. It details the types of responsibilities covered by that position. The *job description,* however, applies the elements of the position description to a particular job that is held by a particular individual. For example, if the position description specifies "catalogs children's materials," the job description may be written "responsibility for cataloging of children's materials, utilizing OCLC and QuickCard as appropriate"; this latter language clearly states the mechanisms available to that particular library and underscores the staff member's ability to use computer-based systems.

The two examples given in figure 7.1 represent typical job descriptions for the cited positions. There is an assumption of a larger staff than may be present in many small libraries; however, whatever the library size, the prin-

FIGURE 7.1 | Examples of Job Descriptions

Assistant Librarian (who also serves as children's librarian)	Library Assistant (acting as administrative aide and secretary)
Supervises library in absence of librarian	Under general supervision of librarian, supervises desk assistants and page
Assists with preparation of budget	Acts as secretary to librarian and assistant librarian
Supervises service to children	Assists with typing as needed
Trains library assistants in work with children	Keeps financial records
Selects children's materials	Keeps circulation and other statistics
Supervises library assistant who works with children	Assists with displays and other public relations work
Supervises community work with children's organizations	Works at circulation desk as needed
Is responsible for library's relations with schools	Handles reader complaints about overdues, fines, etc.
Assists in giving reader and reference service to adults and young adults	Answers telephone and gives preliminary assistance to readers during busy periods
Catalogs children's materials	Has responsibility for library routines and makes suggestions for improved methods
Assists in cataloging adult materials	

ciples may be applied as appropriate. Similar job descriptions for each staff member clarify the duties and responsibilities of each position. Details will, of course, vary from library to library, and these variations are not significant as long as the basic principle is kept in mind: Each member of the staff should spend as much time as possible working on tasks that require skills appropriate for the position's classification and salary.

The relationship between different positions can be depicted graphically on an organizational chart, which makes clear at a glance the lines of authority and responsibility. For the small library with, as an example, two librarians and two support staff, student assistants, and some unpaid staff, the organizational chart may look something like the one shown in figure 7.2.

The job descriptions and the organizational chart are subject to modification. The talents, experience, and abilities of each staff member must be used to the fullest in a small library (as in any library), and duties may be redistributed when there is a change of staff. A new desk assistant, for example, may be able to make beautiful displays—a talent the library cannot afford to disregard. When duties are reallocated, it is important that they be consistent with job classifications; moreover, classification of positions should be reviewed when a significant change occurs. Ideally, each staff member's job description should be reviewed annually at the time of performance

FIGURE 7.2

Sample Organizational Chart

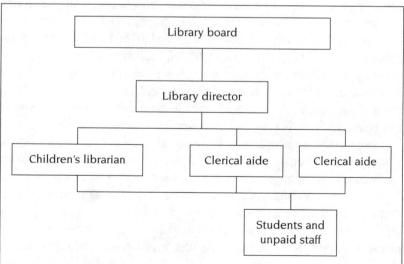

review; this is an opportunity to keep the job description consistent with the job itself as it naturally evolves over time and with the skills and talents of the staff member.

Libraries must comply with local, state, and federal affirmative action rules and regulations. Equal opportunity must be given to each candidate for a position, and documentation of the process should be carefully constructed. The language of any advertisement should be submitted to the appropriate municipal office to ensure that it is in compliance; the community may have an affirmative action or personnel officer who oversees the hiring process for the entire jurisdiction. In addition, a set of hiring procedures should be developed, including a set of criteria that will be applied by the search and screen committee to each application. If these criteria can be assigned to a point system, the selection process is simplified.[2]

Once prescreening of applications is completed, the finalists (or "short list") are considered again, and the decision is made regarding which candidates will be invited for interview. Today, telephone interviews are becoming common, usually as a preinterview but occasionally as the only interview. Where finances permit, it is beneficial to both the library and the candidate to conduct a face-to-face final interview. During any type of interview, a single list of questions should be asked of each candidate to assure consistency and fairness.

Interviews typically are structured with introductory remarks by the chair of the search committee concerning the library, the position, and the community. Questions are then asked of the candidate, and an opportunity is also given for the candidate to ask questions. As with the prescreening process, a rating system should also be applied to the interview, once again in the interests of consistency and fairness. Gathering references is a critical piece of the hiring process; however, since everyone's time is limited, it is considerate to request reference letters only of candidates who are finalists and will be interviewed; to ask for letters for every potential candidate can be a significant burden for those who must write the letters. It is also important to check references by telephone in addition to asking for letters. Many persons given as references will be more candid with oral remarks as opposed to written comments. Ask the same questions of each reference.

Once the new employee has been hired, providing a period of orientation is an essential next step. It can be very beneficial to both the new hire and the library to provide an opportunity to sample various job assignments in different library functions; such a broad orientation provides a useful context in which the new staff member can relate his or her job to overall library operations. Finally, there are the housekeeping tasks of completing forms, issuing keys, and so forth.

Evaluation of Staff ◯

Effective library service rests to a great extent upon the competence of staff members. Even an excellent collection cannot meet customer needs without the interface of expert staff. In managing personnel, it is imperative that there be a procedure in place so that rewards are dispensed when earned and persons who cannot do satisfactory work will be removed from the staff. While it is always pleasant to distribute rewards, it can be difficult (and more so in a small community where everyone knows one another) to go through the steps of discipline leading to possible dismissal.

The entire process of evaluating performance should not be a negative experience, however. The intent is one of planning and goal setting, examining the past year's performance in this context and setting goals for the coming year. It should be more than an exercise; this is a wonderful opportunity for growth and development.

The Probation Period for New Hires

Of course, personnel problems can and do arise. One way the library can protect itself in some measure from future allegations of unfair or arbitrary action is through establishing a probationary period for all new employees. For a new hire, there is usually a six-month probation period for support staff and a one-year probation for professional staff, during which time periodic reports of performance are gathered. If civil service regulations apply, the intervals are predetermined. Fairness requires that a new employee be told where deficiencies exist so an attempt may be made to remedy the situation. Reports should be given at intervals in writing so they can be referred to if there is any doubt that a problem exists. These reports should include a statement of the duties of the job and the qualifications needed, the way in which the individual performs the duties and measures up to the qualifications, and a general comment recognizing good work and pointing out where improvement is needed. Thus, if dismissal is necessary, a basis exists and can be explained if the employee requests a hearing; such a hearing is the employee's right.

Annual Performance Review

After the initial probation period for new staff, personnel reports are usually made on an annual basis. Every staff member is entitled to a performance review; a review is not a "report card," but rather an opportunity to engage in a planning process that is directly related to the individual's work. Achievable goals and objectives for the next year are developed; progress toward the past year's goals and objectives is assessed. The performance review should be a positive experience and an impetus to personal and professional growth. Feedback is an essential part of the communication process, and this is an important entitlement for staff.

A correctly structured performance review serves several important purposes; it

creates and maintains satisfactory levels of performance

identifies needed improvements and areas for growth

creates a dialogue between supervisor and employee in the context of goal and objective setting

provides an opportunity to sit back and assess the job and how it may have changed over the past year—resulting in a revision of the position description

establishes criteria for suitable rewards for excellence (and initiates a process for dealing with inadequate performance)[3]

Performance review is an essential component of personnel management and should be taken very seriously. Supervisor and staff member together prepare a list of reasonable goals and objectives for the staff member each year. These are related, of course, to the library's general objectives and to its specific annual operational plan. If, for example, the library's specific objectives for the year include "reaching at least fifty additional children through story hours and a summer reading program," it will not be difficult to set down appropriate personal objectives for staff members working with children. To ensure that it is reasonable, some conception of how the objective might be carried out will already have been formulated before the objective is adopted. Therefore, the children's librarian will be prepared to agree that, for example, a certain number of day care centers and school classes will be visited regularly, that a target number of visits from those centers and classes to the library will be scheduled, etc.

Not every staff member has this measure of obvious control. In the case of a reference librarian, for example, it is difficult to predict how many questions will be received and answered. What can be cited in measurable terms are the efforts that will be made in terms of outreach, SDI (sending out packets of information to respond to identified needs of community members), and publicity and personal training endeavors.

Like the formulation of policies, the setting of personal objectives gives a staff member more freedom on the job within the parameters of those agreed-upon objectives. Operating within those guidelines, the staff member can go about meeting objectives in his or her own way. The annual performance review conference should concentrate on the objectives and the extent to which they have or have not been fulfilled. As with the library's plan, the purpose of review is not to cast blame but to determine why certain objectives were met early, late, or not at all and to use this information to set more realistic objectives for the next year. This type of annual review thus releases whatever creativity and initiative the staff may possess, while at the same time it imposes on the supervisor a need to make sure that the objectives agreed upon are clearly stated and understood by both parties.

As a part of the review—and certainly throughout the year—employee expectations must be considered. Correlating well with emerging perspectives on job design, these expectations, which can be stated as generalizations, reflect attitudes and feelings that are present in today's worker:

1. "Let us make sure we (supervisor and employee) both understand what it is you (supervisor) expect of me." This is a simple request for an understanding of the ground rules, of the expectations against which performance will be judged.
2. "Leave me alone." There is a strongly felt need for a personal territory, for a place of one's own, and for acknowledgment of the right to organize and perform one's own work within the limits of prescribed guidelines.
3. "Help me if I ask for help." While not a contradiction, this statement simply implies the need for an environment in which questions are encouraged when uncertainty exists.
4. "Tell me how I did." Every employee is entitled to feedback, either praise or constructive criticism.
5. "Reward me in accordance with how I did." A tangible reward system is viewed as a sincere indication that the feedback was really meant.[4]

Disciplinary Action

In every organization, there are times when a probationary period does not detect problems that may surface at a later time. Once a new employee's probation is past, it becomes more difficult to remove that employee from the workforce, but it is certainly not impossible to do so. Where union or civil service regulations are in place, those rules must be followed precisely. However, in general terms, there are several options that the manager should consider, remembering that all actions must be documented in writing and placed in the employee's personnel file:

Coaching A series of regular conferences can be scheduled at which the needs and requirements of the job and the employee's shortcomings are clearly identified. In a method similar to the one used in the performance review, mutually agreed-upon objectives are set. At each successive meeting, these objectives and any progress (or lack thereof) are noted. In some cases, this is the only step necessary to get the employee back on track. A valuable part of the coaching process might be to encourage an employee—for his or her own benefit—to seek employment elsewhere.

Education It may be that a suffering job performance is the result of inadequate knowledge or skills. Putting the employee in contact with appropriate educational opportunities may solve the problem.

Transfer When transfer is an option, it can be used as a point of discussion between supervisor and employee. Perhaps a different work setting would solve the problem.

Discipline When other methods are not proving to be successful, various disciplinary actions can be initiated, beginning with writing a letter that outlines the problem, sharing it with the employee, and then depositing it in the employee's personnel file. Subsequent warnings must also be documented in detail so a case can be built if dismissal is required. Where allowed, a fine might be levied. Farther down the disciplinary road, temporary or long-term suspension is a yet more serious development.

Termination This is the end of the line and the ultimate disciplinary decision. Before reaching this point, all intermediate steps must have proven unsuccessful, and all required regulatory actions, including appeal, must have taken place.

It is never pleasant to work one's way through the disciplinary maze, but it is a necessary component of personnel management. If sufficient attention is given to the hiring and probationary phases of employment, with adequate screening procedures and job descriptions in place, then many of the problems that could occur later can be averted. Personnel management is not unlike juggling, and it is easier to keep the few balls representing the early employment phase in the air than the many balls that are necessary as problems arise.

Organization of Work

In the public sector, a common method for dividing work among a staff and thereby determining the qualifications needed for each position, including the salary to be paid, is the creation of a classification and pay plan. Such a plan accomplishes the following:

1. It gives the most specialized work to the most highly skilled staff, thus assuring the taxpayer that highly paid people are working at an appropriate level and that more-complicated work will be competently done. This means, for example, that the librarian should spend most time on professional tasks and should help out at the circulation desk only occasionally as part of keeping in close touch with customers or in emergencies. Similarly, the desk assistant, often without college or professional training, should normally not be expected to do reference work, except for an occasional directional or simple question. Failure to observe this division of labor principle creates potential problems: A personnel officer may classify a job too low if its holder works below grade too long a time; a librarian who spends too much time on work not requiring special education may be unhappy; and the support staff member who does a good deal of reference work (for example) may wonder why the librarian's salary is higher. The issue of accountability is also present; it is inefficient and probably ineffective for a staff member to spend much time on work that is either above or below the level appropriate to his or her position. Certainly, it does not make sense for a higher paid staff member to spend significant amounts of time doing tasks normally assigned to a lower paid position.
2. A classification and pay plan enables library salaries and classifications to be coordinated with the salaries and classifications of the other public service personnel of the entire jurisdiction, thereby placing library positions in relationship to other public positions.

When this classification occurs for the first time, it usually improves the library staff's salaries, assuming that there are clear-cut grades in the library that are linked to comparable grades in the municipality. A personnel office (where applicable) will study what is done in the library, what qualifications are required for doing the work adequately, how much supervision is required, or how many employees are supervised by the holder of a position. After this study it will be possible to determine where, in the total public service, a library desk clerk (for example) will be best classified and where a librarian is best placed. Most personnel officers making their first close inspection of library work are surprised to learn of its complexity. It is important in this encounter that the librarian clarify the type of work done and what education is required to do it effectively. If, for example, the personnel officer perceives that reference work consists chiefly of looking in the dictionary or city directory, it will be difficult to make a case for the true complexity of such work. In these days of comparable worth, carefully constructed job descriptions written in clear language and without jargon and updated annually are essential tools in the pursuit of fairness and equity.

3. Job classification requires a statement of duties for each position and related job descriptions based on samples of time spent (calculated over a period of time). After these time samples have been taken, the librarian may recognize that there are some misassignments. For example, the amount of time spent by all staff with the public may turn out to be a lower proportion of the total work time than is desirable. Thus, the preliminary step of sampling of time should be taken before there is any suggestion of classification, and adjustments should be made even when no official outside classifier is expected. (A side benefit is that the librarian will be able to determine how staff time is being allocated—valuable information needed to assign costs to library services as a part of program budgeting and planning.)

Without violating the basic principles of personnel management, it is possible to give extra compensation to staff members with additional educational qualifications, provided the additional training adds to the value of the staff member. Art training, a year in business school, a year or more of college, a year or more of relevant nonlibrary experience, relevant continuing education—all these added experiences can enhance a staff member's usefulness, even though the job description may not require them. One way to recognize such additional education or experience is by means of a salary differential, such as a step increase for a year of relevant education/experience or its equivalent. The library should establish and follow a regular policy, approved by the board and committed to writing, and avoid making exceptions unless the situation is extremely unusual and can be justified.

A classification plan is normally correlated with a pay plan showing maximum and minimum salary ranges. Five steps with regular increases are common, with the step increase either a fixed sum or a percentage. The latter is more often found where there is civil service or centralized personnel administration. The library described in figure 7.1 might have a plan such as that shown in figure 7.3. No dollar amounts are given in the figure since it would be difficult to give "typical" salaries because these amounts vary and also become out of date very quickly. The chart's purpose is to show how a salary and classification plan for a particular library may be set up. It should be noted that during periods of inflation, step increases are often supplemented by cost-of-living increases.[5]

Levels of Staff

Typically, libraries will have some mix of professional and support staff. Within the principles discussed previously, each community library administrator must determine the staffing needs for that library.

FIGURE 7.3

Sample Salary and Classification Chart

Number of Positions	Class	Working Title	Salary	Step Increase
1	Librarian	Library director	$000–000	$000
1	Library associate	Children's librarian	$000–000	$000
2	Clerical I	Clerical aide	$000–000	$000
2	Student	Library page	$000/Hr.	$000
X	Unpaid	Volunteer	N/A	

The Professional Staff

If the budget allows three or four professionals (less common than it used to be), it may be possible to have at least one age-level specialist, such as a youth services librarian. The interests and skills of the library administrator, who will and should always take part in providing public service, will necessarily determine the skills needed in the rest of the staff. If the director is good at reference work or children's service, there will be less need for additional specialists in these areas, although there will have to be staff members who will supplement the director's areas of expertise. The community study and the objectives derived as a result will be the chief guides in the decision as to the types of expertise needed on the staff. Where the staff consists of the director and one or two aides, the distribution of effort must be significantly different. Therefore, while the community study may indicate a need for a high level of service and the consequent staff to provide it, the library may realistically have to make this a goal to be achieved incrementally over time.

On a small staff—and in many small public libraries, the library director is the single professional staff member—it is important to remember that total specialization is rarely possible. The excellent cataloger who cannot assist at the reference desk, or the children's librarian who is unwilling to fill in at the adult reference desk while the director is working on the budget, is not the type of person wanted, however talented each may be in his or her chosen area. In interviewing prospective staff members, it is important to make sure that they can be flexible in their duties. In fairness to the new employee, it is also necessary that he or she be aware of what is expected in the way of adaptability as well as what is offered in terms of specialization and authority in the specialty.

In the past, numerical standards were established that tied the number of staff and proportion of professionals needed in a community to the size of the population served. For example: One staff member, exclusive of maintenance staff, for every 2,000 people in the community served, and two nonprofessionals (clerical and paraprofessional) for every professional. Today, it is widely recognized that staffing patterns are more appropriately tied to community needs and to the services that emerge from an analysis of those needs.

There is a range of opinion concerning the necessity for formal library school training. In spite of the undoubted fact that one can always point to highly successful untrained people and to less-successful librarians with full credentials, the weight of logic is on the side of professional training. The most common danger for the small library is that it may become ingrown—a possibility that becomes a virtual certainty when there is a succession of librarians without experience or training elsewhere, each one training the next. The perspective and background of the professional facilitate the opportunity to spot areas for improvement, introduce new methods, and help the library truly become the window to the world of information for the community.

However, in this real world, many communities cannot afford a library school graduate with a master's degree. Indeed, many smaller libraries are open less than forty hours per week, and in these small communities, it may be fiscally impossible (although admittedly desirable) to hire a fully qualified librarian with graduate preparation. This situation has led, in the state of Wisconsin, to the establishment of a formal structure of certification for public library directors. This structure uses community size as a determinant and assigns educational requirements accordingly. Figure 7.4 outlines the relationship between community size and required education. The structure takes into consideration both the needs and the fiscal constraints of the community and provides a workable compromise. In addition, mandatory recertification requirements are also in place, covering five-year intervals.

FIGURE 7.4

Relationship between Community Size and Educational Requirements for Public Library Administrators in Wisconsin

Grade	Community Size	Educational Requirements
I	6,000 or more	Bachelor's degree; fifth-year degree from ALA-accredited program
II	3,000–5,999	Bachelor's degree; 3 semester credits in each of these areas—public library administration, selection of materials, organization of materials, reference
III	under 3,000	Successful completion of 54 semester hours (postsecondary), half of which must be in the liberal arts and sciences; successful completion of a basic library management course

Donald K. Lamb, *Certification Manual for Wisconsin Public Librarians* (Madison: Wisconsin Dept. of Public Instruction, 1994), 2–3.

Support Staff

The importance of support staff in the small library can scarcely be over-estimated. Support staff are, in every respect, full members of the library team. Therefore, their selection and training is very important; job descriptions and routine performance reviews should be standard practice.

Members of support staff are normally recruited locally. The standing of the library in the community contributes much to its ability to attract good local personnel. The library director and trustees must try to make library job opportunities as challenging and attractive as possible so that people with a wide range of backgrounds will want to work in the library, even with the prospect of evening and weekend hours.

A number of terms are used, sometimes interchangeably and confusingly, to indicate library support staff. *Paraprofessional* normally refers to people who assist with professional work and who often have some college education. *Library technician* is the term used to describe graduates of a two-year college program, often offered at a community college, who are given preparation for specific library technical tasks, such as circulation work, bibliographic searching, simple catalog routines, care and use of audiovisual equipment, and so forth. The small community located near a community college offering this training may be able to find and employ a library technician, although such personnel may be more commonly available near urban centers. *Library associate* or *preprofessional* are terms that may be given to someone eligible for and expected to be working toward admission to a graduate library school. *Library trainee* is another term that describes the college graduate, and such an individual may actually be a part-time library school student.

Also part of support staff, *clerical assistants* include those who work the circulation desk and staff such as the typists, secretaries, and bookkeepers that are also found in the business community. In the library, this group, usually in addition to circulation duties, may also work on physical preparation of materials for use—marking, mending, and the like. *Pages* (or *shelvers*) are usually part-time high school or college students who work after school and have as their main task the shelving of materials, although they, too, may be given other tasks from time to time.

This confusion of terms can be perplexing and, for the purposes of this book, all of the terms will be subsumed under the phrase *support staff*. One additional group of library workers will also be included: *unpaid staff*, often referred to as *volunteers*. These unpaid staff members are of great importance to library operations, particularly in the small library where the staff complement is often undersized. Unpaid staff have a traditional reputation of being undependable, but this myth can be defused if appropriate measures are in place—such as job descriptions and performance reviews. When unpaid staff are treated as valuable and contributing members of the library team, working within the same parameters (except a paycheck) as paid staff, attitudes can be very positive. No library can afford to disregard the important benefits that unpaid staff bring to library operations, and it must be a two-way street of perceived mutual benefits.

Compensation

Professional salaries should be set high enough to attract a competent professional staff. More and more library associations are establishing statements concerning minimum appropriate salaries, and this information can be an important guideline for funding authorities. Officials in search of a salary yardstick sometimes survey salaries paid by neighboring libraries. This survey, while seemingly logical, may not always present a true picture. If a librarian in a nearby town is untrained and settled in the community after years of service, or if the librarian is married to a locally employed spouse, the librarian may well have a lower salary than a replacement for the same position would require. The librarian who refuses to ask for an adequate salary is thus not only creating a problem when the time comes to seek a successor but is also making it harder for neighboring libraries to recruit. Salaries for beginning library directors should be comparable to those paid to other municipal managers with equal qualifications on the basis of the current market situation. In some communities, the salary scale for teachers in the local schools is used as a benchmark.

Support staff salaries are usually based on prevailing scales for similar jobs in the community. Turnover is expensive due to additional training time and loss of service efficiency. The library must be able to compete for and hold good local personnel. High school graduation is an appropriate minimum requirement for desk personnel, with business courses or other relevant education included or added, if possible. Support staff must present a good appearance, speak and write correctly, meet the public politely and with friendliness, deal with complaints in a calm and businesslike manner, and have some acquaintance with the content of library materials. In addition, they should be able to keyboard, use word processing and spreadsheets, keep statistics, and be accurate and systematic. Computer skills have become essential to staff competence. Top-level support staff may also have supervisory responsibilities. When competent support staff are found, salary money is well spent to keep them.

Compensation need not be restricted to monetary considerations. The creative library director will develop mechanisms for providing "perks" and enrichment opportunities for deserving staff. Rewards can be totally unrelated to economics and may include such strategies as allowing flex time and compensatory time, providing a desk with a view or with privacy, encouraging additional educational opportunities, providing interesting projects, and so forth. There are many ways to stimulate staff enthusiasm and performance; it is a continual challenge for the library director.

Fringe benefits are another part of compensation that can add up to as much as 30 percent or more of the salary line. Examples of fringe benefits include sick leave, retirement packages, vacation and other forms of paid leave, and medical insurance. These are important morale factors that may be decisive in staff recruitment and retention. In establishing fringe benefit packages, it is important that trustees investigate what is available for similar positions in the area, unless, of course, fringe benefits are standard across all municipal positions.

Working Conditions

Hours of full-time work are generally thirty-seven to forty hours per week, and some small libraries are able to meet this standard while others, as mentioned earlier, are not. Regardless of the local situation, an important principle must be stated: The hours that the library is open per week are not directly related to the hours of employment for library staff. Much of a library's everyday work must go on behind closed doors and, in fact, is more efficiently done when the library is not open to the public. It is unrealistic to expect the staff to engage in planning and other management-related activities during hours when the library's customers are demanding and deserving service. Trustees who do not understand the imperative for off-desk thinking and planning time need to be educated and convinced of this management reality.

Evening and weekend hours pose a challenge to personnel management. In some libraries, a slightly higher rate of pay is offered to those working these shifts; in others, union contracts specify how—or if—such hours are to be staffed. In most libraries, however, evening and weekend hours are just "part of the way things are," and staff members share in providing this service. However, it is assumed that the establishment of library hours has been determined as a result of data gathered during the community study and that such hours reflect the time and convenience needs of residents.

Working conditions include more than hours worked, however. Heating and cooling, lighting, cleanliness, and an attractive ambiance all contribute to staff—and customer—satisfaction. A welcoming atmosphere with pleasant surroundings can do much for staff morale and attitude. In addition, if the library director's management style is supportive of staff participation in decision making, the resultant empowering of individuals' talents and potential can be a true stimulant to library service.

Not usually considered under "working conditions," but perhaps the most personally important "condition" is the design of the job itself. In today's workplace, job design is rapidly coming to encompass the following characteristics:

greater employee control over his/her own work and how it is performed, with evaluation based on results and not on methods

opportunities for social interaction

the opportunity to produce whole units of work and thus to promote a sense of accomplishment

use of a variety of skills to provide both learning experience and growth and to avoid boredom

the provision of feedback to the employee, so that his or her work can be considered within the overall perspective of organizational goals and objectives; the employee must have some understanding of what difference his or her being there and trying makes[6]

This emphasis on employee empowerment transcends but does not eliminate the importance of adequate physical working conditions. It will have critical impact on employee satisfaction and ultimately on effectiveness of service.

Continuing Education for Competence and Advancement

Opportunities for continuing education are available through universities, library associations, library systems, vendors, and other sources. These opportunities may be credit or noncredit in nature, but all have their place in the lifelong learning process.

The Issue of Competence

Every employee in every position has a need to continue his or her education. Regardless of job responsibilities, the information industry is continually changing, and each employee must keep current with these changes. Some changes affect a job directly; others affect the environment in which the library operates. Therefore, continuing education is an ongoing ethical imperative. The important issue is to match an employee's learning needs with appropriate educational events. The library director can be a valuable counselor in this regard.

Continuing education, like preservice education, will automatically have to interface with an individual's life priorities and needs, as expressed in Abraham Maslow's hierarchy. Maslow's rank ordering of needs proposes that this hierarchy is progressive, that until the more basic levels are fulfilled, a person will not strive to meet higher needs. The five levels that he postulated are illustrated in figure 7.5. These levels are usually portrayed as a pyramid, with level five as the peak, attainable at intervals but too "pointed" to perch upon for long periods. In other words, level five is a goal to strive for, a goal that is attainable but from which one slides down from time to time.

The implications of this hierarchy are important for the supervisor's understanding of human behavior. If an employee's survival needs (level one) are not adequately met, all energies are directed toward staying alive and upward progress cannot be expected. It is therefore incumbent upon the library director to regard employees in their three-dimensional wholeness, taking the entire individual into account. A holistic view results in more humane and, ultimately, in better management.

Advancement

In the small public library, opportunities for advancement in terms of actual promotion will be rare, since there are so few available positions. How-

FIGURE 7.5

Maslow's Hierarchy of Needs

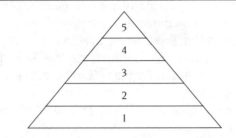

1. Physiological needs: such as food, water, shelter
2. Safety needs: stability and security
3. Social needs: "belongingness," intimacy, and love
4. Esteem and ego needs: self-esteem and the esteem of others
5. Self-actualization: self-realization and self-accomplishment

ADAPTED FROM: Abraham Maslow, *Motivation and Personality* (New York: Harper and Row, 1954).

ever, there is a particular aspect of promotion that can be considered: career ladders. The principle involved suggests that employees should not be placed in dead-end positions but that opportunity for advancement and on-the-job training should be offered. Modern personnel theory expands the concept of career ladders from the traditional vertical promotional advancement to include horizontal ladders that encompass the idea of enrichment. Horizontal ladders are particularly valuable in the environment of the small public library, where vertical promotion may be limited. Strategies for horizontal movement may include job sharing, job exchange, or special projects, any of which carry the opportunity for expanded horizons and additional learning.

As discussed earlier, for every position in the library certain educational requirements should be stated. While there is some philosophical support for job advancement through experience, the importance of adequate educational preparation should not be discounted. If staff members lack the educational qualifications for advancement but are ambitious and wish to make library and information studies a career, what can the administrator do to assist them? The following possibilities may suggest additional strategies:

1. Encourage planned reading and study.
2. Encourage course taking for credit if possible. If noncredit courses are available and fulfill local educational requirements, facilitate the

taking of these courses. Arrange schedules to assist such a program, and provide tuition reimbursement when possible.

3. Use the resources of the library and its network to obtain information about educational opportunities in a variety of formats, using telecommunications technologies where available. Investigate alternative offerings through open universities, external degree programs, College Level Examination Program (CLEP) examinations, and weekend college classes.
4. Obtain information about scholarships and other financial aid from the same resources.
5. Assist by writing recommendations and making use of any other contacts that might help.
6. Suggest to the Friends of the Library that they consider using some of their funds, or raising funds, for scholarships.

If the employee already has some college credits or an undergraduate degree, the problem becomes considerably easier, but most of the same steps can help such a person to continue undergraduate work and move on, if appropriate, to a school of library and information studies. Experience in a library and a recommendation from a librarian are both helpful in gaining acceptance from a school. For minority applicants to both graduate and undergraduate programs, often special programs and financial aid are offered.

While not all library positions require graduate education, and while there are many skills that can be learned on the job to some extent, what one receives from graduate training goes far beyond the "how to" that a supervisor can transmit to an intelligent and willing employee. If a library trains its staff from within, and promotes such trainees to supervisory roles, it is less likely that the library will move forward in the adoption of new techniques and ideas. The school of library and information studies gives perspective, a sense of the whole field of knowledge and its transfer—from producers (authors, publishers, filmmakers, musicians, and so forth) to intermediaries (librarians, teachers, the media) to the ultimate consumer. This is the field in which the librarian operates, the field of communication. One must know not only what is communicated but also how to communicate.

In graduate school other educational qualifications come to the fore. Verbal and written communication abilities are important qualifications for the librarian. A person who works as intermediary between the creative energies of producers and the needs of customers must have a good command of speaking and writing skills. In some geographical areas, the librarian will need to be fluent in one or more languages other than English.

While the suggestions noted above do not necessarily conform to the vertical career ladder pattern, they will offer the employee a much better chance for a career that will be satisfying to the individual and satisfactory to the employer in the following ways:

1. Employees who have completed all the educational requirements will feel more at ease and more accepted. They will feel competent and consequently have more self-confidence.
2. Employees with a good general education supplemented by professional education will be equipped to do a good job and will not have gaps and a constant need to catch up.
3. The knowledge and skill acquired through graduate school are readily transferable to any library job requiring them.
4. Because of the perspective and theoretical knowledge obtained in graduate study, the employee is able to judge more critically what is done, recommend changes, develop managerial ways of thinking, and thus prepare for higher positions.

Personnel management is both an art and a skill. While there are processes and procedures to be learned, successful human interaction requires good listening skills, clear communication, a sense of empathy, and the ability to make decisions. This chapter began with a discussion of library staff as the library's most significant resource; it is imperative that the library director learn well how to manage people and direct considerable energy and commitment to this end.

Thoughts for the New Millennium

Do I recognize that staff cost is the largest item in my budget? How can I make sure that staff is acknowledged by my board and by the funders as my library's most important resource?

In terms of accountability, what steps have I taken to maintain and improve the competence of my staff and myself? Have I successfully made the case for funding for continuing education and conference attendance?

Does my library have a personnel policy? Is it reviewed annually?

Is performance review an annual event? At that time, are job descriptions reviewed and updated?

Does my library have standardized procedures for hiring, evaluation, coaching, disciplinary action, and termination?

How good is the teamwork in my library? Is a professional attitude expected of all staff? Are volunteers regarded as unpaid staff and members of the library team?

Are there issues that need to be addressed regarding compensation? Working conditions? Benefits?

Notes

1. Adapted from Virginia G. Young, ed., *The Library Trustee: A Practical Guidebook,* 4th ed. (Chicago: American Library Assn., 1988), 174.
2. Darlene E. Weingand, *Managing Today's Public Library: Blueprint for Change* (Englewood, Colo.: Libraries Unlimited, 1994), 80.
3. Ibid., 81.
4. Herbert S. White, *Library Personnel Management* (White Plains, N.Y.: Knowledge Industry Publications, 1985), 127–8.
5. See *American Libraries* for an annual survey of salaries.
6. Ibid., 125–6.

8

Operations in Support of the Library's Products

As discussed in chapter 4, the library's products typically fall into three categories: collection, services, and programs.[1] Occasionally a library will create additional product lines, such as food service, a gift shop, and so forth, but the three lines of collection, services, and programs are the staples of every library's operation. (See figure 4.1.) Within each of these product lines, specific products will be designed and the profile might look something like the following:

Collection: books, periodicals, films, recordings, videos

Services: circulation, interlibrary loan, homebound visits, reference, Internet access

Programs: story hours, film and video series, literacy tutoring

The library's products have been determined and developed in response to identification of community needs. The cost of producing and providing these products has been calculated to provide cost/benefit ratios to aid decision making. The most appropriate and effective channels of distribution have been selected. Once promotional communication strategies have been put into place, it is time to focus on those technical mechanisms that will enable the planning and marketing efforts to become reality.

Behind the scenes of every library must occur a variety of activities necessary to the support of the library's products. Using the product lines, support activities can be classified as illustrated in figure 8.1. These activities vary considerably in the amount of skill and time required. This chapter discusses the basic operational functions that undergird the development of

FIGURE 8.1
Activities in Support of the Library's Products

Collection Support	Services Support	Programs Support
Selecting materials (e.g., books, periodicals, newspapers, documents, recordings, videos, films, software)	Developing circulation policies and procedures, incuding record keeping, overdue notices, and so forth	Selecting materials for use in story hours
Placing orders for these items, and the variety of paperwork connected with order records		Purchasing craft supplies, puppets, etc.
Receiving ordered materials, clearing of order records, checking of invoices, payment or authorization of payment of bills	Training staff in automated system use and protocols, as appropriate	Selecting films and videos for programs
Cataloging and classification of new materials	Developing interlibrary loan policies and procedures	Training staff in operation of audiovisual equipment
Preparing materials for circulation	Recruiting volunteers for homebound service	Training literacy tutor volunteers
Weeding the collection—systematic withdrawal of outdated and no-longer-needed items	Training staff in reference interview techniques	
Sending materials to be bound and maintaining records	Training staff in online search protocols	
Taking inventory of the collection at intervals		
Developing evaluation criteria		

those skills necessary for effective collection management, beginning with selection of materials. These functions focus on the collection and, through the collection, support both services and programs.

Collection Management

Several functions make up the overall management of the collection. These functions include making selections, weeding, deciding on replacements, and developing evaluation criteria.

Selection

Chapter 5 discussed the library's material selection policy statement and the kinds of general decisions that it contains. On the basis of these principles, which, in turn, are firmly rooted in community study and library objectives, a library will select its materials in appropriate formats. It is wise to view the library's holdings as "information packages," rather than "books" and "audiovisual." With the proliferation of possible formats to house information, the library can no longer be considered simply a place for books. The information package concept allows for both present formats and future developments in technologies.

The selection process itself, although it concerns itself to a large extent with newly issued materials, also covers selection of gift items to be added, replacement of lost or worn-out items, and systematic collection building by subject area. In addition, effective collection management also acknowledges resources beyond the library's walls to which customers can be referred as needed. The existence of such external resources should influence the purchasing strategies of the library.

There are seven categories of selection aids:

- current sources for in-print materials
- publisher/producer catalogs, flyers, announcements
- current reviews
- national bibliographies
- online databases
- recommended lists
- subject bibliographies[2]

These aids help library staff to make informed decisions regarding available materials. If a specific title is no longer available, used-book and remainder services can be useful in locating possible copies.

While a small library may not be able to afford to collect all the following formats and genres in the depth that might be desired, membership in a system and interlibrary loan networks can do much to expand the world of opportunity. Some libraries make the mistake of focusing almost exclusively on print materials, not recognizing the important contribution that a wide range of formats can provide. Further, there is much research to support the concept of preferred learning styles—that each individual prefers to learn in very personal ways, some preferring to learn through reading, others through listening, viewing, or "hands on" experience. Therefore, it is imperative that the librarian view the budget as a "materials" budget rather than a "book" budget and purchase materials/information packages as appropriate to respond to community needs and library objectives.

NEW BOOKS

Selection of new books is one of the most important of professional tasks, and one that calls for considerable knowledge of authors, illustrators, publishers, and other vendors. When collection work can be done jointly by the member libraries of a system, drawing on all the knowledge and skill found in their combined staffs, the entire group benefits. If this level of collaboration is not possible, informal networking can still provide a useful support system. New books are selected from library lists and reviewing media. A library that is a member of a system may have access to an examination room in which new materials are displayed; this benefit can be a valuable addition to the reviews and lists. If an examination room does not exist, the librarian must depend to a large part upon review media and recommendations from the library's customers. Selection is made easier and more focused by the staff's knowledge of the community and the library's goals and objectives.

PERIODICALS

Sometimes overlooked by the small library, periodicals are an important source of information and are easy to access because of indexes. Much useful and accurate coverage by subject can be added to the library through periodicals, although the cost of subscriptions in recent years has made the selection process even more significant and challenging. Many libraries tie their periodicals selection decisions in part to whether titles are included in those indexes carried by the library. Indexes may be electronic, such as InfoTrac, or paper, such as the *Readers' Guide to Periodical Literature*. Therefore, in addition to those popular and readable magazines that customers enjoy reading and browsing through, the library purchases other indexed magazines that add important informational coverage that the community will need. Back issues will be kept as long as needs and space exist; many libraries use microform and CD-ROM technologies to retain back issues in a minimum space.

NEWSPAPERS

Except for current issues, newspapers are often held on microfilm. The local papers should be preserved, and an extra copy may also be clipped for important local material not found in other sources. If possible, the library should consider subscribing to a nearby metropolitan paper and to such titles as the *New York Times* and the *Wall Street Journal*. Sometimes a system can afford the index to the *New York Times* and may also, either directly or through referral, offer the service of the computerized index to that paper and others.

GOVERNMENT PUBLICATIONS

Because of the complexities of ordering and indexing, government publications are often avoided by small libraries. The federal government, however, is a major publisher of authoritative and valuable documents. Its current lists should be obtained and used for ordering pamphlets, some periodicals, and occasional bound volumes and CD-ROMs. Some extremely valuable reference materials can be obtained from this source, and it should be noted that more and more government publications are appearing in electronic form. Further, although the small library cannot have a comprehensive collection of government publications, one or more libraries in every state serve as official government repositories, and publications can be secured from these resource libraries through interlibrary loan.

RECORDINGS

Another important component of library resources is a collection of recordings. There are a variety of possible formats and genres found in library collections:

Formats

    compact discs, or CDs

    audiocassettes

    digital audiotape

    phonodiscs (popular for many years, but now infrequently collected)

    eight-track tapes (once popular, but no longer produced)

    reel-to-reel tapes (used more by audiophiles than the general public)

Genres

    music—classical, semipopular, current popular, jazz, religious music,
        marches, children's music, well-known performers both vocal
        and instrumental, operas and operettas, musical comedies,
        New Age

language recordings—recordings to assist people in learning foreign languages for travel or in greater depth; some may be designed for use with print materials

drama—Shakespearean plays, other drama, sound effects for the use of local drama groups

poetry—readings by poets of their own work or other poetry readings

documentary recordings—real-life speeches and events of importance; reconstructions of historic events

business—topics such as stress management, time management, working with difficult people; advice on investments, how to manage effectively, customer service

nature—bird calls; sounds such as waterfalls, surf, rainfall, thunderstorms, running brooks

"talking books"—useful for the visually impaired, persons with learning disabilities, commuters, or merely for individuals busy with chores such as wall painting, ironing, and so forth; includes educational texts and popular fiction titles available in both cassette and CD formats

VISUAL MEDIA

Most topics found in print media can be found in one or more visual media. Visual media expand the possibilities for information access. There are a variety of formats available:

Videos—cover any subject area from popular movies to educational and self-help topics (have effectively supplanted films in most libraries); useful for circulation to customers and for library programming; most popular in VHS videocassette format

DVDs—digital videodiscs are the newest format and can be used with dedicated playback equipment or computers with DVD drives

Films—generally cover a wide range of subject areas (once commonly found in both 8mm and 16mm in library collections; now often superseded by videos)

Slides—art prints, travel scenes

Film strips—children's stories, "how-to" information (infrequently collected today)

COMPUTER SOFTWARE

Found in many library collections, computer software programs are usually for in-library use but also occasionally available for check-out. Here, as in audio and visual media, it is critical to know what formats and equipment are available in community homes and schools. With more and more technologies emerging, appropriate purchase must be tied to community needs and interests.

Copyright issues are present with all information packages. The provision of "fair use" applies to usage in the home or in educational situations. For computer software and other media, licenses can frequently be purchased that allow for circulation and/or public performance; some software, such as shareware, may carry no restrictions.

PAMPHLETS

Libraries will need pamphlets but should avoid ordering overly commercial or biased ones simply because they are free or inexpensive. Some pamphlets will help balance a collection on a controversial issue. However, ordering from some propaganda organizations will place the library on a mailing list, and additional floods of material may appear.

OTHER MATERIALS

In addition to the previously mentioned formats, other materials are also part of some library collections. These varied materials may include

Art prints—a variety of artistic styles, usually available for check-out for lengthy periods of time

Games—educational, recreational

Globes—terrestrial, celestial

Maps—flat, relief

Microforms—microfilm, microcard, microfiche

Mixed-media packages/kits—combinations of print, audio, visual, and so forth

Music—printed performance and study scores

Toys—stuffed animals, educational games, blocks, and so forth

Tools—hand tools, possibly basic power tools

Weeding

Because small libraries are continually in need of more materials, librarians sometimes find it hard to convince taxpayers and officials, occasionally even other librarians and trustees, that some materials must be removed from the collection. Questions are likely to be asked, especially when the materials to be withdrawn seem to be in good condition: Why is this discarding necessary? Is it not a waste of taxpayers' money? If the materials were not used enough to be worn out, was not a mistake made in purchasing them in the first place?

A research library is justified in keeping, for the scholar, many materials that may be used only once in a decade; the small library must be weeded and pruned, lest the weeds overrun it altogether. Pride in the number of items in the collection, reluctance to discard public property that may have some monetary value, the faint possibility that someone may ask for a title that has seen its day—all these considerations must be firmly suppressed in favor of the overriding importance of having a library that is alive, attractive, and usable.

What to weed, what to keep, and what to replace do not have easy answers. Experience in the use of the collection, knowledge of the community, and use of standard lists can provide some of the answers. The librarian must also keep in mind the varying rates of obsolescence in different fields. New knowledge is being added in most scientific fields at a rapid pace; thus, many science materials become out-of-date relatively soon. Some technical and geography-focused materials also age rapidly, while others have a longer life. Materials on the repair of cars, refrigerators, radios, and television sets are not necessarily useless because newer models have come on the market and newer materials describe their operation. Older cars, refrigerators, radios, and television sets may still be in use in the community; community analysis can help with these types of decisions.

Subjects that change more slowly include many of the humanities, but even here caution is necessary. No library should feel that it has adequately covered the later Roman period, for example, because it has a copy of Edward Gibbon's *The Decline and Fall of the Roman Empire* or any other single work. Gibbon may be available as a classic, but the librarian should be aware of new research into the period that has modified some of the earlier conclusions. In general, some classics should be kept. However, if the library has only poorly produced versions, regardless of format, these should be replaced if possible with new and attractive purchases. It is also not necessary to buy or keep every minor work of every great writer, filmmaker, artist, and so forth.

A regular process of weeding must be established. Whatever the local preference for systematizing the weeding process, it is vital that some procedure be put into place; it is all too easy to let this important function drift over time.

Replacement

Replacement goes hand in hand with weeding. Shabby, dirty, torn books; films or video with numerous splices or damaged sections; audio materials that skip, jam, or have variable sound quality—all these need to be discovered during a systematic weeding process. Frequently, customer comments will target an item that needs to be replaced. The easy and sometimes automatic reaction is to replace the item if it is still available for purchase. However, two questions should be asked and answered before identical replacements are ordered: Does the library still need material on this subject? Has newer or better material been produced that should be substituted? Only if the first answer is "yes" and the second "no" should identical replacements be considered—and even then, the question of appropriate format should be addressed.

Evaluation Criteria

Many factors need to be considered when making selection decisions. These criteria include factual correctness, content organization, intended use, technical qualities, appropriateness of format, physical durability, and, the foundation of all decision making, community need.

Since selecting new materials for purchase and the activities of weeding and replacement are all parts of the larger process of collection management, they should be consciously correlated. Most libraries order new materials from the regular selection aids familiar to all library school graduates and practicing librarians. Some of these are *Library Journal* and *School Library Journal, Booklist, Wilson Library Bulletin, Public Library Catalog, Schwann Catalog* (for recordings), *Ulrich Periodicals Directory,* and NICEM (National Information Center for Educational Media) directories. NICEM Net (http://www.nicem.com) allows the searching of the entire database by subject, age level, and media type and is an audiovisual equivalent of *Books in Print.*

Since money is scarce, librarians tend to select materials that they know will be in demand and reserve judgment on standard titles that would be useful but are not needed immediately. They realize that several good general titles on a subject often may appear during a given season, and they prefer to wait to choose among them. Thus they develop a file of titles for future consideration, many of which may never be bought if the purchase of currently in-demand titles consumes too great a proportion of the budget.

A procedure that is used in some libraries helps to prevent this possibility. The librarian continues to order regularly the current and popular titles from the usual vendors. Standard titles that may be useful are noted and filed in a "wait" file according to a single classification system, such as Dewey categories. Each month a different classification section is worked on. If, for example, in a Dewey-based file, the 300s are scheduled in January, then during that month the 300s sections of the shelves and recording and visual media areas are weeded, bibliographies consulted, the wait file checked, and replacements ordered. In February, another section is evaluated. In summer, the large categories of fiction and children's materials may be scheduled. If the library follows such a plan, the budget is divided among current and popular titles and standard works, the collection is kept fresh and up-to-date, and the staff learns its resources and is able to provide better service.

Developing the Collection

In addition to overall management of the collection, there are processes through which materials are secured and processed for use. These processes are time-consuming and need to be continuously monitored with the goal of streamlining wherever possible. In this section, discussion will focus on the procedures for securing materials.

Acquisition

The three common sources of vendors from which libraries order materials are jobbers, local dealers, and publishers/producers. Each of these sources has its advantages and disadvantages.

The *jobber* is a wholesaler, an intermediary between the distributor (seller or library) and the publisher/producer. A jobber's warehouse will contain multiple copies of the current and back publications of many publishers/producers. A jobber will thus be able to handle most of the library's wants. A jobber gives a good discount, as a rule, and service is acceptable. Once the library has learned the jobber's procedures (how orders should be placed, in what sequence listed, how often reports will be sent, and so forth), acquisition is simplified; because only one company's procedures must be complied with, paperwork is reduced. For most libraries purchasing general materials, a good jobber is the best choice.

The *local dealer* is a local merchant (i.e., book, audio, or video store) to whom the board may wish to give the library's business. The dealer may press for this patronage. Being nearby, the local dealer on occasion can supply emergency needs quickly. The dealer will usually welcome library personnel who want to use the dealer's bibliographies and lists or browse among the stock. To counterbalance these plus factors, a number of disadvantages should be considered. A local dealer's stock is not usually large enough to take care of the library's needs. For example, even the college bookstore in a college town will not have everything the small public library needs. Since the library will be ordering single copies of most titles, the bookstore would be put to a good deal of additional work and would probably not benefit as much as the proprietor had anticipated. Service would probably be slower for the bulk of the materials than it would be with a jobber, and the discount would probably be lower.

Purchasing directly from the *publisher/producer* may occasionally appear to offer advantages. Some publishers/producers give libraries a higher discount than do jobbers, since the intermediary is eliminated. The small library, with its modest budget, cannot command a high discount from either jobber or publisher/producer as a rule, although a system of small libraries may be able to do so through economies of scale. Publishers/producers have difficulties handling the business of many individual small libraries, each purchasing single copies. They are not normally equipped to handle such business as efficiently as the jobber, whose sole function is such distribution.

The chief disadvantage in dealing with publishers/producers, however, lies in the need to adapt to and communicate with so many vendors. Each has different procedures to be followed, and when correspondence is necessary—about unfilled orders, incorrectly filled orders, imperfect copies, and so forth—there are many publishers/producers with whom to communicate, rather than the one vendor.

Another instance of dealing directly with a publisher/producer occurs when a firm has traveling representatives or sales staff who visit libraries to present the forthcoming list of titles. Librarians may enjoy these visits and become well acquainted with the representatives, thereby exposing themselves to the temptation to purchase more of one vendor's wares than may be warranted.

Service given by vendors varies, and the librarian and board need to assess advantages and disadvantages carefully and avoid the temptation to select on the basis of discount alone. If a purchasing department is involved in the decision, it may be necessary to explain the other factors involved: speed and accuracy in filling orders, prompt and regular reports on items not yet supplied, and ease and economy in procedures—correct invoices, alphabetized bills, and so forth. A cut-rate vendor who offers a large discount may cause the library to pay more in time than the high discount is worth. The librarian has a responsibility to seek out a vendor whose discount is good but whose service is also at a high standard.

However, good service from a vendor is not a one-way street. Incomplete orders from the library; wrongly spelled authors' names; omitted dates, editions, or publishers/producers; or illegible carbons of multiple-copy order forms will not endear a library to a vendor. Such practices are poor business procedures. They are as unacceptable to the vendor as poor services on a vendor's part are to a library. Even the library that is fully automated has the responsibility to proofread and verify all submissions to vendors.

There will, inevitably, be some variations in the general ordering pattern, depending on the type of material ordered.

Audiovisual materials and periodicals should be ordered from vendors specializing in these materials. Periodicals should be ordered from one agent, who should be able to handle claims for undelivered issues.

Pamphlets may be ordered from a vendor. Some may have to be ordered directly from the publisher.

U.S. government publications should be ordered directly from the Superintendent of Documents in Washington, D.C. If possible, make a deposit from which payment will be deducted; this simplifies the ordering process. A jurisdiction's representative in Congress may be able to obtain some documents free of charge. The state library agency can suggest the best method of obtaining state documents. Many state library agencies themselves list and distribute these items. Local documents are identified and obtained through the librarian's knowledge of local government and acquaintance with local officials (another example of the value of such contacts).

Privately printed materials of local interest will have to be ordered directly from the publisher.

The occasional title that the librarian is not sure will be needed or appropriate may have to be ordered on approval, with the privilege of return. This privilege is commonly granted to larger libraries; the small library should request it only when necessary.

Ordering, Receiving, and Paying Procedures

For the vendor the essential element of the materials order is the accurate indication of what the library wants. For the library it is the record that tells what is on order (information that is checked against materials received and used to avoid unwanted duplication), the vendor to whom each order has been sent, and the date of each order (so that older orders may be checked or canceled). Whether using manual or automated procedures, many libraries find that a multiple-copy order form is best adapted to these purposes. Its various parts can be used as

the order itself sent to the vendor (The vendor may use it in any way that fits the procedures—filed by title or publisher/producer, held for delayed orders, and so on.)

the record of the order in the library's alphabetical manual or computer file (If the record contains the name of the vendor [or, if the library has one regular dealer, only the names of the occasional exceptions] and the date of the order, such a record fills the library's needs reasonably well.)

a form for purchasing catalog cards (if used) for the ordered material

When materials are received from a dealer, it is necessary to open the boxes and check immediately to determine whether the box contains the materials listed on the invoice (the list enclosed that is supposed to correspond with the box's contents) and whether the materials are actually the ones ordered by the library. Obvious imperfections should also be noted at this time, but most libraries have abandoned the practice of detailed in-spection as too costly in staff time. These operations should be performed before any stamping of ownership, marking, or pasting is done.

Dealers' bills should be paid as promptly as possible. Sometimes the bill is identical with the invoice—that is, a copy of the former has been used to supply the latter. If not, the bill must be checked against the invoice to ensure that the library is being billed only for materials actually received. Needless to say, no library pays for an item until it has been received either by the library itself or by the processing center authorized to receive it. Occasionally there may be an exception to this rule, as when a subscription to an important set of books, recordings, or videos is paid in advance because it can be ordered in no other way. Such exceptions should be kept to a minimum and made only when the publisher/producer or dealer involved is known to be reliable.

Preparing Materials for Use

Readers of this chapter who are not familiar with libraries may be astonished and concerned at the amount of work necessary to keep a library supplied with materials and to prepare them for use. Materials must be easily accessible to users, and several actions must be taken for this to happen.

Cataloging and Classification

An especially time-consuming task, requiring professional skills, is that of cataloging and classifying each item so that users will find what they want through the catalog or shelf arrangement. So costly in time is this operation that libraries are doing less and less original cataloging. Only unique or unusual items may have to be cataloged on site. Libraries today use one or more of the following services that centralize the work of describing and classifying the majority of materials issued:

1. They contract with OCLC (or other computerized system) to supply copy. A local terminal online to the database is required. Some states have developed statewide databases that interact with the OCLC database. In some instances, local computer programs have been designed that allow even the smallest library to convert its printed records into machine-readable form, subsequently to be included in

the statewide database and ultimately in the OCLC database. OCLC will also supply cards for libraries using a card catalog.

2. They use descriptions, call numbers, and subject headings—adopted or adapted—from one of the several selection aids that include them (e.g., *Booklist*) or from the item itself (e.g., cataloging-in-publication).

3. Libraries using card catalogs either purchase cards from the Library of Congress, purchase cards and perhaps physical processing from a library supplier, or use a processing center at the state agency or one operated by a system.

These outside sources of cataloging records save considerable staff time. Interaction with computerized databases also provides increased access to records beyond the scope of the local library.

Processing Centers and Commercial Services

Advantages of using outside technical services are obvious. Chief among them is the saving of time. More time is available for public service, at no cost in effectiveness of service. The time spent by many small libraries in individual preparation of the same titles has long been deplored as wasteful duplication; each library has been doing the same checking, the same classifying, and the same cataloging. It seems eminently reasonable that these tasks are more efficiently performed centrally. When centralized, the work can be done by experts, with the advantages of machines and equipment that improve efficiency. A centralized service will have access to both the Library of Congress printed records and online cataloging services. If materials are purchased centrally, there also may be an increased discount because of the larger volume of orders.

In selecting an outside processing service for the library, the following factors should be considered:

1. *Cost.* The sum paid for the service is easy to compute and may at first glance seem high to the librarian and especially to the trustees. Much more difficult to estimate, but a part of the total picture, is the cost of the local work that the service replaces. An honest check of the total staff time that goes into processing, and the salaries that such time represents, is likely to prove to be an eye opener. Of course, trustees and municipal officials need to be educated to a higher level of awareness—one that recognizes the importance of customer interaction and community outreach—since too many lay people equate the work of librarians with that of clerical workers. The

cost of supplies and equipment is also a factor but a minor one. The value of the library service that could be given during the processing time cannot be measured in dollars and cents; nevertheless, it must be taken into account and is, indeed, the chief factor to be considered. Another intangible often overlooked is the value to the library, in service and efficiency, of the space occupied by processing work. Comparative costs of the various services available must be weighed, with consideration given to the variations in the amount and quality of service as well as the actual price.

2. *Quality of service.* A number of factors affect the kind of service the library needs. The type of cataloging and classification supplied is the major quality consideration. Further, the service that provides the most detailed cataloging and the longest call numbers is not necessarily the best. In considering the library's needs, the librarian must remember that the function of the catalog and call number is to make possible the quick location of specific items and to make easily accessible the information inside those materials. The services under consideration should be measured against their effectiveness in performing these functions for the particular library concerned. Fullness of descriptive cataloging may contribute little, and length of call number may even prove to be a hindrance. Further, as more and more library catalogs transform into online catalogs, the dominant quality considerations include accuracy, speed, ease of access, and down time.

3. *Coverage.* If the prospective service(s) is limited as to the titles or types of materials supplied, usefulness is correspondingly limited. If the materials available through the service(s) include all or most of those the library would purchase, this limitation causes no problem. If, however, many important titles are not supplied, then the service under consideration could be viewed as only a supplement to local processing. The commercial service selling processed books, for example, may not handle all the books the library needs; if such a supplier is used, the librarian must guard against the temptation to buy only what the supplier has available. To do so is, in effect, to allow the supplier too great an influence in library materials selection. The librarian's eye, in terms of selection as well as in every aspect of library operations, must always remain focused on the customer and on the needs of the community.

4. *Speed.* While relative speed of receipt of materials is a factor to be taken into account in comparing vendors, speed is sometimes given too much weight by small libraries. Certainly the library does not want to wait too long for its materials, and prompt service is excellent. However, all too

often delay in receipt of materials is the reason for reluctance to use an out-side service at all. Small libraries doing their own processing can, it is true, have the best sellers available very soon after they arrive; processing centers seldom provide them as quickly. On the other hand, the processing center usually receives and sends on the greater proportion of new materials long before the library itself could have managed to prepare them. The relative importance of getting the best-selling book or video into the hands of an avid customer a week or two sooner, on the one hand, and the value of add-ing the bulk of the materials more rapidly, on the other, should be considered in relation to the library's overall objectives. Another time factor to take into account is that the outside service usually continues throughout the year without a pause, while the library's own cataloging may be held up by vacations, illnesses, and change of staff.

Among the problems that will face the librarian who wishes to use a processing center are the following:

1. *Obtaining the agreement of trustees and officials.* Librarians who have wished to turn to outside processing report that it is sometimes hard to justify the cost. It is difficult for lay citizens to understand why catalog-ing and materials preparation should be, as it seems to them, so expensive. A price that is low to the librarian may appear high to board members or municipal officials. They find it hard to comprehend what is so complicated about cataloging and classification and why any reasonably well-educated person cannot assign call numbers and make author, title, and subject en-tries for materials.

This reaction is not surprising. It is the same as the reaction of the gen-eral public, probably including the librarian, to the cost of having plumb-ing fixed, the television set repaired, or tonsils removed. One pays for training, experience, and judgment and for the investment made in ac-quiring knowledge and in purchasing and keeping up-to-date the tools of the trade or profession (including staff development). Work performed without knowledge is unsatisfactory in its results. A librarian inspecting a library cataloged and classified by an amateur can spot immediately defects that cannot fail to be reflected in poor service. While changing public per-ception is certainly challenging, it is essential that this change take place. Nothing will happen, however, until the librarian becomes an effective communicator, making it clear to funders and community how needs have been identified and how the benefits that the library provides addresses those needs.

Obtaining board and official approval of outside processing is more likely to be successful if considered in the context of total library planning. If community study, through a full marketing audit, has revealed needs that are not met and services that are not being given, the release of a sizable portion of staff time and possibly of some library space becomes meaningful in terms of what can be accomplished with this time and space. Technical processes are not an end in themselves but a means to public service. Subscribing to an outside processing service should be presented, therefore, not as an end but as a means of providing some of the public services the library has been wanting to give. Boards and officials who share the library's objectives are likely to respond favorably to a proposed change that gives the opportunity to accomplish those objectives.

2. *Adapting the collection to the new service.* Rarely, indeed, does the library that receives materials processed outside find that these materials correspond exactly to those previously prepared by the library's own methods. Classification of biography, arrangement of fiction, use of pseudonyms, and where check-out cards are positioned are examples of some frequent variations. In adapting to the new processing service, the librarian must look forward and not backward. As time goes on, more materials and the most frequently used materials will be the new ones coming in from the processing center. It is shortsighted to change the new materials to fit the old; if changes are needed, they should be made to adapt existing materials to the new method. However, the librarian should guard against the temptation to make changes solely for the sake of neatness and consistency. Only changes that are necessary for public service should be considered, and these should be as simple as possible.

Circulation routines are probably not seriously impeded by variations in the position of check-out cards. Materials that may be withdrawn in a year or two are certainly not worth the expense of any significant change. Cross references in the catalog and shelf list may well suffice to take care of variations in entry, subject headings, and classification. Dummies, or other notification, in the former location referring to the new location symbols bring old and new together and may be adequate in most cases to carry the library through the period of transition.

3. *Adapting the staff to the new service.* While in theory the librarian may have an excellent plan for using the number of hours released by outside processing, it is not paper plans but real people who would be affected. How is the employee who has devotedly done all the cataloging for years going to be transformed into an instant reference librarian or out-

reach worker? How is the time between customers that the desk assistants used for stamping, pasting, and jacketing going to be made available for the clerical work involved in the expanded service program? Librarians faced with these practical problems find little help in the surveys and studies that necessarily consider time and staff in the abstract.

Since each library's staff is different, to lay down rigid procedures for the changeover is not practical. The suggestions made earlier in connection with changing staff attitudes toward public service may be helpful. The problem of the transformed catalog librarian is not unique; like thousands of workers, this staff member is being displaced by a type of automation and needs to be retrained and oriented toward another type of library work. The fact that the process may be difficult for the employee and not easy for the librarian should not be a reason for failing to make the change, any more than the need to retrain and reassign workers prevents a business or industry from automating a process. In a small library, the transition is made easier by the fact that the employee has undoubtedly been working all along at a number of other library tasks that are familiar and comfortable.

An important strategy in dealing effectively with change is the validation of the important previous work that staff has done so well; this work has laid the sturdy foundation for the change that is about to occur. No one likes to think that what one has been doing for years has suddenly become meaningless or obsolete; rather, work flow is a continuum that moves from one practice to another, each change building upon the previous good work.

Projecting and executing a major change is a task that calls for considerable administrative skill. The librarian will probably be confronted not only with human relations factors but also with the need for a restudy of staff duties. The skills needed for the expanded program may be available for development in staff members who have not previously had the opportunity of serving the public. The librarian will undoubtedly undertake some of the new work personally. Taking full advantage of released time requires careful planning. Using the desk assistant's time, for example, might call for a revision of circulation procedures or for a change in the arrangement of space behind the circulation desk. The temporary use of time logs that chart the amount of time each employee spends on each task (see figure 4.3) can help the librarian analyze both tasks and the experience/salary of the person performing each task to determine what changes need to take place. A time log also provides important data for calculating the cost of the library's various products and services.

Processing New Materials

Materials preparation requires considerable handling, no matter what the system. It is an area that especially repays study leading toward simplification. A specific work area and the use of a number of simple devices can greatly speed up work. If possible, materials should move from work station to work station on an assembly-line basis, even if all stations cannot be staffed at the same time. Transfer of materials from tables to trucks and back to tables is wasteful and should be eliminated. If work space prohibits assembly-line layout, however, the use of trucks is certainly preferable to the practice of hand-carrying loads of materials from one point to another.

Even in larger systems and processing centers, the preparation of materials is partially an item-by-item operation. In the larger unit, circulation cards and pockets (if used) can be machine duplicated, and the use of pasting machines and a carefully planned layout may result in economies beyond the reach of the smaller library. Some libraries that are in the process of automating circulation functions no longer use card pockets and rely instead on the bar coding strip on each item plus a reminder "date due" slip. Bar codes (on both the item and the customer's library card) are read by light pens in the automated system, and the data enters directly into the system's memory.

Collection Control

A variety of activities keep the collection in good condition and up-to-date. This ongoing maintenance is essential to good collection management.

Binding, Mending, Withdrawing, and Replacing

When an item is in poor physical condition, the library is faced with decisions on two levels. The first is professional and has to do with the importance of the work to the collection. It involves determining whether the item should be kept at all: whether it has been superseded by other titles, whether its popularity has waned, whether there are enough copies left in the library, whether its availability through interlibrary loan or cooperative arrangement will suffice, or whether it is the most appropriate format for customer needs.

If the item is important enough to keep, the second decision—this time a technical one—needs to be made. Can and should the item be repaired, or should a new copy be ordered? In the early days of public libraries, when salaries were so low that many who worked in libraries were almost volunteers, the relative value of materials and of staff time was markedly different from the situation today. It was then worthwhile to devote hours to the mending of materials to preserve them, even when replacement copies could be purchased. Occasionally a library still follows this practice, with questionable economy. It must always be kept in mind that today 60 to 80 percent of the library's budget is staff cost, and this valuable resource needs to be used wisely.

When an important and unobtainable book has become worn and cannot be rebound, mending may be required. For example, a biography of local significance may already have been rebound and yet need further attention. Its paper may be so brittle that further rebinding is impossible. In such cases, careful mending may be justified. Normally, however, mending should be kept to a minimum. If a book is worth keeping, it should usually be replaced or rebound. Which procedure to follow will depend on several factors. A rebinding is normally sturdier than the trade binding and therefore more satisfactory if hard wear is anticipated. On the other hand, rebound books may be less inviting in appearance than new ones, and their inner margins may be decreased, making reading difficult. The cost of good library binding is not low; it sometimes approaches the original cost of the book itself.

Audio- and videotapes and film may be spliced to prolong use. However, the quality of the splicing and the number of splices that accumulate over time affect the item's performance and ultimate usefulness to the customer. Because phonodiscs scratch so easily, many libraries have turned to alternative audio formats, such as audiocassettes and compact discs (CDs). However, even though one format may be easier to care for than another, the playing equipment that is available in the community must be the primary determinant when various types of software are considered.

Inventory

Many small libraries take annual inventories, a practice impossible for most larger libraries because of the cost involved. Such frequent inventories may not be justified by results. Normally, the librarian who works closely with the collection becomes aware of missing materials without having a formal inventory and can check to make sure that they are gone before ordering replacements. If the library has the misfortune to lose a great many materials through direct theft rather than through the circulation process, an inventory may be needed. Additionally, measures to control future unauthorized "borrowing" should be considered. There are many effective security systems on the market today; however, the time and cost factors involved in adding security strips to materials must also be taken into consideration.

Inventory is also probably needed if the library has grown haphazardly without proper organization. If, for example, a new librarian finds materials in the collection that do not appear in the catalog as well as entries in the catalog for which there are apparently no materials, an inventory may have to be taken. In general, however, the librarian should carefully weigh the value of frequent inventories against the cost in staff time and disruption to service.

Efficiency Procedures

In all activities in which there is routine and repetition, much can be accomplished by a serious effort toward work simplification. Questions should be asked about each process in effect:

Is this process really necessary?

Is it more time-consuming than the alternative routines that would be needed if it were not done?

How much does it contribute to service?

If a process is necessary, the next questions are

Is the present method efficient?

Would a rearrangement of work space make the process easier and faster?

Is the work done by a staff member whose training and salary are appropriate for the job, or can it be done by someone with less training and skill?

Could it be broken down into several operations and performed more efficiently as a result?

Could it perhaps be done by machine?

Would different furniture and equipment improve efficiency: a lower table, more trucks, a high stool on wheels?

As a result of asking questions like these, many libraries have been able to bring about remarkable improvements. Some have abandoned long-cherished records: the accession book, for example, has almost entirely vanished from the scene. Sometimes the changes have been extremely simple—the acquisition of an adding machine or calculator, the rearrangement of a workroom, or even the expenditure of a little more money for supplies. Once the staff has developed the habit of asking "why" and looking about for better ways of accomplishing work, surprising results can be obtained.

Circulation

Circulation work often takes too large a proportion of time in a small library, especially when compared with substantive assistance to customers. For example, during slack hours when there may be only one staff member on duty, it is circulation work, not outreach, that occupies that person's time. Objectives cannot be met without sufficient staff to give direct service—the larger the proportion of time that goes to necessary but unproductive tasks, in terms of objectives, the fewer objectives that can be accomplished.

To many customers, circulation work is the chief task of libraries. This mistaken notion should be examined. Why do we charge out books? The answer is, of course, to know where they are if they do not return when due. When we consider what a high proportion of items charged out comes back before the date due, the amount of time spent on circulation gives us pause. Much of the work done is never used because it is unnecessary. All that time is spent to identify the small proportion of borrowers who do not return their materials on time.

Is there any way to avoid wasted motion? Libraries are subject to fiscal accountability, which does require that some sort of circulation control be normal practice. However, in a small community in particular, the vast majority of readers return their materials on time or shortly thereafter. Therefore, a close look should be given to the issue of collecting fines. Since staff cost is the major item in the library's budget, it is imperative to actually cost out the staff time, postage, and so forth that are expended in the effort to collect fines. In many libraries, more is lost than gained from this activity. In addition, there can be improved public relations for the library that adopts a no-fine policy. This is not to say that control of the collection is waived; rather, in many libraries, a bill for the total cost of the missing item is sent to the customer after one or two months have passed. If the item is then returned, the intent of the bill has been accomplished, and no fine is assessed.

A library needs to know, from its circulation system, only two, or at most three, facts: Who has a given item that is overdue? When was it due? How many items have circulated on a given day? Other breakdowns, such as spot checks of circulation of specific materials for evaluation purposes, must be made manually if the library does not have an automated circulation system. Where the automated system is in place, reports can be generated easily and inexpensively.

In the small library that has not yet automated its circulation functions, simplified methods, including mechanized and photographic systems, eliminate some of the tasks formerly performed. For example, these libraries have eliminated

1. maintaining a user file by name (and spending a good deal of time changing addresses) because they photograph a borrower's identification with address
2. maintaining a file of borrowers by card number
3. slipping or carding returned books
4. stamping dates due in two or three places at the time of loan because they use prestamped date-due slips
5. maintaining separate stamps and records for several lengths of loan because they have only one loan period for all materials (thus saving time and avoiding error)
6. requiring the renewal of books because of a too-short loan period because they have longer loan periods without renewal

Other ways in which the circulation process may be streamlined include

1. sending fewer overdue notices by waiting a week or two longer or by eliminating fines altogether (Most overdue materials are returned within the first two weeks.)
2. reducing the number of checks of desk staff's work by supervisors (After a staff member has learned circulation routines, the cost of checking is greater than the cost of occasional errors.)

3. turning over to the customer some of the work formerly done by staff (Self-service checkout systems are now on the market and have been adopted by many libraries.)

Benefits of such simplified routines, in addition to the major one already noted—the saving of time for more vital work—include the return of circulated materials to the collection faster than before. This advantage makes wanted materials available more often and almost has the effect of an increase in the materials budget. In addition, simplified routines promote better public relations with regard to circulation. The public's common assumption, that circulation is what librarians do, may be modified. Furthermore, the irritations connected with long waits at desks, receipt of notices when materials have already been returned, necessity to return materials before they are completely read or used, or the need to renew because of a too-short loan period—all these would be reduced. All these aspects of library red tape contribute to the public's image of the library as a fussy, inhibiting sort of place.

While the small library can eliminate many of these time-expending practices through the installation of an automated circulation system, this advance may not be feasible for all. In many areas, the library system installs the automated system and member libraries contribute to the cost. Under this arrangement, every member's total holdings are entered, and all circulations are recorded in the terminals in each member library. (Although customers themselves could make this record through a self-service station, this is not yet common practice in small libraries.) Each member library can tell at any time where any of its own books are and who has them. Overdues can be called up at any time, and some automated systems provide a printout that can be used as the notice. Furthermore, the computerized system has great advantages for the cooperating libraries in the sharing of resources: A library not owning an item and wishing to borrow it can determine from the terminal not only what member library owns it but even whether the item is checked out.

Automated systems are, of course, more expensive than manual systems; however, hardware costs have a history of declining, particularly as use increases. Librarians and trustees should become knowledgeable about automated systems and watch both developments and costs carefully. As soon as is at all reasonable, the library should investigate purchasing such a system. The overall benefits definitely outweigh the additional cost. The continual advances in technology can free staff from spending time on rote tasks and allow them to focus on more customer contact and service.

Thoughts for the New Millennium

Does my library have a collection development policy? Is it reviewed annually and updated as needed?

Is there a process in place for regular weeding and replacement?

Has thought been given to streamlining selection, acquisition, and processing procedures? What are the possibilities for additional efficiencies?

Has a community analysis been done to identify customer buying preferences and learning styles?

What formats are in my library's collection? Do I think of the collection as containing information packages, rather than "books"? Should adjustments be made in buying patterns as I build the collection?

When I think of the products offered by my library to the community, do I consider appropriate referral to other agencies as an important component of collection management? Do I follow up on these referrals to make sure that customers' needs have been met?

Are there issues that need to be addressed regarding any of my library's operations?

Notes

1. Darlene E. Weingand, *Marketing/Planning Library and Information Services,* 2d ed. (Englewood, Colo.: Libraries Unlimited, 1999), 81–98.
2. G. Edward Evans, *Developing Library and Information Center Collections,* 4th ed. (Englewood, Colo.: Libraries Unlimited, 2000), 106–8.

9 Library Systems and Cooperative Arrangements

The local public library is a node in a global information network and a window to the world of information. This message has been stated several times in this book, but it bears repeating here. Although library history correctly portrays public libraries in small communities as being very community specific in terms of materials and services, the scope of libraries and information transfer has evolved so dramatically that no public library exists any longer in a vacuum, and all have real or potential connections to a universe of information.

While it is clearly necessary to determine the goals and objectives of the small library from a realistic perspective on available resources, whatever limitations might be identified apply primarily to what is to be offered on or through the library premises. The small library of today is no longer constrained to forgo altogether those services that it cannot afford to offer locally. Thus, the functions of referral, networking, and interlibrary loan come to the fore. In the small library, these functions expand the range of possible services to include a variety hitherto only offered by libraries of much larger size.

Library Systems

Today's small libraries have connections that their predecessors of several decades ago might not have imagined. First, the small library is increasingly a member of a library system. That system, in turn, may be connected with one or more networks. These connections have been established so that every citizen, no matter where he or she may live and no matter what the size of the local library, can have access to the materials and information needed to carry on business, studies, or personal interests. For the small library, these connections are invaluable.

References to resources and services available to the small public library through system membership have been scattered through these pages. Here, as a convenience, a summary of system activities and programs that might enhance and expand the small library's offerings will be given. However, while the movement toward systems and cooperation has developed to a great extent, not all libraries have taken advantage of the possibilities or even explored them. The benefits of system membership are so pronounced that it is incumbent upon every small library to investigate membership as part of the planning/marketing process.

The system movement has been, on balance, quite successful, even though it cannot be considered either perfect or complete. Some systems are still too small and too weak. Some have organizational problems; some have financial difficulties. These problems should not be ignored by the small public library, whether it is a system member or not. Those within systems can work toward improvement—in organization and communication or by seeking additional sources of funds. Those libraries considering membership in a system must, of course, balance potential benefits against any disadvantages that can be identified. However, if the former are solid and increasing and the latter made up of problems that can be tackled and solved, membership will still be a good choice. Not too many years ago the question of system membership was truly a question, often thoughtfully debated and sometimes rejected. Today, however, the need for cooperation and networking has become an imperative rather than an option.

Organization of Systems

Although statutory law affecting the structure and legal basis for systems varies from state to state, there are four general types of systems that can be cited: *consolidated, library district, cooperative* or *federated,* and *network* or *multitype.*[1]

A *consolidated system* may include a large metropolitan library and its branches plus one or more counties. Another model might cover the legal merger of two or more library jurisdictions, often crossing county lines. The board of trustees is generally operational, setting policy, securing funds, and carrying out other legal responsibilities as provided through statutory authority.

A *library district system* is one in which two or more county districts, through the decisions of their respective library boards, form an administrative library system governed by one board. Membership of the board is composed of the trustees of the individual districts forming the systems.

A *cooperative* or *federated system* is one in which improved library service is created by joint action of a group of libraries or library districts by formal agreement or contract to provide certain specified materials, services, or processes for member libraries. Each library or district is governed by its own library board. The common materials and activities are usually coordinated and planned by an advisory board. Federated systems may also be established by statutory action.

A *network* or *multitype system* is an advanced form of the federated system, in which all types of libraries (public, school, academic, and special) in a given geographic area agree, by formal agreement or contract, to provide certain materials and services to the member libraries. In recent years, multitype legislation has appeared in some states as a precursor to such network development, and frequently a system that has been created to link public libraries expands its focus to include all types of libraries.

Limitations and Benefits of System Membership

Benefits can most clearly be recognized in the context of local limitations, for it is in the improvement and enhancement of local services that system membership can have the most impact. Among the most easily identifiable limitations at the local level are the following general categories.

BOOKS

Coverage by subject may be spotty and lacking in depth in a small library. Some subjects may be not represented at all. Topics needed occasionally by one or two citizens cannot be covered locally. Foreign language materials may be limited in terms of both scope and depth. Older, out-of-print items are generally not available.

In contrast, systems sometimes purchase collections of books for long-term lending to members. A librarian may be able to select 150 to 300 titles not held locally and keep them on long-term loan for six months or longer until local readers have the opportunity to use them. The books then go back to the system to be borrowed by other members, and the local library makes another selection. In another scenario, the system will not actively create a collection but will designate a large library within its boundaries to serve (with reimbursement) as a resource library. Systems often have substantial reference collections, far beyond those possible locally. Through a central system collection or through resource sharing among members, or both, systems may make frequent and speedy loans on request to meet the needs of individual users. Fast communication of requests is generally provided, increasingly through the use of fax. Union lists or shared computer networks among members are also often found. Delivery trucks owned by the system usually bring an item within a few days, or a commercial service may perform the same function. Systems usually also perform the service of sending on to a statewide network or other source requests they cannot fill at the system level.

PERIODICALS

Magazines may be the primary source of up-to-date information for most customers. It is the rare small library, however, that can provide trade journals for local workers; professional journals for its teachers, physicians, lawyers, and other specialists; and scholarly journals for the retired scholar or author working at home on a scholarly project.

Systems that include or have ready access to a large collection are usually able to send photocopies of articles in particular journals and magazines if the issue itself cannot be lent. Such photocopying would be, of course, subject to the "fair use" provisions of the copyright law.

AUDIOVISUAL MATERIALS

As more libraries move from film to video, the limitation of purchasing high-cost films is less pronounced, but even videos may range into considerable cost—particularly educational sets or series. The emergence of digital video (or versatile) discs (DVDs) into the marketplace offers yet another option for library collections. Recordings—whether phonodisc, cassette, or compact disc—may individually be within local purchasing capability, but a full collection of classical or popular titles and vocal and instrumental music is generally not possible.

Collecting these media is a frequent and most helpful service of systems. While one small library cannot possibly justify the expense of sizable sums for such materials, a system of twenty to thirty libraries that together serve a larger combined population will have enough use of these important materials to justify collecting them for shared use among the members.

STAFF

It is not always possible for the small library to afford a trained children's librarian, a skilled cataloger, a capable reference librarian, and a computer technician. These most frequently found specialties, plus an administrator, normally exhaust the small library's staff budget and skills. Few small libraries have an audiovisual specialist; a public relations expert; a librarian skilled in service to business, to the handicapped, or to other special groups; or a continuing education consultant. As computers have increasing impact on library operations and services, having access to a technology expert has become more and more essential.

The system itself will have a director with administrative skills who can assist the small library. There will also be, either employed by the system or available through one of its members, skilled reference staff to whom the local library's unanswered questions may be channeled. Systems frequently employ children's specialists and other age-level service librarians, depending on the needs of the member libraries. These librarians function as consultants and help with collections and service and train local staff. Subject specialists and service librarians who specialize in a target customer market (for example, business, people with disabilities, ethnic groups, or the homebound or institutionalized) may be available either through the system or through a member library. Quite common to systems are audiovisual librarians and public relations personnel. The former develop the media collection and assist the member libraries in using the expanding variety of media resources. The latter prepare publicity (newspaper, radio, television, and so forth) for the system as a whole and may be available to assist local libraries with their own publicity. Frequently there will be a consultant designated to serve the member libraries' continuing education and staff development needs; in some cases, the state requires the system to provide such services.

ADMINISTRATIVE SKILLS

The director of the small library manages library operations and shares in general library work. The board, made up of busy people, usually gives generously of its time and skills. However, modern budgeting, measurement, accountability, and other management skills continue to grow in complexity. Studies may be needed. Help in planning, reorganization, or building may be desirable.

In addition to the availability of the skills of the system director, other administrators whose libraries are members will attend meetings and may have skill and expertise to share. A system may receive grants from funding agencies for the purpose of special studies and experiments with new services; in some states, state and federal monies are distributed via the systems. In either case, the small library may be a recipient of such distributed funds.

To these categories, every librarian can add other needs of the small library. Not every one of these needs can be met by system membership, but many can.

The Small Library as a System Member

It is important to realize that the system is not an outside operation that takes over the administration of the small library. If this does occur, the "small library" ceases to be an independent unit and becomes a branch library. In some circumstances, this option may be open and may offer some benefits. In the context of this volume, however, the independent small library is assumed to continue as an autonomous unit, which is usually the case. As such, it joins the system voluntarily after a careful consideration of the benefits offered. As a system member, it participates in the decisions made for the system and often shares in the selection of any system staff. However, while the library becomes a system member, it continues to enjoy autonomy in its own local operations. That is not to say that the existence of the system will not affect the local operation. If the system or another member is building a collection in a special area, the local library may not feel the need to provide as much locally on that topic. If the system offers shared cataloging, the local library will be able to release time and space formerly given to cataloging and to undertake or expand some other locally needed service.

System membership for the independent public library may, and probably will, call for some changes in routines, will require attendance at meetings, and will expect the local library to share its resources as well as the benefits from sharing the resources of others. These changes and their cost in time and materials will be weighed against the benefits: the value of the in-service training workshops offered by the system; the advice of system specialists; the areawide publicity; the availability of many more specialized materials, which may be delivered within a day or two or may, because the system's members are often geographically close, be borrowed or used in person at a neighboring library by the customer who needs them.

These benefits are great, as is evidenced by the rapid increase in the number of systems and cooperatives among today's libraries and in the number of libraries that join them. Today, there is a trend toward multitype systems whose members include not only public libraries but also college, university, school, and special libraries (corporate, museum, historical society, medical, law, and so forth). This broadening of the membership increases the resources and expertise available and increases the small public library's potential.

Another reason for the increased interest in cooperation in today's library world relates to the shrinking pot of resources. Decreasing tax funds drastically reduce what the library dollar will buy, and the library, unlike a commercial enterprise, cannot pass the increased cost on to the customer. In the library's case, the customer is the taxpayer, and today's taxpayer is neither willing nor able to continue to support all public services to the extent that has been possible in the past. If the library expects to be able to continue to offer all the services formerly available—and to meet the increasing expectations of its customers—it is going to have to do so through the cooperative efforts of a system or through some other form of referral.

Costs of System Services

In many states, funds for systems come from state or federal sources. Even so, there may be some payment required of system members. Whether it is called a membership fee, a form of matching funds, or a direct payment for specific services—such as centralized materials processing or a share in an automated system—it will require funds from the local budget. It is sometimes difficult, therefore, for local officials and taxpayers to understand why the profession sees systems as an economy.

The answer is that while the local library does not save money in the sense of having less cash outlay to make, system membership does "buy" services that would cost much more if provided locally. For example, the system's children's librarian who works with staff members of fifteen member libraries helps them all with selection of children's materials, story hours, summer reading clubs, and other group services. The centralized cataloging service performs the cataloging (usually of many of the same titles) for all the members, thus saving the local library the cost of cataloging time. The local collection may be supplemented by long-term loans and individual request service for materials, selected from a collection for which the system pays far more than any of the individual libraries would be able to pay. Thus, while the local library is not "saving" money in the sense of being able to reduce its budget, it is receiving far more for its money than before.

Economy of scale, a major principle in use in a system, can be illustrated by the example of a book that may be used by one person in a population of 1,000. The same book may be used quite heavily enough to warrant its purchase in a city of 100,000. However, in a town of less than 10,000, its purchase is less certain, especially if it is relatively expensive. Therefore, the creation of a larger customer base through system development enables the purchase of materials that might otherwise not be available. Continuing this example, if the book would be so seldom used and so expensive that even the system could not justify its purchase, the network and interlibrary loan can be called upon when a customer makes a request for the book.

State and National Networks

The library system is an important first ring in a series of concentric links that extend beyond the local jurisdiction. These links connect state and national levels and, as society becomes more global in nature, are reaching out into the international marketplace.

State Networks

Beyond the library system lies the *state network,* a term usually used to describe a statewide structure for the referral of requests for materials and information beyond the borders of the system. One accepted definition of a network is computer-based—that is, the locations of materials (and sometimes information, as well) are stored in a database to which the nodes of the network have access. In some cases, the network will also provide the means of communicating among nodes. However, the term *network* also tends to be used for any channeled communication system among libraries for the purpose of interlibrary loan or cooperative reference or cataloging service.

Within most states, each system (at minimum) is a node in the network and thus will have access to a terminal that connects it to the computer database with location information, to a communication system such as e-mail or fax that permits it to send requests along a prescribed channel, or to both. Thus, if a local library is a member of a system, its customers' requests will be checked

1. at the local library; if it is not found there, then
2. at the system's headquarters or resource center, which may have a record of holdings of system members; if it is not found there, then
3. on the statewide network, which usually includes, but is not confined to, the state library agency's library (Normally, it will have access to all the major collections in a state, including specialized ones.); if it is not found there, then
4. beyond the statewide network to the national network

National Networks

As statewide networks develop in most states, the national networks are increasing in both number and capability. National bibliographic databases can provide impressive benefits to any size library. Many librarians working in small libraries can find the use of a bibliographic utility to be cost effective as a means of enhancing their existing service with a higher quality product.

A bibliographic database is a commercial or nonprofit organization that provides a variety of services including cataloging, interlibrary loan, acquisition programs, authority control, retrospective conversion services, archival tapes, access to specialized collections, and so forth. Beginning in the late 1960s, when small groups of libraries began experimenting with MARC (MAchine-Readable Cataloging) records supplied by the Library of Congress (LC), the movement grew as a group of academic libraries in Ohio developed a cooperative, time-sharing system in 1967, which provided access to a MARC database and collected the input cataloging of all member libraries. Originally named the Ohio College Library Center (OCLC), this cooperative has changed its name several times but is popularly still referred to as OCLC. MARC records from LC have been added on a regular basis by contributing libraries, and today United Kingdom MARC records (UK MARC) are also included—a good example of international linkage. A range of services is provided, including a microcomputer-based serials control system, a circulation control system, and an online public access catalog (OPAC) system. OCLC is a major source of catalog data for libraries worldwide.[2]

Evolving alternatives to OCLC have included RLIN, a combination of databases and computer systems developed by the Research Libraries Group (RLG) to serve the materials-processing and public service requirements of RLG's members and many nonmember institutions.[3] WLN (originally the Washington Library Network, later the Western Library Network) is a regional bibliographic utility developed in the Pacific Northwest.

While networks generally coordinate bibliographic access services on a state or regional basis, some networks provide such additional services as e-mail, microcomputer training, cooperative purchasing programs, authority control, and tape processing services. Some major networks providing these services are NELINET, SOLINET, AMIGOS, BSR, and CLASS.[4]

Amplified Reference Service

There are also national networks that extend the reference capability of the small library. As discussed earlier, the small library has a budgetary capacity for a limited collection; this results in a capacity to respond to customer information requests that may not satisfy local needs and expectations. While library systems and state networks are excellent resources for referral of questions that cannot be handled locally, interaction with national networks can bring a wider circle of resources to the library.

Computer databases and telecommunications linkages have opened new vistas in reference services. Such interaction may involve a computer, modem, and telephone lines or cable—with the corresponding significant cost of line charges. Today, however, databases such as ERIC, DIALOG, LISA, and various Wilson indexes can also be purchased in CD-ROM format, offering even the smallest library an amplified reference capability without expensive line charges. While it is true that CD-ROM technology offers the "feel" of online, it must be remembered that the currency of the citations may be three to six months old as opposed to the immediacy of telephone-linked online. However, most customer requests can be satisfied with this level of currency; only the most specialized customers require total immediacy, and these requests can be passed on to the system level.

The librarian and board of the small public library may doubt that such complex services are useful or necessary locally. However, the numbers of customers, present and potential, who would either require or appreciate this extended service are growing as society becomes more technologically sophisticated. Every community, regardless of size, contains some of the following citizens: college and university professors, graduate students, research and development workers in manufacturing, other research workers, the press and other mass media personnel, government workers, business managers—and the list grows. These individuals may be presently in school, in the workforce, or retired (but with continuing professional interests and activities). The availability of major resources beyond the system and through networks will be important for these customers.

For the small library, the point is to know that the resources exist and to make every effort to let the community (especially customers with specialized and sophisticated needs) know that they are available and can be obtained through the local library. Another essential point must not be overlooked: It is not enough that the librarian knows about these extended resources; every staff member (paid and unpaid) who may be on duty at a public desk should know that this wealth of resources can be tapped by a process that begins at that very desk.

Cooperation with Other Libraries and Agencies

Every small public library has the opportunity to engage in direct cooperation with other libraries and agencies, either within the same community or within a reasonable distance. Possibilities include school media centers, college or university libraries, special libraries (corporate, medical, legal, church, and so forth), and a variety of local agencies (such as preschools, YMCAs, scout troops, United Way, and so forth). It is important that personnel in these organizations know one another on a professional level and that they meet periodically to determine how library service can be designed to benefit their customer groups and how responsibilities can be shared. For example, in terms of public library and school media center cooperation, decisions can be made regarding the following:

1. teaching the use of the library, the catalog, periodical indexes

    Who should teach these skills?

    When should they be taught?

    What coordination would help?

2. arranging for class visits to the public library and public librarian visits to school classes

   How and when can such visits be arranged?

   What should be accomplished? By whom?

   What preparation is desirable on the part of the teacher, the school media specialist, and the public librarian?

3. agreeing on the amount of help students should receive from public librarians and school media specialists

   How much can students be expected to do without assistance?

   Is it possible for the librarian to defeat the purpose of the assignment by giving too much help?

   When is the teacher expecting too much of the student in view of existing material?

4. consulting before assignments are given

   Is adequate material available? For how many students?

   Is it suitable in content and reading level?

   Is it where students can readily find it, or does it require searching through reference books that only the librarian can be expected to know?

   Can materials be gathered through interlibrary loan and displays created to facilitate the connection between students and materials?

Such questions help to clarify the planning process for both types of libraries, individually and collaboratively. Similar questions can be negotiation points between any set or group of libraries and agencies as methods of cooperation are being discussed.

In a small community, it is sometimes possible to share collections among libraries, to some extent. If the public library would like to subscribe to two literary magazines but can only afford one, perhaps the local school or academic library would take the other so that the citizens will have access to both subscriptions. Any sharing mechanism must, of course, be predicated upon the development of policies and procedures that allow citizens access to both libraries. Sometimes, as with a corporate library with proprietary materials, an open-access policy cannot be adopted, or perhaps there are legal restrictions that would need to be changed. It is worth the time to investigate what is possible and to develop strategies to create an open-access environment whenever possible.

Interlibrary Loan

Interlibrary loan is an important way for libraries to share resources. As funding becomes more limited, the issue of ownership versus external borrowing becomes increasingly important. The key to effective library service in this new century is access; whether that access is satisfied by on-hand materials or interlibrary loan is becoming less relevant. The development of collaborative relationships with other libraries and agencies and participation in established interlibrary loan networks—these are the strategies that serve the goal of access. A recent national survey reported that approximately 760 library networks and cooperatives existed in the United States.[5] These are formal networks, and this figure does not include the many informal connections that have been developed between libraries and other agencies.

For the small public library, the library system will be the conduit through which interlibrary loans are requested. Even so, there will be costs to the local library that must be considered during the budget planning process. Such costs involve staff time; network and communication costs, such as telephone services, e-mail, modem, line charges, network fees (if applicable); photocopying costs; supplies; maintenance and equipment; delivery costs; staff training; and supervision time. These cost categories are representative of the interlibrary loan process; exact costs and procedures will vary from situation to situation. The local library should consult with the system representative to calculate more-precise figures.

These costs, while potentially too high for some small libraries to accept, may prove to be a cloud with a growing silver lining. As the Internet becomes increasingly available in libraries of all sizes, that technology may provide a solution to high-cost interlibrary loan. Although copyright issues need to be addressed, some documents may be downloaded from the Web—an impact upon both cost and speed of access.

However, even the smallest public library, once its holdings are included in an electronic network, may become a supplying library as well as a requesting library. Many unique titles can be found in local collections. The National Interlibrary Loan Code provides general guidelines and helps to regulate borrowing and lending between libraries. These guidelines are summarized in figure 9.1.

FIGURE 9.1

National Interlibrary Loan Code Guidelines Summary

The Requesting Library	The Supplying Library
Should establish and maintain an interlibrary loan policy for its borrowers and make it available	Should establish and maintain an interlibrary loan policy, make it available in paper or electronic format, and provide it upon request
Should process requests in a timely fashion	
Should identify libraries that own and might provide the requested materials	
Should check the policies of potential suppliers for special instructions, restrictions, and information on charges prior to sending a request	Should process requests within the time frame established by the electronic network; requests not transmitted electronically should be handled in a similar time frame
Is responsible for all authorized charges imposed by the supplying library	
Should send requests for materials for which locations cannot be identified to libraries that might provide the requested materials accompanied by the statement "cannot locate"	Should include a copy of the original request, or information sufficient to identify the request, with each item
Should avoid sending the burden of its requests to a few libraries	Should state any conditions or restrictions on use of the materials lent and specify any special packaging or shipping requirements
Should transmit all interlibrary loan requests in standard bibliographic format in accordance with the protocols of the electronic network or transmission system used	
Must ensure compliance with U.S. copyright law and its accompanying guidelines; copyright compliance must be determined for each copy request before it is transmitted, and a copyright compliance statement must be included on each copy request	Should state the due date or duration of a loan on the request form or on the material
	Should package the items so as to prevent damage in shipping
Is responsible for borrowed materials from the time they leave the supplying library until they have been returned and received by the supplying library; if damage or loss occurs, the requesting library is responsible for compensation or replacement, in accordance with the preference of the supplying library	Should notify the requesting library promptly when unable to fill a request, and if possible, state the reason the request cannot be filled

The Requesting Library	The Supplying Library
Should request a renewal before the item is due; if the supplying library does not respond, the requesting library may assume that the renewal has been granted for the same length of time as the original loan	Should respond promptly to requests for renewals; if supplying library does not respond, the borrowing library may assume that the renewal has been granted for the same length of time as the original loan period
Should return materials by the due date and respond immediately if the item has been recalled by the supplying library	May recall materials at any time
Is responsible for following the provisions of this code; continued disregard for any provision may be reason for suspension of borrowing privileges by a supplying library	May suspend service to any requesting library that fails to comply with the provisions of this code

Requesting library notes from Mary Jo Lynch, "Some Basic Figures," in *Whole Library Handbook* 2: *Current Data, Professional Advice, and Curiosa About Libraries and Library Services*, comp. George M. Eberhart (Chicago: American Library Assn., 1995), as quoted in *Reinvention of the Public Library for the 21st Century*, ed. William L. Whitesides, Sr. (Englewood, Colo.: Libraries Unlimited, 1998): 47–8.

Supplying library notes from "National Interlibrary Loan Code for the United States," RQ 33, no. 4 (summer 1994): 477–9, as quoted in *Reinvention of the Public Library for the 21st Century*, ed. William L. Whitesides Sr. (Englewood, Colo.: Libraries Unlimited, 1998): 48–9.

For libraries interested in a more in-depth investigation of interlibrary loan in terms of planning, process, and expenses, see the *Interlibrary Loan Practices Handbook* by Virginia Boucher.[6]

As the chapter opened, comment was made that the public library is a community's window to the world. By recognizing its role as a node in that global information network, being actively alert to potential opportunities for cooperation and collaboration, and participating in all possible linkages that are available and appropriate, the local public library becomes that window for its customers.

Thoughts for the New Millennium

Does my library belong to a library system?

What are the benefits that my library receives from the system? Are those benefits clearly communicated to my board? To the funders? To the community?

Have I given thought to the relationship between the cost of system membership, the actual cost of benefits received, and the intangibles?

What specific benefits can I identify regarding the categories discussed in this chapter:

books	staff
periodicals	administrative skills
audiovisual	

Are there liabilities to system membership? If so, what are they? Have these issues been addressed with the system administration?

What networks are present in my state? What use does my library make of these networks?

What national networks are available to my library? How are they used by my library?

Are there other, better ways that my library could take advantage of these state and national networks?

What possibilities for cooperation and collaboration with other libraries and agencies are present in my community? Has my library taken advantage of any of these partnership opportunities? If yes, are there others that should be investigated? If no, how soon can we get started?

Notes

1. Gene Martin and Frederick J. Raithel, "Library Systems," in *The Library Trustee: A Practical Guidebook,* 4th ed., ed. Virginia G. Young (Chicago: American Library Assn., 1988), 115.

2. Neil F. Doherty, "OCLC," in *International Encyclopedia of Information and Library Science,* eds. John Feather and Paul Sturges (London: Routledge, 1997), 323.

3. Edie M. Rasmussen, "Research Libraries Group (RLG)," in *International Encyclopedia of Information and Library Science,* 402.

4. Liz Bishoff, "Bibliographic Utilities," in *The How-to-Do-It Manual for Small Libraries,* ed. Bill Katz (New York: Neal-Schuman, 1988), 219.

5. Lisa S. Payne, "The Library Environment," in *Reinvention of the Public Library for the 21st Century,* ed. William L. Whitesides Sr. (Englewood, Colo.: Libraries Unlimited, 1998), 46–7.

6. Virginia Boucher, *Interlibrary Loan Practices Handbook,* 2d ed. (Chicago: American Library Assn., 1996).

10 Outlets for Library Service in the New Millennium

The public library is the sum of its services. It is more, much more than any physical outlet: It is the connection point between the customer's information need and the world of information. In the process of serving as this connection point, the public library may use a variety of outlets: buildings, kiosks, mail service, telephone reference, bookmobiles, and the growing number of electronic networks, such as computer systems and cable television. The outlets that a library manager selects to serve as distribution channels will contribute significantly to the services offered.

First, a library that offers distribution channels that are convenient, easy to use, and comfortable in ambiance creates an environment that is an inducement to library use. Second, distribution channels that are readily accessible and efficient in operation make possible the effective utilization of the library's resources by both customers and staff. In addition, a library that combines effectiveness, efficiency, and appeal creates for itself an image that is subtly but quite definitely different from that created by an inefficient and difficult-to-access method of distribution.

Many a library has limited its vision to what could be offered within the limitations of a single building, eventually moving on to an improved building, taking the same materials and the same staff, yet discovering that its local prestige had risen remarkably simply because the public had judged the product by the package. Imagine what could be possible if the packaging served as an extension of the product, offering maximum effectiveness to each customer.

Electronic Access

The local public library, hopefully cooperating with a library system, is responsible for providing and coordinating access to knowledge, information, and diversity of ideas for its community. *Access* includes the location of any buildings or other physical facilities, the hours of operation, bibliographic access to the library's materials, and demonstrations of technologies that may enable new avenues of access. While the traditional access point for the public library has been a building, for an increasing percentage of the community, electronic access has become an essential benefit. Many libraries offer the community the ability to dial in to the library's online catalog, place holds on materials and request pickup locations, ask reference questions via e-mail, and so forth. While the small public library may have difficulty offering these benefits by itself, through its system membership many things may be possible.

Public libraries have been affected by the increased accessibility of information technology in a number of ways, including[1]

Library operations are becoming automated. Even the smallest public libraries are automating circulation and providing Internet access for the community. While not universally true as yet, the trend is certainly in this direction, and libraries are using technology as soon as it is possible to do so.

Fewer distinctions are being made between library functions, which requires more cross-training and reeducation. While any change requires the upgrading of skills, the changes related to technology occur with greater frequency, and continuing education for staff is a mandate, both practically and ethically.

Libraries and librarians worldwide are sharing and accessing data seamlessly across computer platforms. The ability of library staff to locate the information that customers require has dramatically improved through the use of technology. The barriers of time and distance have dissolved as librarians can connect with resources far beyond their local communities.

Customers are obtaining more-equitable access to information. The library is truly the community's window to the world of information. Through technology, access to global information has increased dramatically, and the importance of the library in the smallest community should reflect this improvement.

Of course, all present and proposed electronic library practices should be firmly rooted in the library's mission and vision plus what has been learned through analysis of the community. The library that has not actively embraced planning and marketing processes may leap without thought into a technological whirlpool. Investments in technology are not a one-time cost. They are ongoing, and there are corollary costs that must also be considered. Indeed, there have been cases where libraries automated and forgot to include the cost of printer paper and maintenance in their budgets. The digital world is attractive and effective, but the library needs always to think of possibilities in terms of what is appropriate locally, given identified community needs and funding resources.

While the cost of electronic access is always a factor, the benefits are considerable, and in some instances, print resources can be discontinued when electronic sources are available. Customer expectations will also increase, however, and the demand for additional, faster, and more user-friendly electronic resources will escalate. When new technologies and systems of access are introduced, the role that the library plays in the community will also change. For example, customers will need to be educated in how to use an online catalog, how to access the Internet, how to place holds electronically, and so forth. In addition, existing policies will need to be reviewed and revised as appropriate; new policies may need to be written.

However, despite the real concerns about cost, resources, and the like, the issue of access is paramount. Some families will have the personal assets to enable them to afford Internet access in the home; others see such a possibility as a distant or unrealistic dream. The public library is in the unique position of being able to "level the playing field" for the citizens of the community by making Internet access available to everyone.

The Library Building

Electronic access brings certain virtual attributes to the public library, but the library as place is still very much an important community treasure. Community pride in its library building is generally very high—whether or not individual citizens have ever been inside. Since the importance of the library building carries both practical and psychological significance, it is critical that the facility be designed carefully and with sensitivity to community needs. The physical environment of the library can influence the activity within its walls, staff attitude and efficiency, and customer comfort and ease of use.

The physical facility housing the library's services also has a direct effect on access. The exterior of the building provides the first criterion that many people use to judge the library. An unattractive building, poorly maintained, with peeling paint, scruffy grounds, and sloppy signage will influence usage and funding. As with the concept of image in many areas of life, the face that the library presents to the world may initially be a physical face.[2]

The public library building should present a compelling invitation to enter, read, listen, view, and learn. The building should be sufficiently flexible to respond to changing use and service patterns—yet be expandable to accommodate collections growing in scope and variety of formats. Buildings should be designed for maximum efficiency—both for users and for staff.[3]

Decisions for the Library Board

Unless the library is fortunate enough to have a building that is large enough, functional, and physically attractive, the librarian and trustees should do whatever is possible to achieve a more effective setting for library service. When a library needs new quarters because of lack of space, poor-quality physical conditions, or the need for a better location, there are many questions to be considered:

> Is a new building necessary? Should the existing structure be remodeled? Is it possible to remodel a suitable building originally constructed for another purpose? What about rented quarters?
>
> Where shall the new or refurbished library be located?
>
> Where will money be found for any of the various options?
>
> What alternative distribution outlets could be used? (If the situation seems to warrant distributing service among two or more physical outlets or electronic or other possibilities, these choices will affect the size and planning of the new or remodeled building.)

Whether an operational or advisory body, the library board will have significant responsibility when a building project is under consideration. The board will provide oversight and direction for the building project, just as it does for the library's policies. Both legal and fiscal authority may be part of the board's role. The board may be vested with the actual responsibility and authority, or it may need to identify and work closely with the governmental unit or office that is legally responsible. The steps that are outlined in figure 10.1 may occur in a somewhat different order in individual communities, but they are typical overall for any library building project.

Undergirding the project, however, must be a thorough understanding of the community's library-service needs based upon the data gleaned through the marketing audit/community study. It is imperative that the board and the staff have a sound knowledge of the community's needs and how those needs affect the library's space needs. While political winds may blow erratically and sudden bequests may provide hoped-for funds, if the board and the staff have not carefully assessed community needs and translated those needs into space requirements, they may be rushed into uninformed or emotion-based decisions. In addition to these considerations, the planners should review the condition of the current building, noting both deficiencies and opportunities for change. With these assessments in hand, the board and other local planners can begin to evaluate options: Does the assessment suggest that the library needs 10 percent more space? 50 per-

FIGURE 10.1 | The Library Board's Role in a Library Building Project

Project Phases	Major Steps
Preproject planning	Make the decision that a construction program is needed
	Select a qualified professional librarian, if one isn't already employed, to direct the service planning to be reflected in the building program
	Study the community, including broad demographic, economic, and other trends as they define library service needs
	Initiate a needs assessment based on the community study

Project Phases	Major Steps
Early groundwork	Direct the campaign to let the community know about the need for new or expanded facilities
	Approve a written building program statement describing present and future building needs
	Appoint a building committee from within the board membership, or if the board is small enough, name a committee of the whole
Decision-making phase	Select and appoint a qualified library building consultant
	Select and appoint a qualified architect
	Select and appoint an attorney
	Select and appoint an interiors specialist
	Select and puchase a site with the advice and assistance of the planning team
	Approve preliminary plans and furniture and equipment layouts
Fund-raising phase	Estimate the cost of operating the new building and seek assurance of adequate operating funds once it is completed
	Secure funds for the project if it is not endowed; activate the campaign, referendum, or whatever is needed financially.
Implementation phase	Approve final plans and authorize the invitation for bids for the building
	Approve construction contracts
	Approve furniture and equipment contracts
	Approve and pay invoices
Celebration phase	Arrange the dedication and open house, with announcements to the public
	Help acquaint the public with the new services and programs now possible and available

ADAPTED FROM: Anders C. Dahlgren and Charles E. Reid, "The Trustee and Library Buildings," in *The Library Trustee*, 5th ed., ed. Virginia G. Young (Chicago: American Library Assn., 1995), 91–2.

cent? 200 percent? Can the present building be renovated? Is an expanded building necessary? As collections evolve into larger percentages of electronic formats, might the library actually require *less* space?

Many factors affect the relationship between physical space and library service. In determining space needs and service projections, the following steps are useful benchmarks:

1. Identify the library's projected service population.
2. Estimate the number of items the library will need in its collection to meet future service requirements, and identify how much floor space is needed to house that projected collection.
3. Estimate the number of seats the library will need to accommodate in-house use of the collection and how much floor space those seats will require.
4. Estimate the number of staff workstations that will be necessary to support the staff's projected routines and how much floor space they will require.
5. Estimate the type and capacity of meeting rooms that the library will need and how much floor space these will require.
6. Calculate an allocation for miscellaneous public- and staff-use space.
7. Calculate an allocation for vestibules, furnace rooms, rest rooms, and other types of nonassignable space.
8. Assemble the estimates for the six types of space into an overall estimate of space need.[4]

In addition, when assessing the present (and proposed) physical facility, the following standards may prove helpful:

The library provides adequate space to implement the full range of library services consistent with the library's comprehensive long-range plan and other service standards.

At least once every five years, the board directs the preparation of an assessment of the library's long-term space needs.

The library building meets state and Americans with Disabilities Act requirements for physical accessibility (multistory structures provide elevators or lifts, as necessary).

Adequate and convenient parking is available to the library's customers and staff on or adjacent to the library's site; the minimum number of required parking spaces may be governed by local ordinance.

The exterior of the library is well lighted and identified with signs clearly visible from the street.

The entrance is clearly visible and is located on the side of the building that most users approach.

Emergency facilities are provided in accordance with appropriate codes; evacuation routes, fire exits, and the location of fire extinguishers are clearly marked; the library has a designated storm shelter.

Lighting levels comply with the standards issued by the Illuminating Engineering Society of North America.

The library provides facilities for the return of library materials when the library is closed; after-hour book depositories should be fireproof.

The library has public meeting space available for its programming and for use by other community groups.

The library has allocated space for child and family use, with all materials readily available, and provides furniture and equipment designed for use by children.[5]

The Building Program Statement

Introduced in figure 10.1, the building program statement is the heart of any building project. Whenever a major capital project is being considered, the library board should prepare a written building program statement. This statement contains the instructions to the architect and includes the following:

1. library space needs, including how the space should be subdivided or organized
2. what is going to occur in each department or service subdivision, including at least a preliminary listing of the furniture and equipment that will be required to support those routines
3. how those departments or subdivisions should interrelate for optimum efficiency
4. other information, such as a brief history of the library, a summary of library goals and objectives, a description of the current building,

or a preliminary projection of the construction budget and the operating budget in the expanded facility[6]

The building program statement may be written by the librarian, by a building consultant, or by both as a joint effort. In some communities, one or more library trustees who have expertise and interest may also want to become involved. When the statement is written, it should be reviewed and approved by the entire board, and copies should be shared with the municipal funding authority. (Local legalities may require that the latter authority also formally endorse the program statement.)[7] Figure 10.2 presents a generic outline of a building program statement.

FIGURE 10.2   Generic Outline of Building Program Statement

Section	Explanation	Details
I. Concise history of the library	Several paragraphs summarizing the library's history and role in the community	
II. Philosophy of library service	The library's mission statement	
III. Library goals, objectives, and strategies	The plan to meet the present and future library and information needs of the citizens within the library's service area	
IV. Proposed facility	The spatial needs to accommodate the provision of expanded resource collections and service areas necessary to reach the objectives outlined above; a list of every functional area in the proposed facility	What is the required usable square footage? What happens in this area? How does this area relate to other areas? How many members of the staff or public will be housed or accommodated in this area? What are the environmental requirements?

Section	Explanation	Details
IV. Proposed facility (cont.)		What are the utility requirements? Data transmission for computer terminals? Electrical outlets? Telephone? Water? Other?
		What furniture and equipment must be present in this area?
		What library materials need to be housed in this area? Include print resources, films, filmstrips, recordings, audiocassettes, compact discs, videodiscs and cassettes, microforms, and any other nonprint collections
		Are there special programs or items requiring built-in equipment or furnishings?
		What floor covering should the area have?
		Are there other special requirements? Lighting? Security? Humidity control? Visual supervision? Other?
V. Project budget	Should include both funding sources and estimated budget	A breakdown of fund sources
		An estimated budget including the best estimates for planning and consultation fees, architectural fees, site acquisition, site preparation, construction, furniture and equipment, and contingencies
VI. General statements	Such topics as directions to the architect, preferences of the building planning committee, or matters that remain unresolved	Accessibility requirements
		Book depositories
		Building materials (ease of maintenance)

(continued)

FIGURE 10.2

Generic Outline of Building Program Statement (*continued*)

Section	Explanation	Details
VI. General statements (cont.)		Built-ins as part of the general design specifications
		Compact shelving (advantages/ disadvantages)
		Energy conservation issues
		Fenestration (location of windows; operable or fixed glass)
		Heating, ventilating, and air-conditioning (HVAC) systems (humidity control, location of mechanical room, location of thermostats)
		Landscaping
		Lighting (natural or artificial; types of artificial light; required lighting levels)
		Open space versus walled areas
		Parking for staff, public, handicapped, delivery vehicles
		Plantings (interior and exterior; ease of care)
		Provision for future expansion
		Shelving (wood or metal; height, depth)
		Multipurpose spaces/meeting room(s)/children's program area

ADAPTED FROM: Lance Finney, "The Library Building Program: Key to Success," *Public Libraries* 23 (fall 1984), 79–82.

It is important to remember that, like the analysis of the library's various environments that comprise the marketing audit, the building program statement is a snapshot of "now" and must therefore be considered a working document that must be revised if conditions change.

Steps to Improved Library Facilities

While this chapter cannot offer a comprehensive guide to space planning and design, many indicators can provide ideas and encourage further study. As an overview, the steps given in figure 10.3 are a framework for facilities planning, whether the desired outcome is new construction or renovation.

Although these are important steps, there are also other factors that affect the total environment. A new building, remodeling, energy conservation, bond issues, accessibility for use by citizens with disabilities—these are but some of the possible considerations facing a library manager. Many

FIGURE 10.3

Steps to a Successful Building Program

Steps	Activities*
Orientation/ literature review	Examine the literature relating to building planning Attend building workshops Interview librarians and trustees who have recently completed building expansions
Needs assessment	Assess community needs and present facility inadequacies Make an initial estimation of space requirements for future service needs by projecting collections and services that will be needed by the community twenty years into the future Prepare a report based upon data gathered in the marketing audit Present the report to the board for approval
Evaluation of alternatives	Explore various options, including new construction, an addition to the existing building, remodeling unused parts of the existing building, or converting another existing structure for library use
Building program statement	Include the elements listed in the sections above State what the library hopes to accomplish in an expanded facility Describe the overall space requirements

*Activities are those of the library director unless otherwise indicated.

(continued)

FIGURE 10.3

Steps to a Successful Building Program (*continued*)

Steps	Activities*
Building program statement (cont.)	Classify the identified need into functional departments or areas Describe potential interrelationships among areas
Project team	Assemble a team composed of representatives from the trustees, the library director, the architect, a library building consultant (optional, but recommended), the municipal funding authority, an attorney, and perhaps representatives from building inspectors, Friends groups, and interior designers
Site selection	Consider visibility and access (of primary importance), availability, costs, property size, and expansion possibilities as well as parking
Construction finance	Prepare cost estimates and a budget, including allocations for general construction, plumbing, mechanical work, electrical work, special construction features, site acquisition, site preparation, architects and professional fees, furnishings and equipment, and moving expenses—plus a contingency fund equal to at least 5 percent of the estimated construction contract Secure funding through municipal appropriation or borrowing, private fund-raising, federal construction grants (i.e., LSCA), and/or a referendum/bond issue
Architectural implementation	Review the architect's plan in fulfillment of the building program statement, including a schematic design of interior and exterior requirements plus the details of cooperation with structural, mechanical, and electrical engineers Present the complete set of working drawings and specifications for board approval
Interior design	Periodically reveiw the plans developed by either the architect or interior designer as they evolve simultaneously with the structural plans As plans near completion, prepare a detailed list of furniture and equipment to be purchased Begin the bid solicitation process

Steps	Activities*
Plans analysis	Present the plans at various stages of their development to the board for formal approval to detect errors early in the process
Bidding and contract negotiation	Gain board authorization of a call for bids after board approval of the final version of the plan Place legal notices in newspapers and trade papers Open received bids in a public meeting after technical and legal review of the bids Recommend bids (frequently the lowest ones that qualify) Gain board approval of bids Sign contracts
Construction	Contractor: maintain legal responsibility for activities at the site and the obligation to complete the project as specified in the plans Architect: act as the library's representative and technical expert Board: continue with overall responsibility for both construction and payment of bills
Moving in and dedication	Make early plans that consider the size of the collection, the amount of existing furniture to be moved into the new building, the distance to travel, and available funding Have a dedication ceremony recognizing the contributions of everyone involved in the project Publicize the new facilities and services
Postoccupancy evaluation	Board: following a short period of operations within the new facility, evaluates the building's functionality, improvement of services, adaptations from the original concept, and anticipates additional changes

*Activities are those of the library director unless otherwise indicated.

ADAPTED FROM: *Wisconsin Public Library Trustee Handbook* (Madison: Wisconsin Dept. of Public Instruction, 1989), 40–5.

of the details of library construction are beyond the scope of a book such as this one. For example, a multiplicity of decisions about building materials, heating and air conditioning, wiring, and floor covering must be made when the library is being remodeled or rebuilt.[8]

An important factor is the control of noise, whether in the public or behind-the-scenes areas. Noise has an inhibiting effect on concentration and productivity. The optimum control of sound can enhance the quality of other environmental factors to a significant degree. Yet noise control also has its promotional side: There needs to be space in the library where conversation and activity is not only allowed but encouraged. The old image of the library as a "shh-hh" place is just that: old. The public library is an information and community center. As such, the rights of customers both to study in a quiet environment and to share ideas with others must be respected and provided for.

Climate control is another component of physical plant management that can directly influence library usage. It is certainly difficult to work—as either staff member or library customer—in a building that is too warm, too cool, or poorly ventilated. An environment conducive to bodily comfort can provide the opportunity, if not the stimulus, for learning to take place.

Expert advice from both architect and contractor is essential to successfully negotiate the sometimes perilous waters of remodeling or building construction. Many libraries find that hiring a building consultant is a very wise investment, as the special expertise of a good consultant can often save many times the amount of any consultant fee.

This chapter focuses primarily on those general considerations about a building and other library outlets that call for knowledge the librarian is best able to supply. The important ideal to keep in mind when determining what distribution channels are needed in a community is customer satisfaction: What channels will enhance a customer's ability to access the information that is required, at a time and place that are both reasonable and convenient?

Specific Building Elements

Every library contains certain common elements, and whether a new building or a remodeling situation is under consideration, these elements must be present:

The main door should be at ground level, accessible to anyone. Ease of operation is important, since most customers will be carrying library materials.

Signage should be both clear and attractive.

The circulation desk is logically situated near the entry for ease of access. Desk height should be carefully considered and appropriate for staff comfort.

The catalog also needs to be readily accessible by customers and staff. Even if a card catalog is still in use, sufficient electrical outlets should be in place in anticipation of the time when an online catalog will be installed.

Collection space may be divided by anticipated customer use, such as browsing by adults, children, and young adults. Arrangement should meet the needs of the specific purpose and customer group.

Materials to be found within each type of collection space can be interfiled or arranged separately by type of media.

Work areas must be provided for the staff in sufficient size and arrangement to facilitate ease of use.

Administrative office space should be included in even the smallest facility. This space should be separate from work areas and can be used for administrative purposes and for private conferences with either staff or customers.

A staff room, where staff members can retire to relax and eat meals, should include both lounge and kitchen facilities.

Meeting rooms are strongly recommended whenever possible, as this enables various community groups to gather for meetings within the library and facilitates opportunities for mutual cooperation.

Janitorial space can be as small as a closet or as extensive as a complete workshop.

Rest rooms are a necessary component; if separate facilities are not possible, a "unisex" facility may be an acceptable compromise.

Mechanical space must be set aside for various heating and cooling systems, the water heater, and so forth.

Unassigned space is always necessary for storage of miscellaneous items and, in this day of computers, for all those computer-related boxes that must be retained to send equipment out for repair.

These elements are integral to every library setting. When square footage is being assessed, careful consideration of the space requirements of each of these elements must be part of the total planning process.

Before the decision to rebuild or remodel is irrevocably made, trustees and prominent citizens should see slides and pictures of new and remodeled library buildings or, if possible, the buildings themselves. The impact of a viewing, with the pleasure and excitement that arise with the prospect of a new and different library setting, often signals the beginning of a successful building campaign and a new concept of library service as a whole.

Deciding to Build or Remodel

The cost of a new library building is high, and the first impulse of citizens and trustees alike is often to enlarge the present facility. Successful remodeling of Carnegie buildings, or others of the same era, has been accomplished in some places, but the cost may be close to that of creating a new structure. However, community sentiment may be so strong—or the building may be on the historic register—that creative remodeling is the most politically wise solution. Yet, remodeling should be discouraged if the library is poorly located or if it is so constructed that the new layout cannot be functional. For example, remodeling that breaks the area for public use into several small rooms presents problems of supervision and traffic flow. Sometimes it is wiser to find another purpose for a historic library facility and seek to build a new library that will meet present and future needs.

The librarian and the board should do a preliminary survey of the present facility, focusing attention on the major areas of structure, electrical, mechanical, and plumbing—with special attention to the requirements for customers with disabilities. The results of this survey will clearly demonstrate whether remodeling, expansion, or new construction should be recommended. The questions found in figure 10.4 will be helpful during a tour of the present building.

FIGURE 10.4

Structural, Electrical, Mechanical, and Plumbing Surveys

A. Structural Survey	
Access	Is barrier-free access provided to the library, its collections, and services?
Foundation and walkways	Do the foundation or wall surfaces show signs of serious cracking?
	Are there signs of severe moisture leakage in areas above and below grade?
	What is the condition of the mortar in exposed masonry?
	Are outside walks and steps flat and unbroken?
Floors, stairs, and thresholds	Does the floor feel solid underfoot when a loaded book truck is moved across it?
	Is there any apparent deflection in the floor?
	Do interior stairs feel firm underfoot, and are the handrails securely fastened?
	Is there any sign of wood rot or other deterioration in thresholds?
	Do windows close properly without undue pressure?
	Do doors fit squarely into their frames?
	Are there signs of doors scraping the floor?
Walls and ceilings	What is the condition of interior walls?
	Is there evidence that asbestos was used in the construction of the building?
	Is there evidence of periodic flooding in any part of the building?
Roof	What is the condition of the roof?
	Do ceiling beams appear bowed?
B. Electrical Survey	
Lighting	Is the lighting adequate for the tasks performed in all parts of the building? (Consider the impact of computer screens on lighting requirements.)
	Do the lights flicker or dim?

(continued)

FIGURE 10.4

Structural, Electrical, Mechanical, and Plumbing Surveys
(*continued*)

B. Electrical Survey (cont.)	
Electrical	How often do circuit breakers have to be reset or fuses replaced?
	Has it ever been necessary to run additional wiring to accommodate new equipment?
	When was the building's electrical system last renovated?
	Are utility bills increasing significantly?
	Does the building have any history of difficulty with its electrical system?
	Is there room on the switch panel for additional circuits?
Data transmission	Are data transmission capabilities available throughout the building to support computers linked in a local area network or to support circulation terminals and public access catalogs tied into a mainframe?
	Are the electric outlets adequate in number, load capacity, and location for both library and office equipment in use today as well as for the next ten years? Twenty years? (Note the special power requirements of automated equipment of all types.)
The future	Can the lighting, electrical, and data transmission systems be adapted readily to reflect changing use patterns and to accommodate new equipment?
C. Mechanical Survey	
HVAC	How old is the present heating and ventilating equipment?
	Does the present heating and ventilating equipment keep the building at satisfactory temperatures in all seasons?
	Have there been difficulties in securing adequate fuel for the heating system during the past several years?
	What are the energy efficiency ratings?
Climate conrol	Are there areas in the library that evoke public or staff complaints for being too warm, too cold, or drafty?
Insulation	Is there adequate insulation in the ceilings, walls, and floors?

C. Mechanical Survey (cont.)	
Equipment	Does the mechanical equipment transmit excessive noise?
	Are any special problems associated with servicing the mechanical equipment in its present location?
	What does the library spend annually to maintain the mechanical equipment?

D. Plumbing Survey	
Fixtures	Is there an adequate number of toilet fixtures?
	Do the number and kind of fixtures meet requirements for customers with disabilities?
	Are lavatories, toilets, and sinks in good condition with few, if any, chips or breaks in the surfaces?
Water supply	Do the water supply and pressure entering the building seem adequate?
Pipes and drains	Is there evidence of leaking pipes or fixtures in floors, walls, or ceilings?
	Does the library seem to suffer from frozen water pipes more often than other structures in the area?
	Are there floor drains in the restrooms to protect against flooding?
	Are drains chronically sluggish?
	Is there adequate drainage from the roof and the grounds during periods of thaw?
Repair history	How often each year is it necessary to call a plumber?
	Has the library ever undergone extensive replacement or renovation of plumbing and fixtures? If so, when?

ADAPTED FROM: Raymond M. Holt, *Wisconsin Library Building Project Handbook*, 2d ed. Rev. by Anders C. Dahlgren (Madison: Wisconsin Dept. of Public Instruction, 1990), 26–7.

In addition to the questions posed in figures 10.4, there are specific guidelines and requirements related to accessibility that may be enforced by local, state, or national authorities. These requirements should be investigated routinely, as standards and legislation are continually under review.

Costs

Building costs have increased rapidly over recent years, and there is no indication that this rate of increase will slacken. There is no question but that a sizable amount of money is going to be needed for a new or remodeled library building. For major construction, which constitutes the largest capital expenditure ever made by most libraries, several methods are frequently used for obtaining the funds. These include saving for a building fund, borrowing through floating a bond issue, and a lease-purchase arrangement.

Saving for a building fund, the oldest of the methods, may have been a wise choice in an earlier day. With rapidly increasing costs, it is much less practical today. Plans may be made, a site secured, a campaign for funds initiated, and a regular amount scheduled to be held out from each year's budget for the new building. However, the estimated cost will in all probability have increased enormously by the time the sought-for sum is in hand. Unless a wealthy donor or a generous jurisdiction is willing to provide the money very quickly, the "pay as you go" method is not very satisfactory in today's economy.

Borrowing the money by floating a bond issue is the method most often used by libraries. Normally it calls for a referendum and a campaign. Friends of the Library are useful in this situation, to explain the need to the voters and to pay for posters, bookmarks, and other campaign literature. Even with a bond issue, there is a time lag between the date the sum is estimated to be needed and the time the funds are actually available. Bids are often much higher than anticipated, and a modification of plans is frequently necessary. Most libraries, as official services of a city or county, will have to convince the taxing body of the need to place a library bond issue on the ballot. The actual business of marketing and retiring the bonds will be taken care of through normal channels by the jurisdiction. A separate library district will have more to do in connection with the financing of the building.

Where the jurisdiction handles all official bond issues, it may also automatically own all buildings so financed. In such cases, retirement of the bonds will not be charged to the library's budget but will be taken care of by a general debt retirement fund. This minor advantage may be overbalanced by a debt limitation for the jurisdiction, mandated by state law or local ordinance, that prohibits a jurisdiction from incurring debts beyond a certain amount. If so, a vote on a library bond issue may have to await the retirement of other debts.

A lease-purchase arrangement is likely to be the most expensive funding method, but it may need to be considered in times of serious fiscal constraint. However, it is illegal to use lease-purchase for construction of public buildings in some states and localities. Lease-purchase is, legally and technically, as its name indicates, the rental of a building over a period of years with an option to purchase it at the end of that time. In most such transactions, the rental is applied to the purchase price, so that the final rent payment will complete the purchase. A building may thus be built for the library, to the library's specifications, and occupied by the library. Ownership resides in the construction company until the agreement is fulfilled. The rent payments (or "installments") usually amount to considerably more than the library would pay for the same building had it been funded through a bond issue. However, since the payments are technically rent, they do not increase the jurisdiction's bonded indebtedness (and thus run into the legal limitation), even though they materially increase the library's operating budget during the period of the lease agreement.

Energy Considerations

In times past, advice about library buildings to boards and directors has tended to center on principles of flexibility and convenience. Such matters as heating and air conditioning have been important but, having more in common with problems of buildings in general, have been seen as the province of contractors. This fact is still true, but the people responsible for planning a library building today cannot avoid serious consideration of energy consumption and its effect on building costs.

While the future cannot be reliably predicted, it seems probable that practically all utility costs will continue to rise and that considerations of reduction of these costs will loom large in planning. Furthermore, energy costs may affect more than one building plan. The choice of the establishment of a branch or a bookmobile, which formerly might have been resolved in favor of the latter, might have to be rethought in the light of current gasoline prices. If the choice is to build a branch, its utilities bills will be higher than would have been dreamed of a few years ago. What effect future energy issues may have on people's habits of movement is still unknown. If people cease to drive as far and as often, what will this mean for library outlets? One possibility was foreseen in the advice previously given by a number of consultants—that is, to build near a shopping center or to rent space in one. If the future holds a genuine cutback in people's driving habits, it may be more practical for a library to locate near other necessary visiting points, and thus be convenient without a special trip (which may be an important consideration, in any event). Similarly, locating along existing public transportation routes should also be given serious consideration.

A few newer libraries are making use of solar energy. It seems likely that this technology will continue to develop, become more effective, and cost less than other energy sources. Costs of existing types of fuels in existing library buildings are encouraging planners to consider building immediately, before costs of building and utilities rise still further. Such plans tend to call for whatever techniques of insulation are appropriate for the location. To build now may be wise, as long as the builders and planners attempt to design and construct a library building that can be adapted to future developments.

Furniture

Librarians are understandably more adept at selecting materials than at selecting furniture and equipment. In either case, however, part of the librarian's responsibility is to know what is available and what the standards are for selection.

It is tempting, but not necessarily the best route, to take the line of least resistance and order everything from a trusted dealer's catalog. Careful furniture selection must distinguish between those items that must be built according to strict library specifications and those that can safely be selected from a library supplier.

In considering furniture, one needs to look for the sturdy, durable, and functional, but this does not mean settling for the unimaginative or institutional. Library supply houses have developed attractive lines of furniture that are a far cry from the massive and forbidding pieces of a generation or two ago. Tables and chairs need not be manufactured specifically for library use, so long as they are strong, light, and functional. Some libraries, especially small ones, use only round tables of an informal type. Sometimes, oblong tables are provided, along with more informal furniture in a browsing area. In general terms, small tables seating four or six are better than longer ones, as they are more easily fitted into new space arrangements and are generally preferred by customers. (Realistically, two people will sit at a table designed either for four or six, so this need for personal space should be taken into account.) A few study carrels with electrical outlets for computers will be appreciated by customers who will be working for several hours at a time, taking many notes, and using several sources over a period of time.

Some items of furniture must be carefully made and are most logically purchased from a library supplier. These items include shelving, which must be adjustable and accommodate materials of various sizes, and circulation desks. In addition, special racks have been designed to display audiovisual materials of various types and sizes. A carefully planned circulation desk is one of the most important pieces of furniture in the library and should be designed with both the circulation system and the needs and preferences of staff taken into account. Some desks require staff to stand or use a high stool; others are constructed to allow staff to be seated. Sufficient storage space is necessary at the desk as well as accessibility to other work areas.

The library's other desks need not always be "library" furniture. The highly desirable second public service desk, at which reference and reader guidance are given, can come from a business supply house, a school supplier, or a library furniture dealer. Work space for the library's behind-the-scenes functions, such as checking in periodicals, processing and other technical services, and reshelving, may be most effectively provided by built-in, shelf-type workstations along a wall.

Furniture and shelving need to be appropriate to the library's general appearance and functions, yet enhance the flexible use of space. Library objectives will determine what is needed, but the age and nature of the present or projected building will also have an influence.

Equipment

Previous chapters have stressed the importance of staff time in the total library picture and the need to reduce time spent on routine jobs by work simplification and the use of appropriate laborsaving equipment. As in so many other decisions, the librarian needs to choose a road appropriate to the local situation in selecting or rejecting the available equipment and technologies. Some of these, while obviously economical and suited to a larger operation, can be considered but also scrutinized with care. The cost of the equipment itself, plus servicing costs, must be weighed against actual time saved; in many situations, this scrutiny may result in a reluctant admission that a particular type of hardware may not be appropriate.

Judicious selection of equipment requires a knowledge of what exists, an imaginative but realistic approach to its possible use, and some means of comparative evaluation of devices on the market. To learn what exists, the librarian can turn to several sources, such as

> exhibits at American Library Association and state library association conferences to actually see what is available and how it works (while being careful about being oversold by persuasive sales personnel)
>
> listings and advertisements in professional journals, especially compilations such as the "Annual Buying Guide" in *Library Journal*
>
> visits to other libraries and shoptalk with other librarians
>
> office-management periodicals, which frequently list supplies and equipment adaptable to library use
>
> visits to office furniture stores
>
> consultation with interior design specialists

In addition, business operations of many kinds use routines similar to those of a library. The alert librarian keeps eyes open when visiting the bank or waiting at the airport and notes how operations are managed, workstations are set up, and the convenience and flow of customers are addressed. Expensive study and research have gone into these arrangements in the private sector, and valuable ideas can often be transplanted into the library situation.

A New Building

If a new library building is decided upon, a major decision has been made, but even more important ones are to follow. The library is at a turning point in its history, and wisdom and judgment of a high order are required. Two kinds of judgment are needed: that which comes from within, from knowledge of the library's program and activities and the particular community it serves, and that which comes from the outside—the know-how of the building experts.

Choosing a Site

The future of the library is bound up with the future of the community; this is true of all library activities, but especially so in planning a building. A new building will be expected to serve for a long time. How large will the community be in ten years? In twenty? Projected growth patterns are available to help here. In which direction is the community growing, and where will business and shopping activities be centered as growth occurs? What are the traffic patterns, and how are they projected to change? The chamber of commerce and local, county, or state planners should be consulted at the beginning of the planning effort to address these important questions. An attractive and relatively new library building left behind by the growth of a community, or stranded on a secondary traffic route because a wrong guess was made or a shortsighted decision adopted, is a waste of community resources.

If a compromise must be made between a good smaller site and a larger but poorly located one, many librarians would choose the former as the lesser evil, planning for more floor space by incorporating a mezzanine or a two-story structure into the design. Officials are sometimes reluctant to pay the cost of a good location. "If people want to use the library, they'll find it," is a frequent argument, and one that reflects the relationship that the library has with its funding authority. It is true that the population of any community includes a number of people who will seek out the library and use it at whatever difficulty and inconvenience to themselves. This proportion will vary with the nature of the community, but it is rarely large. There is also a group of people at the opposite end of the continuum—those who will not use the library even it if is located next door. This, too, is usually a small fragment of the total population.

The largest group is composed of those who fall between these two extremes. The library that is provided for their use, and for which they help to pay, can and frequently will become a vital part of their lives if it is easy to reach, convenient to their life patterns, and located relative to the shopping and other areas that they visit often. If the funding authority is reluctant to provide a site that is appropriate, there is more "homework" to be done than simple persuasion. It is time that the library look to its excellence of service, its communication with funding authorities, and its explanation of accountability and benefits. This groundwork must precede the tangible negotiations represented by a building project.

Planners and other officials often think of a library as a handsome and appropriate addition to a group of other civic buildings. Such combinations, if planned and harmonious, are usually an attractive compromise. They give people a sense of pride in their community, and they make convenient such official occasions as budget presentations and other necessary conferences with other municipal officials. However, a city hall, a county courthouse, or a museum or municipal auditorium may not be the best partner in a facility that will necessarily be a busy place visited by large numbers of people. Those responsible for site selection must ask, first and insistently, what else there is in the neighborhood that draws people frequently and regularly. In other words, what is the best possible site that will enable the community to realize to the fullest the value of its investment in services, materials, staff, and building?

In site selection as in building planning, the librarian should not rely too much on present use. If the present building is used heavily by children but not by adults, the site may be the reason. A new site is sometimes selected in a park near a playground because it is ideal for children, it provides a pleasant setting for an attractive building, and it has the added advantage of saving money another site would cost, since the community already owns the park site. The result is often a bigger and better children's room that provides excellent service to the community's youth but that does not meet the library's obligation to serve adults as well.

Parking may not be the major consideration in smaller communities that it is in larger ones, but any community has congested central sections in which it is hard to park during business hours. More and more, parking lots are necessary adjuncts to library buildings, thus affecting site size.

The Architect and the Consultant

A good architect—preferably one with experience working on library buildings—is a necessity. The "economy" of avoiding architect's fees is a false economy, for the new building must be well-planned, functional, and aesthetically pleasing. However, the library director and the board must be realists and recognize that the architect will not be a library expert. There are aspects of the planning of a new library building that only a librarian understands. An architect is not likely to know how much space is needed for a workroom, for example, or how large a children's room should be.

Working with an architect in planning a library building is an experience that may come only once to most librarians. For this reason the hiring of another expert—a building consultant—is generally advised. A consultant can be invaluable in contributing information about building plans that have been successful—and unsuccessful—in other places and in evaluating the practicality of proposals for the building being considered. The desired consultant is a person who has had a variety of experiences in advising librarians and boards about building projects of different sizes and types. If the budget absolutely does not permit employing a building consultant in addition to the architect, the state library agency may be able to provide help.

Local Decisions

Even with experts to assist, the librarian and trustees must make many decisions. Reading articles in library and architectural journals; observing with a newly aware eye the arrangements, materials, and furnishings of all kinds of buildings, from banks to public offices; scrutinizing the library services not as they presently are but as they might be—these become important activities for the librarian, board, and staff.

This new look at the library's present operation is most significant. Staff members who work in older and crowded library buildings are not always aware how much of their activity is shaped by their environment. For example, librarians often underestimate needed workroom space because adaptation to crowded working conditions has become so much second nature to them that a little more work space seems enormous. The use pattern of the present building is also a dangerous guide. If there seems to be a tendency for customers to take materials home rather than work in the library, is it because space is inadequate, the lighting poor, or the library noisy, with insufficient separation of age groups and intolerable study conditions? If these circumstances were changed, might not people's habits of use change also? Has the library perhaps adapted to these problems by circulating many materials normally kept for in-house use? If so, the librarian must be on guard to allow adequate space for seating and for the various collections in the new building.

These are common examples of pitfalls in planning; others, less obvious, could be cited. Sometimes a personal sacrifice is called for, as when one of a librarian's most cherished ideas, perhaps a brilliant adaptation to the old conditions, turns out to be inappropriate for a new building. The librarian must consider, "Do we do it this way because we *must* in this building or because in any building this way is best?"

This is also the time to ask long-range questions: Is there a possibility that a part of the operations formerly housed on-site will later be performed elsewhere? Will joining a processing center or using a commercial service free up space from materials preparation? Will storage needs be affected by a library system's provision of low-cost storage space for little-used items or even by efficient and fast system interlibrary loan service? Should the library consider microforms for older issues of newspapers and journals, thus saving space, or is the library system planning a central microfilm periodicals service, again with efficient delivery, perhaps fax transmission? What types of electric outlets are needed for present and future computer configurations, connections with bibliographic utilities, linkages to a system's or state's union catalog, fax transmission equipment, and new or additional microform readers and audiovisual equipment? Is the library likely to offer service through alternative delivery channels, such as a branch, bookmobile, books by mail, or electronic transmission? Will the library need facilities for loading, shipping, and additional operations? These long-range considerations must be factored into all decision making concerning new physical space.

Conversion and Remodeling

In some communities, the library's building project involves remodeling and expanding an existing building. In this situation, the site problem is focused on adjacent properties. Are they available? Are they large enough? How much will they cost? Are they properly oriented toward the existing structure to be useful? Will their use create new problems of access and safety? Do they present hidden problems of geology, topography, or buried objects? The feasibility of an expansion project may well depend upon the responses to these and similar questions.[9]

Converting an existing (nonlibrary) building to library use can be an attractive alternative to new construction. However, several criteria must be met if this remodeling is to be successful; these are given in figure 10.5.

FIGURE 10.5

Conversion Criteria

Criteria	Discussion
Overall size of the structure	Does it meet the space needs of the building program, or will an addition be necessary?
Location of and spacing between support columns	Columns should not interfere with shelving patterns.
Location and number of load-bearing walls	This will contribute to or limit the flexibility of the structure under consideration.
Load-bearing capacity of the floors (the ground floor and any upper floors)	Most shelving requires a floor that will support at least 150 pounds per square foot, and the floors of many nonlibrary structures are not that strong.
Ceiling heights	Ceilings should provide a minimum clearance of 10 feet.
Location of rest room facilities	Rest rooms provided in a commercial building, for instance, are often quite different from those required by a public building.
Location and number of electrical outlets	This will affect flexibility and the amount of added construction work needed.
Location and type of lighting fixtures	Lighting can be used to facilitate work and study, and also to accent or enhance the interior design.*
Location and number of windows	Their pattern may adversely affect the placement of stacks and furnishings.
Condition and type of heating and cooling system	Consideration should be given to conservation issues as well as to customer and staff comfort.*
Investigation of how changing the structure's use may affect the applicable building codes	Building codes are frequently revised and need to be monitored.*

*Added by author.

ADAPTED FROM: Anders C. Dahlgren, *Planning the Small Public Library Building*, Small Libraries Publication no. 11 (Chicago: American Library Assn., 1985), 21.

Acquiring and remodeling a building intended for another purpose has been a satisfactory solution to the space problem for many libraries. While the new quarters may or may not be as functional for library purposes as a new or remodeled library building, they may work very well if the space is unbroken by many bearing walls, and if the floors are able to sustain the significant weight of filled shelving. Thus, automobile salesrooms and supermarkets have been successfully remodeled into libraries, while private houses are less likely to be adequate for library needs. Indeed, there are many instances of conversion of former churches in Europe that have proven to be quite serviceable, and some office spaces, such as credit unions or banks, have also been equal to the task. If this solution is seriously considered by a library, there should be as careful investigation and planning of the entire situation as would be done in the case of a new building.

Rented quarters are sometimes useful, but normally only for a short interim period—while a new building is going up, while a search for a branch site is in progress, and so on. It is unlikely that the major remodeling that would be required to convert a rented facility to library use would be cost-effective in the long term, especially when the facility is not owned by the municipality.

Refurbishing the Existing Building

While not every librarian has the opportunity to have a new building, every librarian can make sure the building now in use is as attractive and efficient as possible. If the structure is an old and familiar one, it is likely that the librarian and trustees no longer see it as it would appear to a newcomer. They may not notice the shabbiness, inconvenience, clutter, and crowded conditions.

The Library's Exterior

The first step toward improving a library's appearance and efficiency is to stand back and take a long hard look. The exterior is the criterion by which many people judge the library. An unattractive building with peeling paint, unkempt grounds, and sloppy signage will ultimately affect both usage and funding. As stated earlier, image is to be taken seriously, and the community will remember and judge the library by the face it presents to the world. Refurbishing the exterior of the library can be a useful project for various youth groups, neighborhood associations, or community groups.[10]

From the outside, is it obvious to all passersby that this is a library? If not, a clear and attractive sign is needed. If the building is set back from the sidewalk and partly obscured by trees in summer, the sign may be needed at the front of the lot, rather than on the building itself. Further, regardless of the exact location of the library, signs featuring the generic library logo of a figure reading, which has been adopted nationally, can be placed on principal surrounding streets, pointing to the location of the public library.

Improvements to the outside of the building depend on the style of architecture, the building material, and the nature of the community. Paint will help some buildings; a cleanup job can improve almost every appearance. Any grass and shrubs should be well cared for. Replacing an old-fashioned entrance with a modern one is effective if there is money for it. A new and lighter door to replace a heavy one is a benefit for both children and older people, since fire regulations usually require that doors open outward. Windows should be clean and should open and close with ease.

The Library's Interior

What impression does the inside of the library building give a newcomer? The interior of the library should be a warm and welcoming place. Elements such as windows, lighting, displays, and the overall appearance of the collection set a definite tone. Staff friendliness, in particular, can light up a room.

However, many a library is dark and gloomy, with a musty, institutional smell. New lighting may be needed to facilitate reading and finding materials. In many older libraries, the furniture and woodwork are dark and massive. The circulation desk is often cumbersome and placed so that it is the first thing a customer sees on entering. Moving the desk to one side of the entrance or, better still, replacing it with a modern one less centrally located will often create a sense of space as well as a much more welcoming atmosphere. Painting woodwork and walls a lighter color lightens and brightens a building, and if furniture cannot be replaced, paint may enliven these pieces as well.

Adequate lighting can work wonders on the library's interior; natural light from clean and shining windows can add spaciousness. Creative use of color and signage provides stimulation or relaxation, depending on the hues and the graphics. Different colored carpets can aid in moving people from one location to another and can differentiate between areas without resorting to the cut-up effect of walls and partitions.

Weeding the collection, eliminating shabby materials, and reclaiming extra and uncluttered space can enliven the look of the library. Weeding may well prove to be more cost effective than adding new shelving, and users are drawn to shelves that hold bright, new-looking materials—plus some empty space.

Some points to consider when looking at the library's interior, suggested by the Buildings and Equipment Section of the Library Administration and Management Association, include the following questions.

Are all public service elements of the building easily located from the entrance?

Will the entrance allow for a book security system?

Distinguished by signs, lighting, color, and furnishings, do these areas stand out: children/adults/YA, catalog, books/audiovisual, reference/information?

Are furniture and equipment used to promote, merchandise, and to display some parts of the book and media collections of the library and announcements of library events?

Are signs easy to see and logical to follow?

Is there sufficient dedicated space available for meetings and programs?

Is there space for small conferences? For quiet study?

Can the meeting room be used after closing with accessibility to rest rooms and a telephone? Is there a kitchen?

Does there appear to be good traffic flow?

Is the catalog accessible from all parts of the library?

Is there an instructional sign for catalog use?

Can the building be easily maintained?

Has provision been made for safety and emergencies: fire safety, emergency exits, emergency lighting, nonskid floors, and safety glass?

Are wall coverings appropriate for the area in halls and around water fountains?

Have steps been kept to a minimum or eliminated?

Are corridors well lighted?

Are finishes easily maintainable and long-wearing?[11]

Most people enter the library to find materials, and the librarian looking critically at the building must ask whether they can find what they want easily. Are directional signs clean and clear? Do they say what they mean in words the user can understand, or do they perhaps point to the "900s" instead of to "travel" and "history" or perhaps to the "charging desk"—a term many users do not understand? Perhaps the materials have been shifted but not the shelf labels and signs. The catalog should be marked and have nearby a clear usage guide, again written in clearly stated language and not in library jargon. The customer should not have to ask where to go to get a library card, where to return books, where to check out materials, where to go for information, or where certain materials are located.

In addition, if materials are so tightly shelved that they are difficult to remove, or if the shelves are so high that the top one cannot be easily reached, the library needs more shelving, more space, or a good weeding. The customer's comfort and convenience should be considered. Space to write and study should also be available as well as a few comfortable chairs for those who wish to use materials in the library.

Familiar objects, such as old pictures, statuary, and other items that may have seen better days, can be replaced with newer items that are attractive and colorful; flower arrangements provided by the local garden club can work a visual transformation. An attractive screen might partition off a corner used for work space; an old, unused fireplace can be covered over or used as a backdrop for plants and flowers. Rearranging standing shelves and tables can provide more usable space, and appropriate curtains or tinted blinds can give a softer touch to an overly austere interior. With the use of imagination, many changes can be accomplished with moderate expense.

Additional Distribution Options

Libraries defined as "small" in this book usually have little need to establish a branch. However, there may be public demand for another outlet, and circumstances may justify considering one. The community may have grown in one direction, so that most of the population lives in a new area some distance from the library. A new outlying shopping center may attract many residents away from the old shopping district. In some cases, the best plan might be moving the library to the new shopping area, but service may still be needed in the older area. The librarian and board may have to give serious thought to a new outlet for the newly evolved area. Other circumstances for establishing a new outlet may be a new superhighway that cuts off half the population from easy access to the library or the annexation of a new area.

Library service may be supplied to a new area in several ways. The simplest and best solution may be cooperation or agreement with a neighboring jurisdiction to give library service to the section needing it. This arrangement will be satisfactory if the neighboring library service is conveniently located for the citizens in question and if it is of comparable quality to the original home library. The neighboring library can be paid outright for its services, or if both jurisdictions belong to the same library system, a cooperative agreement could be negotiated.

The community may prefer a branch library solution, but the board needs to assess carefully whether the budget can be stretched to cover this additional responsibility or whether new funds can be secured. Setting up a branch by dividing the existing collection and the existing staff's time creates two services whose sum may be weaker than the original service. In neither can the customer find the resources of materials and staff that were available before the division. A branch creates new types of expenses in addition to the cost of providing or renting space. Delivery service—involving packing, shipping, and record keeping—is necessary. Materials and requests must go back and forth, as must supplies and equipment, statistics, and memorandums. If the branch has a collection permanently located at the new site, it will need a catalog; if the collection is on a rotating basis, records of what is sent will have to be maintained.

If the library serves an extensive although sparsely populated area, the issue of additional outlets changes. A county or multicounty library may still be a small library by this volume's definition, even though it may serve a sizable area. It is important that consideration be given to ways of reaching people who are not within convenient distance of the main library, which is usually located in the largest town in the region served. It is not enough to assume that people will come in to town on other business and use the library on these occasions. The outlying population should, of course, have access to the largest outlet of their library, but they should also have some entry point to service that is nearer home.

The Bookmobile

For many rural locations where roads are good and the population is within a reasonable distance, a bookmobile has traditionally been the type of outlet chosen. It has certain advantages. It can

bring requested materials from the larger library

offer fresh selections on each trip

be staffed by a professional librarian or a talented paraprofessional who is knowledgeable about the total resources of the library

offer a variety of materials on a variety of subjects to small populations (As the bookmobile is on the road for long periods of time, the collection receives good exposure to a sizable audience.)

On the other hand, bookmobile service also has disadvantages.

Primary is the issue of energy conservation and the rising costs of bookmobile operation because of increased gasoline prices.

A rural bookmobile stops only a short time at any service point. The time of each stop is not only brief, but fixed as to hour. Thus, hours of service are inevitably less convenient for some users. (An in-town bookmobile can stop in a location more often and can stay longer than a rural one. It can test different neighborhood locations and determine the most convenient one. In addition, because it travels smaller distances than a rural bookmobile, an in-town bookmobile uses less fuel and is less costly to operate.)

Rural bookmobiles normally stop only once every two weeks. Even if it is possible to stop weekly, there is little opportunity for rush service.

Reference service is limited, if it can be offered at all. The staff member is busy helping customers and keeping on schedule. Space is limited, and people must move through quickly to allow others to enter. The driver-clerk is occupied with circulation work.

Bookmobiles provide no facilities for sitting down and copying material from an encyclopedia, atlas, or other reference source. To carry copying equipment on the average bookmobile would pre-empt space that could be used for materials.

Normally, returned materials cannot be shelved until the bookmobile reaches home base. It follows that the people near the end of the run have less choice than those at the beginning of it.

In spite of these disadvantages, some of which can be resolved (at least in part) with creativity and ingenuity, a bookmobile may be the best choice for a service area that involves workable distances between service points. With rising costs, it is less desirable to plan for a bookmobile that would spend a significant proportion of its time in transit. This is costly not only in fuel but also in salaries, since little work can be done on a moving vehicle.

The Branch

The small branch outlet is an alternative to consider. It is a common method for serving rural areas in some western states where distances are great and population is sparse. Two types of branches are an outlet in a store or other building the population visits regularly and an outlet that serves only as a library facility. Three approaches are possible:

1. *A portable structure or kiosk* can be purchased and erected in a shopping mall or other heavily traveled site. A *rented store,* if affordable and in a good location, can also be very appropriate. Usually, there is some level of staffing at the site so that materials can be checked out. Staff can be selected from the regular library staff, from a cadre of volunteers, or possibly from student workers. Most commonly part-time workers, these staff members must be viewed (whether they are paid or unpaid) as members of the library's total staff and, as such, have job descriptions and performance reviews and be invited to staff meetings. A larger collection is possible with a rented store than with the other listed alternatives. When reference service is needed, today's technology can connect the remote facility with the regular library via telephone lines or computer link. If the library has an online catalog, the outlet can have access to this catalog. Signs can be posted to acquaint users with the request and reference services available.

2. *An arrangement can be made with the owner and operator of a popular store to house and service a few shelves of books;* payment, on a modest scale, is offered for this space and service. The work required must

be simple, since the storekeeper will not be able or willing to give much time to library service.

3. *A self-service station* can be established that operates on the honor system and is periodically replenished by library staff. Do-it-yourself request forms can be provided, and preaddressed and stamped envelopes for mailing requests to headquarters can be provided.

One advantage of these arrangements is convenience: If a popular store, mall, or other area is selected, everyone in a very small community is likely to visit it and at least have the opportunity to become acquainted with the library materials available there. Another advantage is time: The outlet will be available longer hours than a bookmobile, can be open at times that mesh well with customer needs, and can provide work space for note taking or copying.

Each remote outlet's collection must be changed regularly and frequently. Since only a selected group of materials is available, the customers who regularly visit the site will very quickly have used much of what is of interest. While it may not be necessary to remove all of the materials and bring in a completely new supply, the outlet's staff will know what is still being used and what is no longer needed and can set aside or send in materials to be replaced by the next shipment. In addition, new materials should be sent regularly since new titles are routinely added to the library. In this way, materials that would not circulate enough at an individual remote outlet to warrant permanent placement there can now move among sites and receive full use. This type of fluid collection necessitates record keeping at the headquarters library to call in titles that are in one outlet and requested by another.

Materials by Mail

While far from being complete library service, using mail to deliver library materials offers unique advantages and personalized service. In a typical scenario, a booklet-type catalog is used, containing attractively listed and annotated lists of materials, both print and audiovisual, in broad interest categories. Items are numbered in the catalog, though not with library call numbers. The catalog is available in multiple copies for any interested citizen. Inside are removable postcards for requests, postage paid. There is space for the customer's name and address and for the numbers of books requested. The customer mails in the request and receives the materials in a mailing bag, which is to be used for their return. A mailing label, other request cards, and sometimes other library lists or supplementary catalogs are enclosed.

Books selected for the service are bought in paperback if possible and are purchased in quantity. They are shelved by catalog number, and the business of filling requests is a relatively simple routine procedure.

Mail service has proven to be an extremely popular service in most places where it has been tried. It is convenient and easy to use. There are no constraints of time—the customer may send a request whenever it is convenient. The homebound need not leave home; the rural user need only go to the mailbox to receive and return materials. The service, therefore, has benefits beyond that of reaching remotely located users. Some libraries use it for persons with disabilities or those that are homebound who live in town, setting up criteria for eligibility and publicizing its availability for this purpose. (Note: Using a system of volunteers for delivering materials to homebound customers also works extremely well for many libraries.)

While popularity of the service is acknowledged, increasing postage costs are pricing the service beyond the realistic reach of many small libraries. If it is a service that must eventually pass into an honorable past, it has served many customers with great distinction, and the attributes that marked its success need to be translated into new services facilitated by developing technologies.

Electronic Connections

Developing technologies are making time and distance less and less a problem for library services. In some areas, customers can reach the library catalog, place holds on materials, or seek information from the comfort of home using personal computers or, occasionally, cable television. The future holds increasingly significant development along these lines.

Is the public image of the library one that accurately portrays what the library can provide to its community—or is yesterday's paradigm alive and well? Libraries have been traditionally valued and simultaneously undervalued by their communities. Today, as competitors in the information industry aggressively vie for customer attention, the image that the public library projects takes on added significance. According to the Benton Foundation's report, *Buildings, Books, and Bytes: Libraries and Communities in the Digital Age,* while public support for libraries remains strong, there is a perception that libraries are "behind the curve" regarding information technology and are likely to remain there.[12]

Figure 10.6 illustrates four broadly drawn "images" of public libraries that can be used as benchmarks for staff reflection. Summary characteristics are given and then expanded upon in an effort to consider how improvement might be achieved. For example, the traditional library does, indeed, serve as a physical and cultural space for the community; however, the library may focus on internal operations, and outreach of its services into the community would be a valuable enhancement. For the resisting library, the image of rejecting technology can be modified into a positive approach by using appropriate technology in the delivery of library services and by developing access for the entire community. The adapting library, while the most positive image presented in figure 10.6, can still be improved by underscoring the expertise of library staff and focusing on the customer. Finally, the coopting library needs to strive for balance in mission, roles, collection, and use of technology as a tool as opposed to an all-consuming purpose.

It is important to realize that technology cannot become a substitute for the complex issues of librarianship, such as the library's role in the community, customer access and satisfaction, and identification of and response to customer needs.[13] While technology offers increasingly important tools with which to connect customers to the information they are seeking, technology does not have a life of its own. It is the library's staff that uses these tools to provide quality service. Keeping up with this technological explosion is more than a challenge; it is a requirement for library staff, yet is becoming an unreachable goal due to the rate of change. However, it is essential that librarians make every effort to stay as current as possible and that every staff member's job description include an emphasis on continuing education.

Whether the assessment data—including consideration of electronic technologies—suggest remodeling, expansion, a new building, or development of alternative distribution options, creating the most desirable configuration of physical space and delivery systems to support the library's services is both complex and rewarding. The challenge of doing so can bring together the various facets of library operations into a dynamic synthesis, and it offers the library manager the opportunity to shape the direction of library service well into the future.

FIGURE 10.6

Images of Public Libraries

Images	Summary Characteristics	Ways to Enhance Image
Traditional library	Exists as physical, cultural space Focuses on books, reading Provides public plaza/civic forum May/may not consider technology as central to providing service	Provide outreach into community Add a variety of formats Partner with other agencies, sometimes in their space Promote available technology
Resisting library	Manifests values of traditional library Focuses on information have-nots Focuses on librarian/ customer interaction Has a suspicion of technology	Create value-added image Focus on equity of access for all Use technology in the interaction Build on benefits of technology
Adapting library	Serves as a connecting point to information Presents the librarian as navigator Adapts technology to essential roles Adapts essential roles to technology	Communicate what is possible to customers Develop expertise of librarian to save customer time, money Use library staff as trainers Provide judicious adaptation, with customer service as focus
Coopted library	Has roles out of balance Has lost traditional purpose Devalues the book, reading Embraces, celebrates technology	Make commitment to balance Merge traditional values with changing opportunities Affirm all formats as information packages Use technology that is of appropriate scale

ADAPTED FROM: Figure 1 in Douglas Raber and John M. Budd, "Public Images of the Role of Information Technology in Public Libraries: Alternatives and Controversies," *Public Libraries* 38, no. 3 (May/June 1999): 181.

Rapid changes in technology, in distribution design and function, in publication and reproduction of materials, and in the composition of the community are creating a dynamic environment for public libraries. Entwined within this environment are also many human concerns, including

- concern for all customers—including those who are economically or physically challenged or those who have insufficient information access
- concern for productive and mutually supportive working relationships among staff members and with other members of the community
- concern that the library offers service that is customer centered and competent
- concern that the library serve as the community's window to the world of information
- concern that technology be recognized as life-enhancing rather than life-controlling

While the ways that library staff perform their jobs continue to experience significant transformation, the core values and mission of the public library remain unchanged. As the new millennium begins, the importance of the public library is key to the community's overall quality of life. It is challenging, indeed, for the library and its community to work together to identify needs and design effective responses that improve circumstances for all concerned. This partnership of library and community must rest on a firm foundation of perceived mutual benefit; when the partnership is strong, everybody gains—a true win-win situation.

Thoughts for the New Millennium

How does the technology that my library offers affect my library's role(s) in the community? Do I consider this relationship when deciding whether to add new technology?

What role does the Internet play in my community? What percentage of my customers have home access? For what percentage would the library be the sole access? What can I do to provide information equity to my community?

Does my library's collection management policy include guidelines to determine whether or when electronic, audiovisual, or
print resources will be purchased?

What reference sources are presently available in print format
in my library that might be more effectively used by customers
in electronic form?

Do my present delivery systems respond to customer convenience and needs? Should other options be considered?

Do I regularly evaluate my library's building? What condition
is it in? What improvements could be made? Should consideration be given to a new building, remodeling, or refurbishing?
Are there other options that should be considered?

How healthy is the partnership between my library and the
community?

Notes

1. Fran White, "Technology and Libraries," in *Reinvention of the Public Library for the 21st Century,* ed. William L. Whitesides Sr. (Englewood, Colo.: Libraries Unlimited, 1998), 105.

2. Beth Wheeler Fox, *The Dynamic Community Library* (Chicago: American Library Assn., 1988), 64.

3. *Wisconsin Public Library Standards* (Madison: Wisconsin Dept. of Public Instruction, 1987), 38.

4. Anders C. Dahlgren, *Public Library Space Needs: A Planning Outline* (Madison: Wisconsin Dept. of Public Instruction, 1988), 1.

5. "Access and Facilities," *Wisconsin Public Library Standards,* 39–40.

6. Anders C. Dahlgren and Charles E. Reid, "The Trustee and Library Buildings," in *The Library Trustee,* 5th ed., ed. Virginia G. Young (Chicago: American Library Assn., 1995), 96.

7. Ibid., 96-7.

8. For additional help with these decisions, see Sandra Nelson, Ellen Altman, and Diane Mayo, *Wired for the Future: Developing Your Library Technology Plan* (Chicago: American Library Assn., 1999); Jeannette Woodward, *Countdown to*

a New Library: Managing the Building Project (Chicago: American Library Assn., 2000).

9. Raymond M. Holt, *Wisconsin Library Building Project Handbook* (Madison: Wisconsin Dept. of Public Instruction, 1978), 14.

10. Fox, *Dynamic Community Library,* 64.

11. American Library Assn., Library Administration and Management Assn., Buildings and Equipment Section, *Checklist of Library Building Design Considerations* (Chicago: American Library Assn., 1988), 11–12. This publication contains checklists for the following design elements: site, exterior, interior, accessibility, circulation, children's facilities, young adult, reference facilities, book stacks and shelving, seating, nonpublic areas, convenience facilities, equipment, communication and electrical equipment, security systems, mechanical equipment and noise control, and future considerations.

12. The Benton Foundation, *Buildings, Books, and Bytes: Libraries and Communities in the Digital Age* (Washington, D.C.: Benton Foundation, 1996). Further information can be found at http://www.benton.org/Library/Kellogg/buildings.html.

13. Bernard Vavrek, "On My Mind: Your Public Library Has a Web Page, So What?" *American Libraries* 29, no. 1 (Jan. 1999): 50.

A Library Bill of Rights

The American Library Association affirms that all libraries are forums for information and ideas, and that the following basic policies should guide their services.

I. Books and other library resources should be provided for the interest, information, and enlightenment of all people of the community the library serves. Materials should not be excluded because of the origin, background, or views of those contributing to their creation.

II. Libraries should provide materials and information presenting all points of view on current and historical issues. Materials should not be proscribed or removed because of partisan or doctrinal disapproval.

III. Libraries should challenge censorship in the fulfillment of their responsibility to provide information and enlightenment.

IV. Libraries should cooperate with all persons and groups concerned with resisting abridgment of free expression and free access to ideas.

V. A person's right to use a library should not be denied or abridged because of origin, age, background, or views.

VI. Libraries which make exhibit spaces and meeting rooms available to the public they serve should make such facilities available on an equitable basis, regardless of the beliefs or affiliations of individuals or groups requesting their use.

Adopted June 18, 1948.
Amended February 2, 1961, and January 23, 1980,
reaffirmed January 23, 1996,
by the ALA Council.

APPENDIX

B

Kendall Public Library Long- and Short-Range Plans 1999–2003

Long-Range Plan
Kendall Public Library
Kendall, Wisconsin

Vision Statement

The Kendall Public Library envisions a future in which

- People of all ages will find expanding recreational, informational, and technological resources to connect them to a global body of knowledge;
- The youth of the community will find resources, programs, and services which will offer entertaining and enjoyable activities and experiences, and which will equip it for the larger world beyond the village;
- The library will offer services, programs, and resources which will result in it becoming a focus for a strong sense of community enjoyment, identity, and involvement.

Mission Statement

The mission of the Kendall Public Library is to offer materials, programs, and services which will provide satisfying recreational experiences for people of all ages; learning support for elementary, middle school, and high school students; and opportunities for personal growth and development for all ages, in a pleasant and welcoming environment.

Roles of the Kendall Public Library

Accordingly, the service responses the library focuses on will be:

> PRIMARY: *Current Topics and Titles* The library helps to fulfill residents' desire for satisfying recreational experiences and information about popular cultural and social trends.

> PRIMARY: *Formal Learning Support* The library provides informational resources, personal help, and educational tools that further the progress of students.

> SECONDARY: *Lifelong Learning* The library provides materials that will foster self-directed personal growth and development opportunities.

Needs Assessment/Community Study

Because of the high level of effort just expended by the Library Board and village in the drive for the new building, and because the Director is newly hired, an extensive study of the community has not been done at this time. Rather, a basic level of effort has been chosen for the "looking around" phase. The Director has handled most of this task, with input from Library Board members, one other staff member, and various members of the community. The Director has gathered information from existing and easily-accessed information sources, and has used Workform C (from *Planning and Role Setting for Public Libraries,* Chicago: ALA, 1987) to do this, and to target areas of future necessary information gathering. The Director has also used Workform D *(Planning and Role Setting for Public Libraries)* to identify potential impacts on library services and to determine possible library responses.

Future Forecasting Screens

Any long-range plan must attempt to take into account changes in future community needs, resources, staff needs, and library use.

Community Needs

Despite some political opposition, there has been good village support for the library, as evidenced by the funding of the new building. The village faces the possible loss of its elementary school, which has been a source of community focus and pride. The purpose of the long-range plan is to build on and increase public support for the library by continuing to increase the library's visibility in village life, and to develop collections and services which will position it more firmly as a community asset and a focus of community identity.

Resources

The community will continue to be one primarily of blue-collar, low-income workers and elderly people. However, a good national economy and low unemployment will trickle down to the local level. These factors are already being reflected in rising land values and new homes being built in the area. County reimbursement for non-resident library users will increase the library's materials fund in the near future, and it will be especially important to show careful rationales and planning for expenditures of those funds by that time.

Use

Library use has increased since the move, and will continue to increase due to a more visible location and welcoming facility. Strong interest in the Internet has already been shown and will continue to grow. New formats offered will bring in new customers, as will increased use of marketing techniques to encourage growth.

Staff

As library use increases, it will be necessary to add a part-time clerical worker to the staff. Volunteer help with putting holdings on Wiscat will also be needed. A Friends of the Library group will be actively sought and promoted.

Long-Range Plan Goals and Objectives

Goal 1: The library will provide a current collection of titles in high demand to ensure customer requests are met quickly.

Objective 1: Develop a plan to improve and facilitate total book ordering process by 2000.

Objective 2: Survey customer satisfaction with Adult Fiction collection by 2001.

Objective 3: Increase circulation of Adult Fiction by 5% by 2002.

Objective 4: Increase circulation of YA titles by 10% by 2003.

Goal 2: Materials will be offered in the formats people want.

Objective 1: Increase circulation of audio books by 50% by 2003.

Objective 2: Increase circulation of videos by 10% by 2001.

Goal 3: The library will provide printed informational resources that will support the educational progress of students.

Objective 1: Improve communications between teachers and library by 2000.

Objective 2: Increase Juvenile Nonfiction collection by 15% by 2003.

Objective 3: Develop a Juvenile Reference collection of at least 15 non-encyclopedia volumes by 2001.

Goal 4: The library will provide electronic access and educational software that will enhance the educational progress of students.

Objective 1: Offer Internet and Ebsco/UMI access to students aged twelve and up by February 1999.

Goal 5: The library will provide adult materials on a wide variety of topics of general interest.

Objective 1: Increase the Adult Nonfiction collection by 10% by the end of 2001.

Objective 2: Increase Adult Nonfiction circulation by 25% by 2003.

Goal 6: The library will offer services which will foster interest in lifelong learning.

Objective 1: Organize Adult Nonfiction collection to encourage browsing by 2000.

Objective 2: Offer Internet access to enhance research capabilities in areas of public interest by 1999.

Evaluation Strategies

In keeping with its small staff, the library will use a basic level of effort in reviewing results of its long-range and short-range plans. The Director will use the chart following the short-range plan to informally monitor the accomplishment of on-going activities for herself and the one other staff member. At the end of the long-range planning phase, the Director will use Appendix A to assess how well the objectives were accomplished, and Appendix B to review the goals. The Director will also use Appendices C and D to assess future information needs and review the whole planning process and make recommendations for the next phase.

Long-Range Timeline	1999	2000	2001	2002	2003
Goal 1: Objective 1	████				
Objective 2		████			
Objective 3	████	████	████		
Objective 4	████	████	████	████	████
Goal 2: Objective 1	████	████	████	████	████
Objective 2	████	████	████		
Goal 3: Objective 1	████	████			
Objective 2	████	████	████		
Objective 3		████	████		
Goal 4: Objective 1	████				
Goal 5: Objective 1	████	████	████		
Objective 2	████	████	████	████	████
Goal 6: Objective 1	████				
Objective 2	████				

Short-Range Plan
Kendall Public Library
Kendall, Wisconsin

Vision Statement

The Kendall Public Library envisions a future in which:

- People of all ages will find expanding recreational, informational, and technological resources to connect them to a global body of knowledge;
- The youth of the community will find resources, programs, and services which will offer entertaining and enjoyable activities and experiences, and which will equip it for the larger world beyond the village;
- The library will offer services, programs, and resources which will result in it becoming a focus for a strong sense of community enjoyment, identity, and involvement.

Mission Statement

The mission of the Kendall Public Library is to offer materials, programs, and services which will provide satisfying recreational experiences for people of all ages, learning support for elementary, middle school, and high school students, and opportunities for personal growth and development for all ages, in a pleasant and welcoming environment.

Roles of the Kendall Public Library

Accordingly, the service responses the library focuses on will be:

PRIMARY: *Current Topics and Titles.* The library helps to fulfill residents' desire for satisfying recreational experiences and information about popular cultural and social trends.

PRIMARY: *Formal Learning Support.* The library provides informational resources, personal help, and educational tools that further progress of students.

SECONDARY: *Lifelong Learning.* The library provides materials that will foster self-directed personal growth and development opportunities.

Needs Assessment/Community Study

Because of the high level of effort just expended by the Library Board and village in the drive for the new building, and because the Director is newly hired, an extensive study of the community has not been done at this time. Rather, a basic level of effort has been chosen for the "looking around" phase. The Director has handled most of this task, with input from Library Board members, one other staff member, and various members of the community. The Director has gathered information from existing and easily-accessed information sources, and has used Workform C (from *Planning and Role Setting for Public Libraries,* Chicago: ALA, 1987) to do this, and to target areas of future necessary information gathering. The Director has also used Workform D *(Planning and Role Setting for Public Libraries)* to identify potential impacts on library services and to determine possible library responses.

Short-Range Plan Goals, Objectives, and Actions January 1, 1999 to December 31, 1999

Goal 1: The library will provide a current collection of titles in high demand to ensure customers requests are met quickly.

Objective 1: Develop a plan to improve and facilitate total book ordering process by 2000.

Action 1: The Director will develop a list of popular authors to put on "automatic order" with Baker and Taylor by February 1999.

Action 2: The Director will call both Ingram and B&T to find out about automated ordering software by April 1999.

Action 3: The Director will ask elementary school librarian which reviews, companies, and methods she uses for children's book orders by May 1999.

Objective 2: Survey customer satisfaction with Adult Fiction collection by 2001.

Action 1: The Director will ask WRLS consultants for information and examples of good user surveys during the first half of 1999.

Action 2: The Director will write the survey and determine how to distribute it in summer of 1999.

Action 3: The Director will distribute the survey and analyze the results in Sept/Oct 1999.

Objective 3: Increase circulation of Adult Fiction by 5% by 2002.

Action 1: The Director will use the results of the survey to identify areas of dissatisfaction and need by Dec. 1999.

Action 2: The Director will begin ordering materials in new areas identified as most wanted starting in January 2000.

Objective 4: Increase circulation of YA titles by 10% by 2003.

Action 1: Staff will identify YA titles with spine labels by March 1999.

Action 2: Staff will change catalog cards to indicate YA by March 1, 1999.

Action 3: The Director will order posters to highlight the YA section by March 1999.

Action 4: The Director will ask WRLS for information on YA collections, topics, and titles by July 1999.

Goal 2: Materials will be offered in the formats people want.

Objective 1: Increase circulation of audio books by 50% by 2003.

Action 1: The Director will determine monthly amount to be budgeted for audio books by March 1999.

Action 2: The Director will begin ordering audio books once a month, beginning in April 1999.

Objective 2: Increase circulation of videos by 10% by 2001.

Action 1: The Director will set up an account with B&T's video department in January 1999.

Action 2: The Director will order videos once a month beginning in April 1999.

Action 3: Staff will list and renumber the existing collection.

Goal 3: The library will provide printed information resources that will support the educational progress of students.

Objective 1: Improve communications between teachers and library by 2000.

Action 1: The Director will visit the 6th grade class to hand out library cards and meet class members by December 1998.

Action 2: The Director will visit all elementary classes to promote the Summer Reading Program in May 1999.

Action 3: The Director will examine major textbooks for grades 1–6 by September 1999.

Objective 2: Increase Juvenile Nonfiction collection by 15% by 2003.

Action 1: The Director will examine collection and determine most-needed materials by October 1999.

Action 2: The Director will set up a monthly plan for buying most-needed books by December 1999.

Objective 3: Develop a Juvenile Reference collection of at least 15 non-encyclopedia volumes by 2001.

Action 1: The Director will determine the best volumes to buy by asking WRLS consultants and by reading reviews and catalogs by December 1999.

Goal 4: The library will provide electronic access and educational software that will enhance the educational progress of students.

Objective 1: Offer Internet, and Ebsco/UMI access to students ages twelve and up by February 1999.

Action 1: The Director will write and propose for Board approval an Internet policy by January 1999.

Action 2: The Director will train the staff in Internet and Ebsco/UMI use by February 1999.

Action 3: The Director will write basic directions to be displayed near the computer by February 1999.

Goal 5: The library will provide adult materials on a wide variety of topics of general interest.

Objective 1: Increase the Adult Nonfiction collection by 10% by the end of 2001.

Action 1: The Director will examine the ANF collection and determine the most-needed material by December 1999.

Action 2: The Director will make a plan for orderly buying to fill in by December 1999.

Objective 2: Increase Adult Nonfiction circulation by 25% by 2003.

Action 1: The Director will create at least 4 seasonal nonfiction displays during 1999.

Action 2: The Director will begin working on possible topics/titles lists and displays in September 1999.

Goal 6: The library will offer services which will foster interest in lifelong learning.

Objective 1: Organize Adult Nonfiction collection to encourage browsing by 2000.

Action 1: The Director and staff worker will use signage to identify major subject areas by interest.

Objective 2: Offer Internet access to enhance research capabilities in areas of public interest by 1999.

Action 1: The Director will bookmark Websites for several areas of interest by July 1999.

Action 2: The Director will create handouts of Websites for several areas of interest by September 1999.

Short-Range Timeline	Jan.	Feb.	March	April	May	June	July	Aug.	Sept.	Oct.	Nov.	Dec.
Goal 1: *Objective 1:*												
Action 1	■	■										
Action 2			■	■								
Action 3						■						
Goal 1: *Objective 2:*												
Action 1	■				■	■	■					
Action 2									■	■		
Action 3												
Goal 1: *Objective 3:*										■	■	■
Action 1												
Action 2												
Goal 1: *Objective 4:*												
Action 1	■	■	■									
Action 2												
Action 3			■		■	■	■					
Action 4			■									
Goal 2: *Objective 1:*								■	■	■	■	■
Action 1												
Action 2				■	■	■						
Goal 2: *Objective 2:*												
Action 1	■	■										
Action 2				■	■	■	■	■	■	■	■	■
Action 3									■	■		

Short-Range Timeline	Jan.	Feb.	March	April	May	June	July	Aug.	Sept.	Oct.	Nov.	Dec.
Goal 3: *Objective 1:*												
Action 1	■											
Action 2					■							
Action 3								■	■			
Goal 3: *Objective 2:*												
Action 1									■	■	■	
Action 2												■
Goal 3: *Objective 3:*												
Action 1												■
Goal 4: *Objective 1:*												
Action 1	■	■										
Action 2		■										
Action 3												
Goal 5: *Objective 1:*												
Action 1										■	■	■
Action 2												
Goal 5: *Objective 2:*												
Action 1	■	■	■	■	■	■	■	■				■
Action 2												■
Goal 6: *Objective 1:*												
Action 1			■	■	■	■	■					
Goal 6: *Objective 2:*												
Action 1					■	■						
Action 2									■			

Short-Range Plan	1/1/99–12/31/99
Actions for Goal 1	Date Done
1. Director: Develop automatic order lists	
2. Director: Call Ing and B&T/automated ordering software	
3. Director: Ask grade school librarian about ordering tools	
4. Director: Ask WRLS about user surveys	
5. Director: Write survey	
6. Director: Distribute survey, analyze results	
7. Director: Identify gaps in AFic collection	
8. Director: Begin ordering materials in new areas	
9. Staff: Spine labels on YA titles	
10. Staff: Change catalog cards to YA	
11. Director: Order posters for YA section	
12. Director: Ask WRLS for YA info	
Recommendations:	

Short-Range Plan	1/1/99–12/31/99
Actions for Goal 2	Date Done
1. Director: Determine budget for audios	
2. Director: Begin buying a determined amount of audios per month	
3. Director: Set up account with B&T's video dept	
4. Director: Order videos once a month	
5. Staff: List and number existing video collection	
Recommendations:	

Short-Range Plan	1/1/99–12/31/99
Actions for Goal 3	Date Done
1. Director: Visit 6th grade class/lib cards	
2. Director: Visit grades 1–6 to promote SRP	
3. Director: Examine major textbooks 1–6	
4. Director: Examine Juv NF collection for gaps	
5. Director: Set up monthly purchasing plan for Juv NF	
6. Director: Determine best Juv Ref volumes to buy	
Recommendations:	

Short-Range Plan	1/1/99–12/31/99
Actions for Goal 4	Date Done
1. Director: Write Internet policy for Brd approval	
2. Director: Train staff in Internet and Ebsco/UMI use	
3. Director: Write directions for public use	
Recommendations:	

Short-Range Plan	1/1/99–12/31/99
Actions for Goal 5	Date Done
1. Director: Examine A NF collection for most needed materials	
2. Director: Write purchase plan for A NF collection	
3. Director: Create seasonal displays	
4. Director: Create topics/titles lists and displays	
Recommendations:	

Short-Range Plan	1/1/99–12/31/99
Actions for Goal 6	Date Done
1. Dir/Staff: Identify major subject areas by signage, A NF	
2. Director: Bookmark Websites for areas of interest	
3. Director: Create handouts of Websites	
Recommendations:	

INDEX

Note: Page numbers in *italics* indicate figures.

A

access
  electronic, 189–90
  to information, 229
accessibility, building, 207
accountability, 35, 36
  fiscal, 96, 116–18
  and output measures, 117
  and staff, 120, 131
acquisition, 154–7
actions, 113
  strategies, 50, *51*
administrative skills, and library
    system membership, 175–6
administrators, library, 13
  and board member selection, 24
  certification of, 135
  and fiscal responsibility, 96
  and policies, 78
  as public officials, 13
advancement, staff, 140–3
advisory groups, 32
affirmative action, 126
agriculture, 5
Americans with Disabilities Act, 93
anecdotal information, 117
architects, 214–15
audiovisual materials, 150

  and library system membership,
    174–5
  purchase of, 156
automation, 189. *See also* technology

B

barriers to information, 43
Benton Foundation, 226
bequests, 105–6
bibliographic databases, 179
bidding, 115–16
bills, paying of, 17, 158
binding, 165
board of trustees. *See* library board
bond issues, 208–9
bookmobiles, 223–4
books
  and library system membership,
    173–4
  new, 148
borrowing for building fund, 208–9
Boucher, Virginia, 185
branches, library, 222, 224–5
budgets, 98–9, *114*
  citizen support of, 112
  and cost factors, 56
  and finance, 96–119
  hearings, 98, 112–13
  and library board, 22, 112
  line-item, 57, *57,* 97, 108–9, 111
  long-range planning, 107, 112
  and personnel, 19

budgets *(continued)*
  and planning, 6
  preparing, 106–14
  program, 26–7, 57, *57,* 97,
    109–12
  and public relations, 69
  and service, 54
building (process)
  and architects, 214–15
  board's role in, 191–5
  costs, 208–9
  decisions, 215–16
  elements, 202–4
  program, *199–201*
  program statement, 195–8, *196–8*
  vs. remodeling, 204–8
  site selection, 213–14
buildings, library, 190–8
  exterior of, 218–19
  interior of, 219–21
  new, 212–16
*Buildings, Books, and Bytes: Libraries
  and Communities in the Digital
  Age,* 226

C
capital outlay, 108–9
career ladders, 141
case studies, 60–4
cash, 116
cataloging and classification, 158–9
centralization, 17, 18
certification, 6, *135*
change, 2–3, 49, 227, 229
circulation, 167–9
  automated systems, 169
  desks, 211, 219
  outside the library, 68
classification plans, 18, 131–3, *133*
clerical assistants, 136
climate control, 202
coaching, 130
collection
  balance of, 83–4
  control of, 164–7
  depth of, 84
  development of, 154–8

  management of, 146–54
  as product, 145
  support operations, *146*
  well-rounded, 83
commercial services, 159–63
communication, 62, 64, 142–3
community
  board representation of, 22
  budget support, 99, 112
  characteristics of, 2–3
  college, 4
  company/industry, 4
  growth of, 213
  institutions and organizations, 40,
    219
  interest in library, 3
  market, 5
  needs of, 6, 7, 36, 38, 54, 60, 69,
    113, 192
  small, 1–11
  suburban, 3–4
  university, 4
community study, 10, 54
  and marketing audit, 36, 38–43
  and policies, 85–6
  reflection on, 47
  and staff levels, 134
  and vision, 6
comparable worth, 18
compensation, 137–8. *See also* pay
  plans
competence, staff, 140
computer software, 151
consolidated library systems, 172–3
consultants, building, 215
continuing education
  and change, 189, 227
  for competence and advancement,
    140–3
  in personnel administration, 20
conversion, building, 216–18
  criteria, *217*
cooperation. *See also* library systems
  with libraries, 4, 102, 181–5,
    222
  with local agencies, 35, 181–5
cooperative library systems, 173

copyright
  and computer software, 151
  and interlibrary loan, 183
corporations, 106
costs
  vs. benefit, 58, 110
  and budget process, 56–7
  building, 208–9
  of building new vs. remodeling,
    204
  of collecting fines, 91
  vs. demand, *59,* 108, 110–11
  direct, 91, 110
  of electronic access, 190
  energy, 209–10
  of equipment, 212
  indirect, 57, 91, 110
  of interlibrary loan, 183
  and line-item budgets, 108
  of materials preparation, 159–60
  postage, 226
  and program budgets, 109–10
  and staff time, 57–8
  utility, 209–10
cross training, 189
custom, 13, 14
customer groups, 85–6
customer service, 10, 54

D
data, 48, 56
  and accountability, 117
  assessment of, 227
  primary, 38, 43–5
  secondary, 38–9
  sources of, 39–40
  statistics, *118*
dealers, local, 155
decisions, when building, 215–16
deferred giving, 105–6
demand, 81–2
  vs. cost, *59,* 108, 110–11
democracy, 12
disciplinary action, 130–1
discounts, 155, 156
distribution, 62, 64, 188, 202
diversity, of board, 22, 24

donations, 104–5
duties, staff, 122

E
earmarked tax funds, 100–1
education
  continuing, 20, 140–3, 189, 227
  and poor job performance, 130
  professional, 134–5, 142–3
  requirements, 6, *135*
efficiency, 166–7
electrical system survey, *205–6*
electronic access, 189–90
electronic connections, 226–7
employment, 1, 5–6
  equal opportunity, 126
empowerment, 139
endowments, 105–6
energy considerations, 209–10
equipment, 211–12
evaluation
  of materials, 153–4
  of product design, 62–3, 64
  of staff, 127–9, 137
exterior, building, 218–19

F
facilities planning, *199–201,* 199–204
facilities survey, 204, *205–7*
fair use, 151
farming, 5
federal aid, 101–3
federalism, 12
federated library systems, 173
fees, 90–3, 97
finance. *See* budgets
fines, 90–3, 97, 167–8
focus groups, 44, 45
formats, of materials, 92–3, 147
foundations, 104, 106
friendliness, 2, 121–2
Friends of the Library, 89, 105, 208
fringe benefits, 138
funding
  of building costs, 208–9
  private sources of, 96
  shared, 102

funding *(continued)*
supplementary, 103–6
fund-raising activities, 105
furniture, 210–11

G
general fund, 98
gifts
financial, 104–5
materials, 87–8
goals
and accountability, 117
and budgets, 6, 69, 107, 111
and community analysis, 10
creating, 48–52
and levels of service, 71
and marketing audit, 56
and planning process, 10, *31*
and policies, *74–5,* 77, 80
staff, 128
governance, library, 12–29
enhancing, 26–8
and library board, 16–26
and local officials, 15–16
government publications, 149, 156–7
grantsmanship, 106

H
hierarchy of needs, Maslow's, *141*
hiring, 123–7
homebound, 226
hours
of service, 89–90
of work, 138–9

I
image, library, 218–19, 226–7, *228*
informality, 2, 121–2
information
access to, 28, 43, 229
needs of community, 6, 7, 36, 38,
54, 60, 69, 113, 192
packages, 147
provision of, 38
unexpressed needs, 42
intellectual freedom, 86
interior, building, 219–21

interlibrary loan, 4, 98, 147, 183–5
code guidelines, *184–5*
of government publications, 149
*Interlibrary Loan Practices
Handbook,* 185
internal analysis, 45–6
interviews, 44, 45, 126
inventory, 165–6

J
job classification, 132
job descriptions, 122, 123–5, *124,*
126, 132
for unpaid staff, 137
job design, 139
jobbers, 154–5
justification, budget, 111–12, 113

K
Kotler, Philip, 55

L
laws, 13–15, 76, 97. *See also*
regulations; rules
federal, 13–14
and library boards, 20
state, 13–14, 15, 99
lease plans, 82
lease-purchase arrangements, 209
legislation. *See* laws
levels of service, 65–8, 92, 97
defined, 65–6
librarians
and budget presentation, 112
as department heads, 17–18
relationship with board, 26
responsibilities of, 21–2, *23*
libraries
and access to information, 28
assessment of, 36
county, 5
as municipal departments, 15–16,
17
needs of, 113
primary income of, 97
purposes of, 32–3

Library Administration and
Management Association,
Buildings and Equipment Section,
220–1
library associates, 136
Library Bill of Rights, 86
library board, 16–26
and accountability, 79, 96
advisory, 15, 17–20
and budgets, 100, 112
and building projects, 191–5,
192–3
diversity of, 22, 24
education of, 79, 138, 159
and fiscal responsibility, 96
history of, 21
and justification of outside
processing of materials, 161–2
meetings of, 25
operational, 15, 20–2
and policies, 73, 79
as public officials, 25–6
qualifications for, 24
relationship with librarian, 26
responsibilities of, 21, *23,* 26
selection of members, 22–4
size of, 24
terms, 24
library directors. *See* administrators,
library
library district systems, 173
Library of Congress Division for the
Blind and Physically
Handicapped, 93
Library Services and Construction Act
(LSCA), 93, 103
Library Services and Technology Act
(LSTA), 103
library systems, 4, 171–8
autonomy of small libraries, 176
benefits of membership, 34, 103,
147, 173–6
costs of services, 177–8
limitations of membership,
173–6
organization of, 172–3
and selection aids, 147

and sharing of unneeded materials,
89
and state aid, 102, 103
library technicians, 136
library trainees, 136
licenses, 151
lighting, 219
local government, role of, 100
local history, 84
local income, sources of, 98–101
local interest, 157
local officials, 16
and justification of outside
processing of materials, 161–2

M
macroenvironment, 36
mail, materials by, 225–6
marketing, 54–72
audit, 36–46, *37,* 56, 112
process, 6
service and, 34–6
*Marketing for Nonprofit
Organizations,* 55
Maslow, Abraham, 140
hierarchy of needs, *141*
materials
budget for, 108–9
controversial, 86–7
disposal of, 88–9
formats of, 148–51
gift, 87–8
lost, 91
by mail, 225–6
overdue, 90–1
preparation of, 158–64
repair of, 165
selection of, 78–89, 147–51,
160
unneeded, 88–9
withdrawal of, 164
mechanical system survey, *206–7*
meetings, community, 44, 45
mending, 165
microenvironment, 36
mission, 7, *31,* 33, 56, 69, 229
multitype library systems, 173, 177

N
national networks, 179–80
needs, hierarchy of, *141*
network library systems, 173
networks
    national, 179–80
    state, 178–9
newspapers, 148–9
noise, 202
nonresidents, 92

O
objectives, *50*
    and accountability, 117
    and budgets, 6, 69, 107, 111, 113
    characteristics of, 49
    and community analysis, 10
    creating, 48–52
    and levels of service, 66, 71
    and marketing audit, 56
    and planning process, *31*
    and policies, 73, 77
    staff, 128, 129, 130
    and staff levels required, 134
occupations, information needs of, 41–2
OCLC, 158–9, 179–80
older adults, 60–3
operating expenditures, 108–9, 110
operational plans, 111, 113
operations in support of products,
    145–70, *146*
ordering, 157
ordinances. *See* laws
organizational charts, 125, *125*
organizations, local, 40, 104, 219
orientation, staff, 126–7
output measures, and accountability,
    117
Output Measures for Public Libraries,
    27
outreach, 35
overhead, 110
ownership, sense of, 48

P
pages, 136
pamphlets, 151, 156

paraprofessionals, 136
parking, 214
pay plans, 18, 131, 133, *133,* 137–8
performance reviews, 127–9
    of unpaid staff, 137
periodicals, 148, 156
    and library system membership,
    174
personnel. *See* staff
personnel officers, 18–20, 132
petty cash, 116
planning
    and advisory groups, 32
    and budget preparation, 107, 112,
    113
    long-range, 107, 112, 113
    process, 6, 7, *31*
    SWOT analysis, 46
    team, 31–2, 51–2
Planning and Role Setting for Public
    Libraries, 7
Planning for Results: A Public Library
    Transformation Process, 7, 34
plumbing system survey, *207*
policies, 73–95
    board responsibility for, 20, 22
    changes in, 77–8
    making of, 78–9
    materials selection, 79–89
    personnel, 94, 122–3
    precautions, 77–8
    review of, 77–8
    sets, *74–5,* 76
policy manuals, 73–4
position descriptions, 123–4
postage costs, 226
preprofessionals, 136
price, 10, 56–8, 108
priorities, 7, 33, 58–60, 69, 71, 111
probation periods, 127
procedures, 20, 73, *74–5,* 76, 77
processes, efficiency of, 166–7
processing, of new materials, 164
processing centers, 159–63
product design, 63–5
product items, 55–6
product lines, 55–6

product mixes, *55,* 55–6
products, 10, 54–6
  cost of producing, 56–8, 110, 111
  in program budget, 109, 110, 111
  support operations, 145–70, *146*
programs, 145
  support operations, *146*
promotion, 10, 62, 64
public funds, 98–101
public relations, 62, 68–70
publishers/producers, 155–6
purchasing, 114–16
purpose of library, 32–3

Q
quality of new materials, 82–3

R
real estate taxes, 97, 99, 103
rebinding, 165
receiving, 157–8
reciprocal use, 4
recordings, 149–50
reference service, amplified, 180–1
references, 126
referenda, 99, 100, 208
refurbishing existing buildings,
  218–21
regulations, 13, 97. *See also* laws;
  rules
  exceptions to, 77
remodeling, 216–18
  vs. building, 204–8
rental collections, 82
replacement of materials, 153
resource sharing, 34, 102
responsibilities
  division of, 15, 21–2, *23,* 26
  staff, 122
rewards, 138
RLIN, 180
roles, public library, 7, *8, 31,* 33–4,
  69, 80
rules, 73, *74–5,* 76, 77. *See also* laws;
  regulations
  exceptions to, 77

S
salaries, 18, 133, *133,* 137–8
sales, of withdrawn materials, 89
sampling, 44
saving for building fund, 208
security, 166
selection, 147–51
  aids, 147, 153
  and commercial services, 160
  policy, 147
selective dissemination of information
  (SDI), 27–8
service, 229
  hours of, 89–90
  levels of, 65–8, 92, 97
  from a marketing perspective, 34–6
  responses, 7, *8–9,* 33–4
  staff attitudes toward, 70–1
services, 145
  special, 93
  support operations, *146*
shared funding, 102
shelvers, 136
shelving (furniture), 211, 220, 221
signage, 219, 221
site selection, 213–14
small businesses, 63–5
"smallness," 2, 30
software, 151
space, 194, 204, 215, 216
specialization, 134
specifications, 115–16
staff, 66
  activities, 66, 67
  adaptation of skills, 162–3
  administration of, 120–44
  attitudes toward service, 70–1
  classification of, 18, 131–3, *133*
  disciplinary action, 130–1
  duties of, 122
  evaluation of, 127
  functions of management, 123–33
  and hours of service, 89–90
  levels of, 133–7
  and library system membership,
    175
  performance reviews, 128–9

staff *(continued)*
   personnel files, 130
   personnel officers, 18–20, 132
   policies regarding, 94, 122–3
   policy initiation, 78
   probation periods, 127
   professional, 134–5
   profiles, 120
   salaries, 18, 131, 133, *133*, 137–8
   standards, 134
   support, 136–8
   termination of, 130
   time, 57–8
   unpaid, 136–7
standards
   facilities, 194
   staff, 134
state aid, 101–3
state library agencies, 15, 102, 103,
   215
state library associations, 15, 102
state networks, 178–9
state support, 98
statistics, interpreting, *118*
structural survey, *205*
study carrels, 211
supplementary funding, 103–6
support operations, 145–6, *146*
support services, 110
surveys, 44–5
SWOT analysis, 46, *46*

T
tables, 210–11
target markets, case studies, 60–4
taxes, 96, 98–101, 103
   earmarked, 100–1
   library, 99–100
   real estate, 97, 99, 103
technology, 28, 34, 189, 227, 229
termination of staff, 130
time logs, *58,* 163
time samples, 132
transfer of staff, 130
trustees. *See* library board

U
unions, 4, 130, 139
unpaid staff, 136–7
utility costs, 209–10

V
vendors, 154–6
vision, 6, 7, 33, 56
visual media, 150
volunteers, 62, 105, 136–7, 226

W
weeding, 152–3, 220
withdrawal of materials, 164
WLN, 180
work, organization of, 131–3
working conditions, 138–9

Darlene E. Weingand is a consultant, speaker, and trainer specializing in Library and Information Science Management, based in Hawaii. She is Professor Emerita, University of Wisconsin–Madison, and adjunct professor, University of Hawaii at Manoa. Her areas of expertise include customer service, management, marketing, planning, futures study, library administration, distance education, continuing education, and training. Her most recent books include *Customer Service Excellence: A Concise Guide for Librarians* (1997) and *Future-Driven Library Marketing* (1998).